FV

 St. Louis Community College

Forest Park
Florissant Valley
Meramec

Instructional Resources
St. Louis, Missouri

Mythology

Plattsburgh Studies in the Humanities

Jürgen Kleist
and
Bruce A. Butterfield
General Editors

Vol. 1

PETER LANG
New York • San Francisco • Bern
Frankfurt am Main • Berlin • Wien • Paris

Mythology

From Ancient to Post-Modern

Edited by
Jürgen Kleist
and
Bruce A. Butterfield

PETER LANG
New York • San Francisco • Bern
Frankfurt am Main • Berlin • Wien • Paris

Library of Congress Cataloging-in-Publication Data

Mythology : from ancient to post-modern / Jürgen
Kleist and Bruce A. Butterfield, editors.
    p. cm. — (Plattsburgh studies in the
humanities ; vol. 1)
    Includes bibliographical references.
    1. Myth. 2. Mythology. I. Kleist, Jürgen.
II. Butterfield, Bruce A. III. Series.
BL304.M925   1992   306.4—dc20   91-44219
ISBN 0-8204-1742-4   CIP
ISSN 1061-6012

Die Deutsche Bibliothek-CIP-Einheitsaufnahme

Kleist, Jürgen:
Mythology : from ancient to post-modern / Jürgen
Kleist.—New York; Berlin; Bern; Frankfurt/M.;
Paris; Wien: Lang, 1992
    (Plattsburgh studies in the humanities ; Vol. 1)
    ISBN 0-8204-1742-4
NE: Butterfield, Bruce A.:; GT

Cover Design by Geraldine Spellissy

The paper in this book meets the guidelines for permanence
and durability of the Committee on Production Guidelines for
Book Longevity of the Council on Library Resources.

© Peter Lang Publishing, Inc., New York 1992

Printed in the United States of America.

"Mystic Birth" (1981) by Nina Winkel

Winkel Sculpture Collection
SUNY Plattsburgh Art Museum

Acknowledgments

The editors would like to thank the following people for their support and their help:

Bonnie Burdo, W. Raney Ellis, Bernie Grabczewski,III,
Lizabeth Harnas, Judith Hitt,
H.Z. Liu, E. Thomas Moran, Charles O. Warren

* * * * * * *

Photographs of Sculptures by Nina Winkel:

Table of Contents

Ancient Myths in Modern Contexts

Myth and Society

Myth and the Human Condition

Myth, Science, and Technology

* * *

Preface

"The head of a man is like a labyrinth of a thousand streams of water. . . . Man's head is not a trustworthy implement, nor is it a machine about which we know, with any certainty, what it is good for or is not good for.
". . . codified (or at least established) law. . . only attends to the surface of events—that minutia which history can record—and ignores the flying body—the essence of history itself.
"The heart of a man is like a labyrinth of a thousand streams of liquor . . . ."

> Camilo José Cela, "Postscript: The Head, Geometry, and the Heart," in his novel *Mrs. Caldwell Speaks to Her Son*, trans. J.S. Bernstein (Ithaca: Cornell University Press, 1968), pp. 195, 197, 205.

"The ultimate weaver of world mythology is a woman, and the loom is her body."

> Camille Paglia, *Sexual Personae: Art and Decadence from Nefertiti to Emily Dickinson* (New York: Vintage Books, 1990), p. 585.

With these statements Camilo José Cela and Camille Paglia suggest the central metaphors on which are focused the fifteen essays and one novel-fragment that follow in this collection. Although these sixteen writers—participants in an interdisciplinary symposium on mythology held at SUNY Plattsburgh in March 1991—obviously approach the topic of mythology from the vantage point of many disciplines and for many purposes, they all explicitly or implicitly play with the metaphors of the labyrinth and of the body in order to explain the workings of mythology as they see them.

Paglia's metaphor is, of course, the body itself as mythology—as the loom on which the mythmaker weaves, again and again, in constantly changing patterns and combinations, the stories that interpret, and thus create, the universe. Cela's metaphors—the head and the heart of man as labyrinths, the essence of history as a flying body—suggest the further metaphoric possibility of mythology as the flying body by which the human being escapes, Daedalus-like, from the labyrinth within.

If the universe is—as some contemporary scientists define it—not a mechanical, controllable one, but an ever-expanding, evolving one, and if our metaphors for this universe constantly change but always seem correct, then perhaps mythology—itself expanding and evolving—is the response most in keeping with the universe as we interpret and constantly reinterpret it.

The essays and novel-fragment that appear in the first section— **Ancient Myths in Modern Contexts**—look at the evolution of several historically important myths. Peter Hertz-Ohmes offers a postmodern adaptation of the *Odyssey*, disrupting the unities often found there, and finally questioning the value of any interpretation as a final product of reading this work. In response to the impossibility of locating Odysseus geographically during the ten years after the Trojan War, Hertz-Ohmes suggests a physiological model for the reading of the Odyssey—Odysseus as a virus, antibody, DNA, or sperm, travelling not in linear progression but throughout the body/text's multidimensional space.

In their related essay on the Ulysses myth, Yvonne Jehenson and Natalie Joy Woodall follow the evolutions of Ulysses from Homer's hero of the *Iliad* and *Odyssey* into three parodic versions—that is, versions "set alongside" the original but interpreting Ulysses from the perspectives of later time periods: Vergil's *Aeneid*, Dante's *Commedia*, and Tennyson's *Ulysses*. Similarly, Renée Delgado traces the labyrinth and minotaur myths from their origins in ancient Egypt, through Greek mythology, to their appearances in Cervantes' *Don Quixote* and Borges' "The House of Asterion."

Thomas J. Braga looks at myth as a "return to origins" in his discussion of Mário de Andrade's 1928 "rhapsody," *Macunaíma*, in which the Amazonian Indian mock-heroic folk protagonist Macunaíma travels to São Paulo, discovers that the modern city and everyone in it is merely "the Machine without magic and without force," and finally flees to his Amazonian homeland. In Erich Wolfgang Skwara's "Don Juan as Myth," excerpts from his novel *Pest in Siena*, Don Juan is transformed into a modern credit-card-carrying man struggling to recreate himself once again, playing his old game in the new and unnerving landscape of contemporary Siena.

The four essays in section two—**Myth and Society**—come to terms with the myths that have sustained or failed to sustain nations and international political systems. Edwin Hamblet's "French-Canadian Messianism" and Edward R. Schaffer's "The Myth of American Exceptionalism" both suggest the recurring validity—for at least many French Canadians and Americans—of myths that have evolved through several centuries. Barbara Fischer, in her essay "The Myth of Tolerance," traces the myth of German-Jewish friendship from its emergence during the German enlightenment to its final failure in Nazi Germany. Eberhard Görner, in discussing "Myth and Socialism," illustrates the failure of socialism to evolve successfully in the German Democratic Republic by telling his own forty-six-year story of life under the socialist regime.

Myth and the Human Condition—section three—contains essays on the twentieth-century French writers Albert Camus, Eugène Ionesco, and Samuel Beckett. In her "Terrorism and/or Sacrifice in *Les Justes* by Albert Camus," Armelle Crouzières-Ingenthron discusses terrorist myths in Camus' play, finding that in pursuit of a just cause the terrorist—for Camus—is prepared to sacrifice not only the lives of others, but his own as well. Pascale Perraudin finds that, in Ionesco's plays *The Chairs* and *The Bald Soprano*, the modern "myth of incommunicability" proves itself to be not modern at all, because lack of communication has been the human condition throughout history. Sylvie Debevec Henning—in her essay "Writing the Body: 'Qui tient le/la greffe?'"—discusses the myth of corporeal unity—the myth of the body, or text, as a closed, self-contained or comprehensive system. Here, in an argument clearly parallel to Camille Paglia's, Henning argues for the carnivalesque conception of the body—which "exceeds itself in order to go out into the world," "allows the world to enter it," and is "implicated in a process of transformation and becoming."

In the final section—**Myth, Science, and Technology**—Richard D. Moore argues that science has now taken us beyond the mechanistic, controllable universe, upon which science has been based since Descartes and Newton, to a new universe "more like an organism than a machine," a universe that is evolving, "going somewhere"—a universe that contains a story. Scott R. Smith argues, similarly, that the myth of mind as machine—and thus the attempt to create artificial intelligence—represents "mankind's misunderstanding of self," and that "the phenomena of mind depend on the physiology of one's whole body."

In an essay called "Myths of Re(-)Creation: Mythology in the (Post-) Nuclear World," Thomas J. Morrissey concludes that myths of re-creation—as found in science-fiction stories about life after nuclear holocaust—continue to reassert themselves so strongly that science-fiction writers create and re-create them even as they are well aware that the human species would not survive a nuclear winter.

Finally, Michael Johnson discusses the film *Back to the Future Part II*, which he analyzes not only as science fiction, but as mythology and fantasy as well. Illustrating his point with a palindrome, Johnson argues that human experience has to be read at least two ways, both forwards in linear time and backwards throughout time past, and that traditional myths help one to cope with one's double aspect—or doppelgänger—as one journeys "with oneself through various time frames and dimensions."

In the end, of course, ancient myths are also our new-age myths—a body, labyrinthine within, moving outward into the universe, weaving new stories from old, telling the universal story, always becoming.

Bruce A. Butterfield
Plattsburgh, New York
December 1991

Ancient Myths in Modern Contexts

"Wood Nymph" (1982) by Nina Winkel

Winkel Sculpture Collection
SUNY Plattsburgh Art Museum

Peter Hertz-Ohmes

If Gods Were Hormones:
Fractals, Catastrophes
and
Other Good Things in Homer's *Odyssey*

This paper is at best schematic. It does not pretend to interpret the *Odyssey*. But it will look at bases for interpretation and ask questions about the process leading to interpretation. Finally it will ask whether interpretation *as a final product* is a good thing.

If gods were hormones! The title is of course a come–on. But it is also meant to jolt us into some realizations about the way we read. We read science in one way, literature in another. We seldom relate the two, yet we should. Unless we have been over–academized and too compartmentalized, we should realize that our scientific and our literary paradigms overlap. The humanities must include the sciences and vice versa, for as our mathematical and physical models of the world change, so do our understandings of social, literary, and political models.

The Copernican revolution certainly affected our religious views and made a new literature possible. Descartes, Newton, Locke, Rousseau, Kant, Riemann, Einstein, and Gödel have helped reshape literary and political models as much as have Dante, Shakespeare, Goethe, Freud, and Joyce.

I don't believe in reading the *Odyssey* the way an ancient Greek would listen to it. I want to relate the *Odyssey* to my present life. To do that I have to be able to adapt the *Odyssey* to postmodern ways of seeing the world. If that adaptation is not possible in some way, the *Odyssey* ceases to be a significant part of my heritage.

But not to worry! The *Odyssey* is very adaptable to different bases of interpretation. Let us review three or four generations of interpretive strategy (see Appendix A).

Wilamowitz-Moellendorff, in his influential book *Die Heimkehr des Odysseus* (Berlin: 1927), searched behind the transmitted text for historical facts the way others at the time looked for the historical Jesus or the original sources of the Old Testament. By trying to resolve what he considered irreconcilable inconsistencies in the *Odyssey*, he broke up the work and introduced multiple Homers but in the end he produced a unified historical representation on which the work was supposed to be based.

Karl Reinhardt thought this was tantamount to destroying Goethe's *Faust* in order to find Marlowe and three other versions. In *Tradition und Geist* (Göttingen: Vandenhoeck, 1960), Reinhardt takes a New Criticism approach that treats Homer as a single text-immanent, implied author who holds the *Odyssey* together, regardless of the historical sources. If we look at the conventional sequence of the adventures (Appendix B), we can quickly recognize two aspects of Reinhardt's work. The first is the intentional way in which "Homer" organizes the episodes so that Odysseus loses all his men and arrives in Ithaka alone. The second is the way these same episodes systematically form Odysseus' education, from brash hero to wary and cautious king reclaiming his throne.

Horkheimer and Adorno in turn compare the *Odyssey* to the Robinson Crusoe story, the shipwrecked individual who transfers his own culture into the more primitive Third World. His *hybris* is Enlightenment; he is the embodiment of the consequences of bourgeois ideals. Loss of identity through cleverness allows Odysseus to survive. He is Nobody (Udeis) and hence no threat. He is a beggar in disguise, an undercover agent. Through subversion, self–denial, and self–sacrifice, he continually puts his Self at risk in order to legitimize the profit he exploits from feudal, agrarian, or hunter societies. In short, he is the slippery con–artist and self–made man of Capitalism.[1]

Michel Serres finds in the *Odyssey* the transformation from isolated and non–communicating social/linguistic systems to system-federation and interchange of information across the board. The trouble is, the federation process soon becomes imperial and dominating. From Homer to Virgil!

Thus differences are repressed in favor of a single unifying space–time structure, a single hegemonic geography. Euclidean–chronological coordinates take hold of everything and turn anomalies into irrational, imaginary, or mythological monstrosities to be excluded from a rational, logical world.

"The plurality of disjointed spaces, all different, is the condition of the series that assembles them,"[2] the prerequisite base for Odysseus' journey and itinerary. His story, as he tells it, is the discourse through which the disjointed spaces become unified. Penelope at home reflects this process as she weaves and unweaves her tapestry, so that when Odysseus comes home, the tapestry and the discourse are one and the same.

In effect, Odysseus and Penelope disunite and come together, assemble and dissemble in a mutual play of and with reason, whereas Plato and Virgil later tie the spaces together into the single predetermined imperial space/time order whose rationality has prefigured our era ever since.[3]

Or has it? Riemann in the nineteenth century and Cantor and others began to break down the metric restrictions under which we have lived for two thousand years. Riemann's non-Euclidean geometry, Cantor's orders of infinity, Hausdorff's topological redefinitions of dimension, Hilbert's phase spaces with unlimited flexibility, Gödel's proof that mathematical systems need not be consistent: these redefinitions began to undermine what was at the turn of the twentieth century a static, uniform, homogeneous, continuous, regular and regulated universe. For those in the know, our universe today is again dynamic, inhomogeneous, discontinuous, irregular, and, if I may anticipate, "strangely" attractive.

So we're back to the *Odyssey*, but this time to disrupt, in a postmodern way, the very unities that have been found in that work. We will want to deconstruct the work in two stages. First we will use a physiological approach to show that narrative structure can be spatially and chronologically disparate and still hang together as a text. This concept is not new, but it is worth underlining since so much emphasis is placed on the spacial-chronological coordination of Dublin and Bloomsday in Joyce's *Ulysses*. After that we will shatter the whole-number-dimensional linguistic space/time model we have so long taken for granted, and find examples in the *Odyssey* of antinomies based in fractional dimensional structures or fractals.

You might ask, how did I decide to pursue a physiological model for the *Odyssey*? Very simple. I asked myself where Odysseus had been for ten years after the Trojan War. The usual answers bothered me because they were so obviously variations of the single global geography we have been talking about. Odysseus was supposed to be in the Mediterranean or in the Black Sea, or he had gotten out to the Atlantic through Gibraltar (Skylla and Kharybdis) and discovered America. Big deal! Then what were all the monsters and stuff? Psychological fantasies? Must we admit that this clever and rational hero covered his tracks by making the stories up?

Not good enough. Let's eliminate the human element and look at Odysseus as a probe, an operator in the abstract. What if each adventurous episode were a separate experiment in a laboratory? And what if the work as a whole were some sort of biological organism, a living and breathing text that we could dissect with a knife or a CT scan or a barium enema?

Isn't the metaphor of literary wholeness such a biological one? Some literary critics today still think of the life of the author as equivalent to the life of the text. Others say that the text has to be a whole organism regardless of the author. And some see one literary text in communication with another. In physiology we have a similar situation but without the psychological overtones.

"You [dear reader!] are used to thinking of people as intact entities. The doctor sees that people are made up of component parts; the human body is a well-oiled machine. The cell biologist sees a collection of cells — colonies, really — all living in harmony to produce a supercolony or 'nation' called a 'man,' . . . a pluralistic multi-ethnic society."[4]

The social structure or nation state of cells seems rather obviously an application of the affective fallacy: cells are like humans and vice versa. Nevertheless, what would it get us if we thoroughly mixed metaphors: literary organisms and physiological nation-states? We might get a ride through the body à la Disneyland, or produce a movie in which tiny humans in a submarine are injected into the blood stream of an important person to eliminate a brain clot. Like *Fantastic Voyage* with Raquel Welch. Or Woody Allen's sperm in *Everything You Always Wanted To Know About Sex.*

But this time let's not have a *human* odyssey. This time Odysseus *is* a virus, or an antibody, or DNA, or an actual sperm, whatever the adventure calls for. From the point of view of the affected body (the text as a whole), the succession of adventures in the *Iliad,* the *Odyssey,* and the *Aeneid* takes on a certain simultaneity, in which the linearity of the story is replaced by semi-independent physiological events in multidimensional Hilbert space. And the reader, together with the author, experiments to see what is happening through the performance of probes, monitored in computer language or on a graph or on a TV screen or in terms of specific body reactions. Here are some examples:

a) Simple microbic invasion and antibody neutralization in Kikones.

b) Some kind of virus in Kyklopes cloning to the ram after infecting the cave/cell and destroying the Cyclop's eye.

c) Kalypso as an egg ovulation with Odysseus as the sperm, with a pregnancy of eight months, instead of eight years, and premature delivery.[5]

d) Virgil's Trojan horse story with the already encapsulated cancer cells (soldiers) locked inside the fortified boundaries of a hostile social organism.

e) Cell mutation and antidotes (Moly) play essential roles in Kirke,

f) whereas immunity in the form of inserted ear plugs (gene manipulation in the DNA) save the crew-cells from contagion by Seirênês.

g) When Odysseus comes home, he is an inoculation of friendly antigen that activates local factors against the malignant Suitor cells; the antigen raises everything to a fever pitch, then in a moment of life-threatening crisis restores the body-politic to health.

h) Penelope of course is the heartbeat of the organism.

i) And *the gods are hormone messengers and regulators* that prevent things from getting out of control.

This sort of exercise is quite amusing as well as instructive. Physiology quickly gets rid of residual psychological motivation and allows us to eliminate distracting emotion. Penelope is much less of a sexual martyr if she is the organism's literal heartbeat rather than Odysseus' neglected heart throb! I'm just playing around. A physiologist might make a real case for such modeling, but I won't.

Nevertheless, physiology and psychology, history and linguistics are in the last analysis all out of date these days unless each of these disciplines, together with literary criticism, takes into account contemporary "chaos theory." What do we mean? Perhaps the best approach is to examine, at several levels, the depth of information contained in a simple dynamical system such as a pendulum.

Note (case 1) that when a pendulum swings unassisted, gravity and air friction will eventually bring it to a stop over a fixed point. Thus it is said to be under the control of a "fixed point attractor," the predictable ending point of the pendulum's trajectory. Now (case 2), if the pendulum were in an ideal or frictionless environment (on the surface of the moon, for example, which has no atmosphere and less gravity to slow the pendulum down), it might keep going forever, alternating between two fixed points. As the moon rotates under it, the pendulum would begin to describe a regular and periodic circular or elliptic path. Here the attractor is a "limit cycle," a periodic curve or frequency or wave length. This path is also predictable, given certain initial conditions of the pendulum.

But (case 3) pendulums do not always behave as nicely as they perhaps ought. So when a heavy, free-hanging, earthly pendulum (like Foucault's pendulum in a museum) is given, from time to time, a little extra push to keep it from slowing down and hence to keep it periodic, "strange" things sometimes happen. Thanks to that little extra push, which disturbs the system ever so slightly, the pendulum, after quite a long time, may go erratic, even berserk, unpredictably out of control. When it does this, it is under the influence of what is nowadays called a "strange attractor," for obvious reasons. Such a system is said to have gone chaotic.[6]

Any system that is either static (unchanging) or periodic (changing in a regular or predictable way) contains a strictly limited amount of information. Once in their rut, static and periodic systems cannot tell us much more than is already evident. On the other hand, systems that turn chaotic, systems that become erratic and hence seem to defy predictability, are *too full of information* and, until recently, nobody could figure them out. So they were ignored. Then, with the advent of computers, it became possible to plot many periodic trajectories from given conditions. Could there be a way that a seed of randomness might be introduced into the calculation. But how? What would be the nature of the seed?

And suddenly, an interesting reversal takes place. Forget the periodic trajectories! Let's concentrate on the tiny little push. If for a long time the tiny little push is just that, a tiny little push, perhaps a thousand-fold repetition of the push is the answer. With a computer it might be possible to repeat in terms of simple mathematical functions a cumulative calculation that results, let us say, after ignoring the first 500 tries, in visible evidence of randomization when plotted on graph paper. And indeed, this is the case. In fact, the longer the program runs the more random the results. This at least explains the chaos effect.

But in the midst of chaos, and the longer the program runs, some remarkable images will take shape on the graph paper or on the computer screen. These shapes have come to be called fractional dimensional structures or "fractals," and it is their totally unexpected appearance that revolutionized current thinking about the relationship between complexity and predictability.

"It has generally been assumed that complicated forms must be generated by means of a complicated process. . . . But fractals are at one and the same time highly complex and particularly simple."[7] By means of a relatively simple but time-consuming iteration of selected functions with variable constants, a computer can turn out the regular pattern of leaves or lungs, the irregular pattern of coastlines and mountain ranges, or the complex pattern of ins and outs known as the Mandelbrot set.

Even more remarkable is the fact that the infrastructure of a fractal has, if you zoom in on any fraction thereof, self-similar properties. "For systems under the folding and stretching influence of the strange attractor, any single folding motion of the system represents (though in a unique instance) a mirror of the entire folding operation."[8] We have, therefore, on the one hand the randomizing influence of a strange attractor and on the other hand the regulation implicit in self-simulating scaling mechanisms.

After all this, how does chaos affect our reading of the *Odyssey*? For one, it takes our reading back in time as well as forward. It is a well known fact that ancient Indian ragas are essentially chaotic in their variability, rather than tonal or harmonic. What holds a raga together is a god, a regulator, a tension created between the energy of control and the entropy of existence.

In the same way, some physiologists today postulate the radical idea that heartbeats are chaotic rather than periodic, that variability is necessary to adapt to environmental changes, and that hormones or other regulators, themselves "sympathetically" chaotic, counter the heartbeat's parasympathetic firing rate in a continuous tug of war full of healthy fluctuations.[9] Keeping on course is, even under these conditions, a kind of normalization process, but the old idea of normalization to a periodic ideal may be arresting for the heart and deadly for the organism as a whole.

Thus Penelope's weaving is not as periodic as it looks. "The queen who weaves and unweaves, who makes and undoes this cloth that mimes the progress and delays of the navigator, of Ulysses on board his ship,"[10] reflects in her work not so much the steady waxing and waning of the moon but the perturbations of Mercury, the effects of which undermined theoretically our all-too-periodic Newtonian universe.

A 'fractal process' [like heartbeats] is one that cannot be characterized by a single scale of time (a single frequency), analogous to a 'fractal structure' like the lung, which does not have a single scale of length. Instead, fractal processes have many component frequencies. . . A number of diseases show a loss of the variability associated with fractal structure and fractal function.[11]

The *Odyssey*, it appears more and more evident, is a still healthy work that can easily become infected by subsequent interpretation, if by interpretation we understand a process of normalized closure.

Not only are its images subject to infection, but its language is as well. "Since everybody knows that language is a heterogeneous, variable reality, what is the meaning of the linguists' insistence on carving out a homogeneous system in order to make a scientific study possible?"[12]

The same might be said for the literary critic who attempts to impose a homogeneous system on a given linguistic text. In other words, it is no longer possible for linguists or literary critics to ignore the inherently fractal nature of language configurations.

Fractals, we remind ourselves once more, have uncertain boundaries and are controlled by strange attractors. Strange attractors imply that any given point in the fractal structure may send the next points in diverging directions. No two trajectories in the system overlap or repeat. Thus the system no longer obeys Kierkegaard's Either/Or imperative or logic's True/False, yes/no imperative. No longer is it possible to say definitively whether a given element is "in" the system or "outside" the system. From now on, it will be necessary to recognize that a language text can expand and interfold in infinitely complex ways.

Thus the best we can do in terms of literary criticism is identify or suggest classes of regulators which *for particular readings* introduce a degree of predictability or recurrence into the text. These regulators function like sympathetic hormones in physiological systems and are themselves subject to only partial control by the literary critic's chaotically functioning brain waves.

Although there are limits to such organic models of linguistic structures, and I may have overstepped them already in my efforts to open up discussion, let me conclude by quickly sketching four applications of fractal interfolding to problems we regularly encounter and regularly ignore in classical or modern criticism.

A. The observer and the observed

We have suggested that Odysseus could be considered as probe and camera eye for the experimental observer. But if this is the case, what assumptions are made by the implied reader and/or the implied author? Certainly the observer interferes with the probe, and the probe interferes with its textual environment in ways that give rise to problems similar to quantum mechanical uncertainty. The selection of words for emphasis, the selection of alternative meanings, and the imaging or modeling of the probe's actions are all highly problematic and result in multiple intentionality in the text, where intentionality can be understood as a fractal trajectory with unlimited bifurcation points. Can or should we at least count on a "statistically" normal reading of the *Odyssey*, based on an already normalized text?

B. Mind and body

Odysseus narrates many of his own adventures as he embodies them, but the post-Rousseau, post-Derrida listener might wonder how reliable his autobiography is. In particular, how do Odysseus and Penelope relate? As head to body, as outside to inside, as practice to theory, as operative to controller, as male to female? What psychological systems are inscribed or enfolded whose assumptions reinforce or subvert Odysseus' desire to return home, insofar as he must *first* tell his story?

C. Descriptives and performatives

Sometimes we know all the words but we still don't know what's up, because what is said doesn't describe anything, but, instead, initiates something unsaid. This is especially problematic in the case of proper names. Self-negating Odysseus-Udeis (Nobody) in the Cyclop's episode is a prime example. What is the effect of a name in performative terms if names as "tensors" generate a delirium of fractal spaces? The Udeis-effect versus the Odysseus-effect.[13]

D. Language text and reference world

Why can a language text like the *Odyssey* escape the reference world again and again? What makes ever more interpretation possible? What really is chaotic intensification of language? If we can talk about the language of fractals, can we also talk about the fractals of language? And if we can, does this imply a variety of new and interesting "hyper-texts" that open up to a wide choice of "hyper-orders"?

As far as I am concerned, we have just begun to read the *Odyssey*. Most of the works that are based on this text have, over the centuries, tried to restrict the information it contains within carefully controlled boundaries. I have been suggesting that control is a two-edged sword. We cannot know, consciously, everything that is simultaneously present in word texts, even if we had all the time we needed to explicate all the possibilities in all possible reading trajectories. But we do have the ability to select parameters and perspectives that suit our needs for regulation. If therefore we can learn to live without the finality of a single closed and perfect reading, I have faith that the provisional gods and hormones we have currently chosen will serve us well in our continuing search for their equally provisional successors.

Notes and Comments

1 "The possibility of failure becomes the postulate of a moral excuse for profit. From the standpoint of the developed exchange society and its individuals, the adventures of Odysseus are an exact representation of the risks which mark out the road to success. Odysseus. . . had the choice between deceit or failure." Max Horkheimer/Theodor W. Adorno, *Dialectic of Enlightenment* (New York: Herder, 1972), p. 62.

2 Michel Serres, *Hermes* (Baltimore: Johns Hopkins, 1982), p. 48.

3 "Reason plays Odysseus as he plays it; he is not Virgil, for whom the providential teleological closure of non-reflexive reason has been completed, and hence for whom the future has been decided. . . In the *Odyssey* reason has yet to fulfill its appetite." Michael Clark, "Adorno, Derrida, and the Odyssey: A Critique of Center and Periphery," *Boundary* 2, xvi n. 2 (Winter/Spring 1989), p. 119.

4 Richard Noel Re, *Bioburst: The Impact of Modern Biology on the Affairs of Man* (Baton Rouge: Louisiana State University, 1986), pp. 51-52.

5 Readers interested in "catastrophe theory" should consult René Thom, *Structural Stability and Morphogenesis* (Reading, MA: Benjamin Cummings, 1975), p. 302. "The profound motivation of sexuality is probably not the exchange of genetic material, as is usually supposed, but rather the smoothing of the reproduction catastrophe. . . . The fertilization of an ovum by sperm coming from the exterior creates an organism that is genetically and therefore metabolically different from the mother, thus allowing her to reject this organism by the formation of a shock wave."

6 Chaotic strangeness is clearly a factor in the novel which Umberto Eco calls *Foucault's Pendulum*. But that would be another paper.

7 John Briggs/F. David Peat, *Turbulent Mirror: An Illustrated Guide to Chaos Theory and the Science of Wholeness* (New York: Harper and Row, 1989), p. 96.

8 Briggs/Peat, p. 95. This book has a useful and comprehensive bibliography on chaos, etc.

9 Ary Goldberger, et al., "Chaos and Fractals in Human Physiology," *Scientific American*, v. 262, February 1990, pp. 48-49.

10 Serres, p. 49.

11 Bruce West, et al., "Physiology in Fractal Dimensions,"*American Scientist,* v. 75, p. 364.

12 Gilles Deleuze/F. Guattari, *A Thousand Plateaus* (University of Minnesota, 1987), p. 100.

13 See Jean-François Lyotard, *Économie libidinale* (Paris: Minuit, 1974), section 2, on tensors and names.

Appendix A

Basis of Interpretation

a) Unity of historical representation and the disunity of the work: the problem of *multiple* Homers and *historical* inconsistencies in the Odyssey. [Wilamowitz-Moellendorff]

b) Unity of the story and its single *implied* author Homer: psychological-mythological consistency and a "new criticism," text immanent approach. [Reinhardt]

c) Unity of interpretive ideology: "enlightened" (rational) cover-up of earlier more, primitive civilizations to legitimize exploitation and profit. [Horkheimer and Adorno]

d) Unity of information exchange: topological-topographical unification at some level for the sake of methodological disclosure and open systems. [Serres]

f) Discontinuous, inhomogeneous, irregular dynamical textual systems: chaotic intensification of language with bifurcations, humor, and fractal resonance at all levels subject to the regulating interplay of sympathetic and parasympathetic force fields. [Hertz-Ohmes]

Appendix B

The Odyssey: The 10-year epic is told in 40 days (from Kalypso to end).

Telemakhos (Books 1-4): Telemakhos and Penelope;Nestor, Menelaos; Athena

Adventures (Books 5-12): The hero starts with 12 ships and crews

   Kikonians: plunder and loss, impetuous attack [Book 9]

   Lotus Eaters (Lotophagians): drugs, passivity [9]

   Kyklopês (Polyphemos): lower limits of civilized society, hybris [9]

   Aiolos (wind): potentially friendly powers of nature [10]

   Laistrygonians: cannibal types, one ship left [10]

   Kirkê on Aiaia (Hermes too): love changes men into animals, stay 1 year [10]

   Erebos (Hades): heritage and destinies, Teirêsias [11]

   Seirênês: lure of knowledge (they sing the mind away) [12]

   Skylla and Kharybdis: cruel powers greater than hero [12]

   Helios on Trinakia (sacred cows): loss of men (thunderbolt), Odysseus alone [12]

   Kalypso on Ogygia: immortality, stays 8 years [5]

Poseidon's storm: (18 days to Phaiakians) [5]

Phaiakians (Nausikaä, Alkinoös): perfect civilization, games, stay 5 days [6-8]

Home in Ithaka (Books 13-24): 17 days of anonymous preparation: triumph.

Odysseus as beggar, Eumaios the swineherd, Laertes the father, Eurykleia the nurse, Argos the dog, Telemakhos the son, Mentor the tutor, Athena the goddess, Penelope the wife, and of course the 100 suitors (plus the harper, the bow, and the olive tree bed).

Yvonne Jehenson and Natalie Joy Woodall

Parody
and
The Character of Ulysses

> What is important to keep in mind, however, is that parody—no matter what its markings—is never a mode of parasitic symbiosis. On the formal level, it is always a paradoxical structure of contrasting synthesis, a kind of differential dependence of one text upon another. [Linda Hutcheon, *A Theory of Parody: The Teaching of Twentieth Century Art Forms* (New York: Methuen, 1985), p. 61.]

The character of Ulysses, the Homeric hero par excellence, has intrigued generation upon generation of writers and has invited many interpretations of the man. His story, first told in the *Iliad* and the *Odyssey*, was later embellished by Eugammon of Cyrene in his *Telegonia*, Sophocles in *Philoctetes*, and Euripides in *Trojan Women*. This character has also found his way into twentieth-century literature, as evidenced by the works of James Joyce and Nikos Kazantzakis, to name but two contemporary writers.

Linda Hutcheon posits an interesting theory of parody, which will be used as the basis of this study of the recurring appearance of this literary figure. Whereas parody is generally considered a contrasting of two works, one of which emphasizes the negative aspects of the earlier work, Hutcheon revalorizes the concept by seeing parody as a major form of self-reflexivity, as a form of inter-art discourse. She uses a second meaning of the Greek prefix "para" in "parody" to mean not "counter" or "against" or "in contrast to" but, instead, to mean "beside," therefore suggesting "an accord or intimacy instead of a contrast" (Hutcheon, 32).

By this definition, parody operates as a method of inscribing continuity while permitting critical distance. It is fundamentally double and divided. Its ambivalence stems from the dual drives of conservative and revolutionary forces that are inherent in its nature as authorized transgression (26). Parody is authorized because, as Thomas Greene asserts: "Every creative imitation mingles filial rejection with respect, just as every parody pays its own oblique homage" (1982, 46). Transgression occurs because change entails both cultural continuity and a simultaneous play on the tensions created by our historical awareness of the similarities and differences between two juxtaposed texts. Parody is not a monologic mastery of another's discourse. It is a dialogic reappropriation of the past. The two voices are thereby allowed to be heard (Jenny, 1976, 279).

If parody is to be successful, a process of transcontextualization must take place. Parody is neither pastiche nor imitation. It involves not only a structural "énoncé" but the entire "énonciation" of discourse. This enunciative act includes an addresser of the utterance, a receiver of it, a time and a place, discourses that precede and follow—in short, an entire context (Todorov, 1978a, 48).

As Riffaterre (1980a, 626) and Barthes (1975b, 35-6) acknowledge, however, a reader-decoder must ultimately activate the intertext. That is the objective of the present paper. The writers discussed — Virgil, Dante, and Tennyson — all use the character of Ulysses for specific purposes, thereby parodying the Homeric conceptualization of the hero. The bias of each author, influenced by the period in which he lived, is illustrated by the various Homeric traits displayed by the Ulysses character in each poem.

A short exposition of the nature of the Homeric Ulysses seems appropriate at this point. In brief, what sets Homer's Ulysses apart from other Mycenaean heroes is his combination of intelligence, which is translated into great cunning or deviousness, and his physical prowess. One of Homer's favorite epithets for him is *wily*. Early in the *Iliad*, Ulysses prevents a mass exodus of Greeks from Troy, merely by going from man to man, persuading, threatening, and cajoling, as each man merits (*Il* . 2. 189-210).[1] Later, when envoys are selected to try to entice Achilles to return to the fighting, Ulysses is among them: "And the Gerenian horseman Nestor gave them much instruction, looking eagerly at each, and most of all at Ulysses, to try hard, so that they might win over the blameless

Peleion" (*Il.* 9. 179-80).

Nestor, like everyone else, is well aware of Ulysses' cunning and knows that if anyone can persuade Achilles to cease his boycott, it is Ulysses. Further demonstrations of Ulysses' nature can be seen in the *Odyssey*. While Ulysses' curiosity causes his predicament, his wiliness eventually extricates him from danger when he encounters Polyphemus, the cyclops. Unfortunately, his boastfulness, another trait of the Homeric hero, seals his fate. Most inappropriately, he reveals to Polyphemus his true identity and brings down upon his head the wrath of Poseidon, Polyphemus' father (*Od.* 9. 501-35).[2]

Boasting was an acceptable practice among Homeric heroes, provided that it could be substantiated. In the *Iliad*, Ulysses' behavior on the battlefield at Troy provides ample evidence of his courage and physical prowess (cf. book 11. 473-88). His cunning and audacity are also to be seen in the spy mission he undertakes with Diomedes in book 10. As Diomedes acknowledges: "Were he [Ulysses] to go with me, both of us could come back from the blazing of fire itself, since his mind is best at devices" (*Il.* 10. 356-7). Confused with this sense of adventure, however, is a less admirable display of cold-blooded ruthlessness. Ulysses and Diomedes have no compunction about murdering the Thracian king, Rhesus, and his companions while they sleep, in order to steal their horses (*Il.* 10. 483-514).

Lastly, these traits are demonstrated in the *Odyssey* when Ulysses answers the challenge of the young men as they compete in the games at the court of King Alcinous (*Od.* 8. 94-185). Although many other examples of cunning and of physical ability can be proffered in both epics, the best occurs in the *Odyssey*, when the hero must devise a plan to rid his home of the unscrupulous suitors. With the assistance of his son, Telemakhos, the disguised Ulysses, who has infiltrated the palace, acquires a weapon and kills the young men after depriving them of any means of self defense.

Here a combination of deviousness, as evidenced by his disguise as a beggar, the removal of the arms decorating the walls, the opportunity seized when Penelope proposes the contest for her hand in marriage, as well as the sheer physical strength needed to use the bow effectively—all confirm beyond doubt Ulysses' reputation as the epitome of the Homeric hero (cf. book 21). It was now left to later writers to interpret the hero from vantage points distanced by time and circumstance. Three varying representations will constitute the remainder of this paper.

The *Iliad* ends before the Trojan War concludes, and the *Odyssey* only alludes to the city's demise. It is to Virgil, the author of the *Aeneid*, that we must look to read about the actual destruction. Unlike the *Iliad* and the *Odyssey*, which belong to oral tradition, the *Aeneid* was a consciously and conscientiously written epic, a masterpiece conceived and developed over a span of ten years (29-19 B.C.).

Its avowed purpose was to glorify the Romans, who considered themselves descendants of the Trojans. Virgil, who had no concerns about copyrights or plagiarism, freely borrowed from Homer's works. It is when Aeneas narrates to Dido the sad story of Troy's last day that we see the first evidence of the contemporary revalorization of the theory of parody, for the traits presented so admiringly in the Greek epics — namely deviousness, deceit, and cunning — are used by Virgil to portray Ulysses in a very poor light indeed.

The Trojan War has dragged on for ten long years because the city walls are impregnable. Realizing this, Ulysses first steals the Palladium, the possession of which is crucial to the Trojans for their survival (*Aen.* 2. 163-6).[3] He then devises a plan to make the Trojans destroy their own walls. The appearance of a wooden horse and the disappearance of the Greeks confuse the Trojans until Sinon, a spy, is "captured" and taken to King Priam.

Sinon has allowed himself to be seized in order to gain the confidence of the Trojans. He tells them he has fled the Greeks because Ulysses has plotted his death in revenge for remarks made by Sinon against Ulysses (*Aen.* 2.77-144). The story is believable *and* believed because of Ulysses' reputation for underhanded behavior. The thought never occurs to the Trojans — until it is too late — that the wily Ulysses is even capable of concocting a disparaging story about himself in order to secure the fall of Troy. Complete success is achieved when the Trojans, deluded by this tale, tear down the walls (*Aen.* 2. 189-94). And as if Ulysses has not brought enough havoc to the city, when Sinon opens the horse, the Ithakan is discovered among those concealed in its belly, his presence capping the deceit (*Aen.* 2. 261).

Ulysses, as presented by Virgil through the eyes of Aeneas, displays the same traits ascribed to him in his Homeric characterizations. It is here that parody can best be appreciated. Virgil uses these traits to ennoble the Trojans' plight and to undermine at the same time the achievement of the Greeks. Aeneas, naturally bitter over the loss of his homeland and the deaths of his wife and his father-in-law, Priam, sees only the negative side of the man's personality.

Ulysses has forced Aeneas and his fellow refugees to leave Phrygia and to spend years looking for a new home, again in imitation of what Ulysses himself must do. As Ulysses offended Poseidon and was cursed to wander, so the Trojans have offended Juno and Minerva and are similarly cursed. The difference is that Ulysses brings trouble upon himself, whereas Aeneas' woes are externally generated — that is, as a result of the abduction of Helen and the resulting warfare.

Virgil further parodies Homer in his characterization of Aeneas, whom he patterns after Ulysses, the wanderer, but Virgil makes him, instead, a reticent, hesitant, almost unwilling hero, who must be goaded by the gods to get on with his mission. A comparison to Homer's original story is useful here. For when Hermes visits Calypso to tell her that Ulysses must be allowed to leave Ogygia, Ulysses is found sitting on the shore, weeping and yearning to be on his way home (*Od*. 5. 79-84). Mercury, Virgil's messenger god, has to order Aeneas, who is found contentedly assisting with building projects, to leave Carthage (*Aen*. 4. 222-37). Homer's character has lusted after adventure and action, whereas Virgil's "Ulysses" must be subject to duty and the gods' will.

The desire to get home, no matter what the odds, forms the central theme of the *Odyssey*. Everywhere the hero wanders, he is challenged, whether by witches such as Circe, or by monsters such as Scylla, or by distractions such as the lotos-eaters and the sirens. Virgil parodies this theme by setting Aeneas in various locations in the Mediterranean and then presenting him with signs, clues, or apparitions to convince him that he has farther to go. Virgil even brings Aeneas into contact with the sirens and Scylla and Charybdis, but his encounters produce very different results. Viewing them side by side, one can see the many similarities between the epics of Homer and Virgil. The purpose of each, however, is strikingly different, and the intent is what effects the parody.

At the beginning of the fourteenth century, Dante Alighieri published his epic, the *Commedia*, the most widely read section of which is the *Inferno*. Dante casts himself as the central figure, and his journey through the Inferno and Purgatorio to Paradiso parodies those taken by Ulysses and Aeneas, not only because they attempt to reach a specific destination, that is, "home," but also because all three must visit the Underworld in order to gain knowledge about their destiny.

Dante's depiction of the Underworld, specifically its description of great sinners, is a direct parody of Homer's catalog of Greek women (cf. *Odyssey*, Book 11), and Virgil's catalog of Roman heroes (cf. *Aeneid*, Book 6). The former listing enables Homer to talk about famous Greek heroes, the husbands or sons of these women, whereas the latter permits Virgil, in yet another parody, to continue his campaign of nationalistic propaganda.

Even the Underworld itself is parodied. The Homeric and Virgilian Tartarus is but a part of the Underworld, which also includes Elysium, the ancient equivalent of Paradise. The Christian Dante, on the other hand, changes the text by making sinners go down, while the saved ascend Mt. Purgatory to Paradise. The Underworld, as conceived by Dante, is restricted to a place of torment for the eternally damned.

Although Virgil's motive for composing the *Aeneid* is political, Dante's is theological: he wants to save sinners from eternal damnation by showing them what they face if they persist in their evil behavior. To accomplish this goal, he uses well-known historical and literary figures, punishing each in accordance with the type and severity of the crime. In Canto 26 we find Ulysses among those regarded as evil counselors. He is being punished for stealing the Palladium, for creating the wooden horse, and for persuading Achilles to abandon Deidamia (26. 55-63).[4] The punishment he suffers, imprisonment in eternal fire, reflects Dante's view of those who misuse their influence.

Dante parodies the physical description of Ulysses. The Homeric hero is vigorous and active, as befits his role as military leader. In contrast, Dante's Ulysses says: "I and my companions were old and tardy" (26.106). Why Dante permits himself this characterization is quickly discerned — Ulysses wants one last adventure, and an impending death brought on by old age offers a convenient reason (26. 112-8).

According to the story recounted to Dante's guide, Virgil, Ulysses decides to delay his journey home because he wants to "gain experience of the world, and of human vice and worth" (26. 98-9). To that end, he persuades his crew to venture beyond the Pillars of Hercules, those landmarks set up "to hinder man from venturing farther" (26. 108-9).

This journey was originally the voyage of the Greeks to the Land of the Cimmerians in order to find the entrance to the Underworld — a voyage proposed to Ulysses by Circe (*Od.* 10. 487-95) and undertaken most unhappily by the Greeks (*Od.* 10. 566-7).

Dante parodies the original by having Ulysses himself make this suggestion. In so doing, Ulysses is made to violate the laws of God and humankind by persuading his crew to abrogate their responsibilities to their wives and children, who have waited patiently for them at home. He then compounds his sin by daring to go into the unknown, seeking new experiences merely for the sake of "virtute [=prowess] and knowledge" (26. 118-20). Again, Dante shows Ulysses in his guise of evil counselor. The voyage beyond the Pillars of Hercules ends in disaster and tragedy, for the sailors unwittingly come upon Mt. Purgatory. Because they acquire forbidden knowledge with their discovery, God destroys their ship. All the sailors, including Ulysses, are killed (26. 139-42).

Ulysses' evil counsel has effected the deaths of his companions and brought grief to their families. An even worse sin, however, is committed when Ulysses supposes that he can, with impunity, explore beyond the limits of human experience. The Homeric version, on the other hand, demands that Ulysses and his men return, in order to continue their journey homeward.

Dante's reaction to meeting Ulysses is very interesting. He is eager to see the hero and acknowledges his great fame (26. 64-9). Yet it is Virgil who actually speaks to him, pointing out that because Dante is Italian, and therefore a descendant of the Trojans whom Ulysses helped defeat, the Greek may "disdain thy words" (26. 73-6). The irony is that Virgil too is Italian, in fact Roman, whereas Dante is Florentine. One also recollects that Virgil's description of Ulysses in the *Aeneid* is not flattering. Hence the irony of Virgil's argument that, having written about the Trojan war, he should address Ulysses.

Clarification of this illogical argument is found in the ambivalence of the *author* Dante for Ulysses. Despite Dante's admiration for the classical hero, his Christian intent does not permit him to express this emotion more than fleetingly. Therefore, he must distance himself from Ulysses while confronting him. Is it because his attraction for the classical world is so strong that he fears he too may become contaminated with forbidden knowledge and suffer the same fate?

The technique Dante uses is similarly employed by Virgil and by Homer. Ulysses meets Aias Maior in the Underworld, but Aias refuses to speak to him (*Od.* 11. 553-64). Virgil parodies the incident by having Dido refuse to answer Aeneas (*Aen.* 6. 450-74). The ultimate parody, however, is Dante's, because he wants both to maintain the ancient convention and to ensure that Ulysses has the opportunity to tell his story. He turns the scene around, casting himself as the silent participant. Virgil's presence provides a convenient way to entice Ulysses to speak.

Thus far, Homer's Ulysses has been parodied for political reasons in Virgil's *Aeneid* and for theological reasons in Dante's *Commedia*. The last variation on the Ulysses theme to be examined here is found in Tennyson's poem *Ulysses*, where Ulysses is parodied for moral and ethical purposes.

Tennyson's hero arrives home safely, but by his own admission he is very discontented and unhappy. His return to Ithaka, where he is virtually a stranger because of his long absence, does not provide the same satisfaction as his many adventures have. He describes himself as an "idle king" (l. 1),[5] and chafes at the fact that he must sit home "by this still hearth" (l. 2), as ruler of a people who neither know nor respect him.

He longs to leave Ithaka — "There lies the port; the vessel puffs her sail;/There gloom the dark broad seas" (ll. 43-4) — in order to "drink life to the lees" (ll. 6-7). Remembering past glories he muses: "I am a part of all that I have met" (l. 19). Ulysses' life lacks excitement and action. "How dull it is to pause, to make an end,/To rust unburnish'd, not to shine in use" (ll. 22-3). He therefore proposes one more adventure, theorizing that he might better die doing something than live doing nothing. "Yet all experience is an arch wherethro'/Gleams that untravell'd world whose margin fades/For ever and for ever when I move" (ll. 19-21).

Tennyson seems to create a situation with Homeric antecedents, based on Teirêsias' prophecy in the *Odyssey* — that is, that Ulysses must carry his oar inland until a people unfamiliar with the sea ask him about the "winnowing fan" he bears (*Od*. 11. 117-26). The parody is double-edged because when Ulysses announces that he wishes to "follow knowledge like a sinking star,/beyond the utmost bound of human thought" (ll. 31-2), the reader quickly realizes that Tennyson is relying on Dante's parodic transformation of the Homeric Ulysses, who suffers punishment for a similar desire: "deny not, to this brief vigil/Of your senses that remains, experience of the/Unpeopled world behind the sun" (ll. 112-17).

Tennyson, however, transforms the text once more. Dante's Ulysses is eternally condemned for seeking after knowledge. Tennyson's, on the other hand, reflects his own era—one that glorifies action, revels in progress, delights in the expansion of knowledge. Ulysses' wanderlust illustrates the Victorian zeal for active participation in life, as evidenced by the acquisition of empire.

Overshadowed is the duplicitous, wily Ulysses of Virgil and the curiosity-seeker of Dante. Emphasized is a Ulysses extolled for his adventurous spirit: "You and I are old;/Old age hath yet his honor and his toil./Death closes all; but something ere the end,/Some work of noble note, may yet be done" (ll. 49-52).

Whereas Dante's hero is killed for his counsel to "gain experience of the world, or of human vice and worth," Tennyson's is lauded for this same reason. Ulysses knows well enough that he may not return from this voyage. "It may be that we shall touch the Happy Isles/And see the great Achilles" (ll. 63-4). Victorian that he is, Ulysses is prepared to take the risks. Thus, for Tennyson, Ulysses is an admirable character, and his final words evidence a summation of the Victorian ethic: "that which we are, we are, —/One equal temper of heroic hearts, /Made weak by time and fate, but strong in will/ To strive, to seek, to find, and not to yield (ll. 67-70).

To be truly effective, parody must be apparent to both encoder/ writer and decoder/reader (Hutcheon 27). The personality and the adventures of Homer's Ulysses are so universally known that they provide an excellent reference point for writers who have their own stories to tell and morals to impart. Three authors from three decidedly different time periods and cultural traditions have effectively transformed this story of a Greek hero, thereby making Ulysses coincide with their particular literary requirements. These three works attest to the double-coded richness of parody, to the irrefutable fact that "parodic representations expose [a] model's conventions and lay bare its devices through the coexistence of the two codes in the same message" (Ben-Porat 247).

26

Notes

[1] *The Iliad of Homer*, tr. Richmond Lattimore (Chicago: University of Chicago Press, 1963), p. 81. All subsequent references to the *Iliad* are cited by line numbers in the text.

[2] *The Odyssey of Homer*, tr. Robert Fitzgerald (Garden City, New York: Doubleday and Company, 1963), p. 161. All subsequent references to the *Odyssey* are cited by line numbers in the text.

[3] *The Aeneid of Virgil*, tr. Allen Mandelbaum (New York: Bantam Books, 1971), p. 35. All subsequent references to the *Aeneid* are cited by line numbers in the text.

[4] *Dante's Inferno* (London: J.M. Dent and Sons, 1964), p. 291. All subsequent references to the *Inferno* are cited by line numbers in the text.

[5] Alfred, Lord Tennyson, "Ulysses,"*Tennyson's Poetry*, ed. Robert W. Hill, Jr. (New York: W. W. Norton Company, 1971), p. 52. All subsequent references to "Ulysses" are cited by line numbers in the text.

Works Cited

Aeneid of Virgil. Tr. Allen Mandelbaum. New York: Bantam Books, 1971.

Alighieri, Dante.*The Inferno*. The Temple Classics. London: J. M. Dent, Ltd., 1964 (rpt.).

Barthes, Roland. *The Pleasure of the Text*. Tr. Richard Miller. New York: Hill and Wang, 1975.

Ben-Porat, Ziva. "Method in *Madness*: Notes on the Structure of Parody, Based on MAD TV Satires." *Poetics Today*, 1979, I, pp. 245-72.

Greene, Thomas M.*The Light in Troy: Imitation and Discovery in Renaissance Poetry*. New Haven: Yale University Press,1982.

Homer.*The Odyssey*. Tr. Robert Fitzgerald. Garden City, New York: Doubleday and Company, 1963.

Hutcheon, Linda. *A Theory of Parody: The Teaching of Twentieth Century Art Forms*. New York: Methuen,1985.

Iliad of Homer. Tr. Richmond Lattimore. Chicago: University of Chicago Press, 1963.

Jenny, Laurent. "La Stratégie de la Forme." *Poétique*, 27 (1976), pp. 257-281.

Odyssey of Homer. Tr. Robert Fitzgerald. Garden City, New York: Doubleday and Company,1963.

Riffaterre, Michael. "Syllepsis." *Critical Inquiry* , 6 (1980), pp. 625-638.

Tennyson's Poetry. Ed. Robert W. Hill, Jr. New York: Norton, 1971.

Renée Delgado

The Labyrinth and the Minotaur in *Don Quixote*
and
"The House of Asterion" by Jorge Luis Borges

The labyrinth and the Minotaur are Greek myths rooted in a much more ancient myth. According to Borges in his *Manual de Zoología Fantástica*, the cult of the bull and the double axe (called "labrys," from which labyrinth could have been derived) was typical of pre-hellenic religions.[1] The construction of labyrinthical edifices occurred not only in Greek myths. In antiquity there was a huge labyrinth constructed by King Amenemhet IV (XII dynasty) close to Lake Moeris in Egypt. The reason for the construction of this labyrinth is still a mystery today as it was in antiquity. The writings of Manethon and Pliny in the first century A.D. discuss the question: "Demoteles says that it was the palace of Moteris, Lyceas that it was the tomb of Moteris, many that it was erected as a temple of the sun, which is believed most of all."[2]

The key to the interpretation of labyrinths according to C.N. Deeds is in the ritual and myth associated with them, especially the myth of the Egyptian god Osiris and the rituals that commemorate his assassination and resurrection. It is highly probable that the Greek myth of the Minotaur and the labyrinth of Crete stem from the older Egyptian myth. Yet it is the Grecian myth that was most widely known in Europe and from which scores of reproductions and interpretations have flowed.[3] Virgil and Ovid, and later Dante, brought the myth into literature and moral thought.

In medieval literature in Spain, Juan de Mena wrote a labyrinthical work in both its own structure as well as its content, which contains characters from the Cretan myth and from Virgil's*Aeneid* and Dante's *Divine Comedy*. These last two works, of course, contain labyrinths of their own and allusions to the Daedalian creation.[4] De Mena's was not the only medieval Spanish literary work to mention the labyrinth, nor was Spain the only European country to become obsessed with this structure in its physical and mythological representations. The labyrinth appears, as already mentioned, in the *Divine Comedy* and also in Boethius' *Consolation of Philosophy* and in Chaucer's *House of Fame.*

Labyrinthical structures appeared all over Europe, not only in gardens and paintings but also in church buildings as famous as the Reims and Chartres cathedrals. In her book on the labyrinth, Penelope Reed Doob closely examines these representations, up to and including those of the middle ages. Yet in literature, as in architecture, the labyrinth reached its peak as symbol and structure in the Renaissance and Baroque periods. During the Spanish Golden Age (1500-1700), the labyrinth formed part of the titles of works by Lope de Vega, Tirso de Molina and Calderón de la Barca, three of the most important writers of the times.

Cervantes, although he wrote no work containing in its title the word "labyrinth," writes in a labyrinthical manner, using fiction within fiction, taking his readers down winding and complex paths. He was very conscious of this structure and its multiple implications when he wrote his master-work *Don Quixote* (1605/1612). Not only does this work have a labyrinthical narrative structure impregnated with ambiguity and paradox, as is the labyrinth, but he mentions the structure literally and alludes to the Cretan myth throughout the novel.

The connotations of the labyrinth as a topography of death and resurrection, in the episodes of the "Sierra Morena" and the "Cave of Montesinos" in *Don Quixote*, correspond to the vision of the labyrinth in "The House of Asterion," by Jorge Luis Borges, four centuries later. In this short story, Borges presents us with his transformation of the myth or rather the destruction of it. Here, we will first examine the labyrinth as ritual and myth, then its function in *Don Quixote*, and finally the twentieth-century re-interpretation of this myth in "The House of Asterion."

The Labyrinth

The origin and use of the labyrinth have been discussed since antiquity. In our introduction we cited Pliny as one of many writers and/or historians of antiquity interested in the labyrinthical structure. Perhaps the labyrinth of which Pliny spoke was used in all of the ways he cited: as palace, tomb and temple. It is probable that it was used as all three: the palace of a dead king is his tomb, and the tombs of the kings in Egypt were habitually connected to religious temples, as is true today in Christianity, inasmuch as many churches are also the burial places of important figures. Deeds' essay "The Labyrinth" develops an anthropological study of the origin of this fascinating symbol. He concludes that the labyrinth has its roots in the tomb-temples of Egypt.[5]

According to Deeds, the labyrinth was constructed in order to protect and conceal the dead king-god in its center. Egyptians believed that by protecting his corpse, the life of the dead king-god would be preserved in the after-world. This belief came from a myth whose origin is the god Osiris, assassinated and resurrected. Every year the Egyptian king-god (the pharaoh) reconstructed the ancient myth by a ritual that included a procession with laments, dances, the sacrifice of a bull that represented the Egyptian king-god, and the triumphant resurrection of the king-god upon his exiting the temple/labyrinth. Only the high priests and the royal family participated in the secret ritual at the center of the temple/labyrinth, where the sacrifice of the bull occurred. Part of the ritual included magical formulas and enchantments. It was also customary during this ritual, when the time came, to crown the new pharaoh and consecrate his marriage, which was then consummated in the same temple.[6]

The ritual was a means of renewal. The kings would go to the tombs to fortify their vitality by communicating with their dead ancestors. They believed that their dead lived an immortal life after death and that they stayed within their tombs. During the ritual, magical acts were also performed for the good of the people.[7] This ritual, with the king/bull at its center, could very well lie behind the myth of the Minotaur, half man and half bull. It was believed that, by magic, the sacrificed bull and the king became one. The king as bull would die and then be resurrected on the third day. In the Greek version of this myth, Theseus teaches the Athenians a labyrinthical dance to celebrate his defeat of the Minotaur. This dance, according to Deeds, could have come from the Egyptian ritual. The Greek tragedies of antiquity show an uncanny likeness to the Egyptian ritual and the labyrinth dance taught to the Greeks by Theseus. The Greek tragedies are composed of five parts: contest, death/sacrifice, messenger (death, as in the center of the labyrinth, did not occur out in the open in front of the people but, rather, it was announced by a messenger), lamentation, and resurrection of the dead.[8] These parts resembled to a significant degree the Osirian ritual and the labyrinth dance.

The Labyrinth in *Don Quixote*: The Sierra Morena

The image of the labyrinth appears clearly in the first part of *Don Quixote*, in the chapters about the Sierra Morena. Salvador Jiménez Fajardo, in his article "The Sierra Morena as Labyrinth in *Don Quixote*," studies the labyrinthical element but excludes from it the anthropological and mythological implications of the symbol.[9] The Sierra Morena as topographical labyrinth becomes apparent when Don Quixote sends Sancho to Dulcinea and advises:

> But the best way to avoid missing me or going astray yourself will be for you to cut some branches of the broom that are so plentiful about here. Strew them at intervals here and there as you go until you reach the open country. These will serve as landmarks and signs by which to find me when you return, just like the thread in Theseus' labyrinth.[10]

These last words without doubt refer to the Cretan labyrinth, at the center of which lay the Minotaur. Theseus left the labyrinth successfully because he used a thread upon entering that led him back out after he killed the Minotaur. Don Quixote suggests that Sancho imitate him so as not to get lost in this other labyrinth, the Sierra Morena.

Fajardo speaks of the double at the center of the labyrinth and of the mirror images that are presented in the chapters dealing with the Sierra Morena. This play with doubles occurs not only with Quijote/Quijano, the Knight and the hidalgo, but also with the other characters who come into the Sierra Morena: Ginés de Pasamonte is also Ginesillo de Parapilla, thief and writer; Cardenio is both a madman and a gentleman; Dorotea is both a lady and Princess Micomicona. All the other characters in the Sierra Morena have double roles as well. Strangely enough, or perhaps not so strangely, some of the doubles are also mirrored images of the self. Cardenio appears to be a madman and is actually mad with love, and Dorotea, who pretends to be a princess in distress, is actually a lady in distress. This doubling corresponds to that aspect of the labyrinth that invokes the double self.

Quijote/Quijano is another mirrored image at the center of the labyrinth. He is a monstrous figure, a monstrously anachronic one. He inspires fear as well as laughter and admiration. He is at once a gentleman and a clown, as the Minotaur is at once a prince and a freak. There are also similarities between Don Quixote and Theseus. Both are warriors who enter the labyrinth, sword in hand. Each hopes to leave the labyrinth with the aid of the woman he loves. Don Quixote says he will be freed from his self-imposed penance by a letter from Dulcinea, and Theseus uses the thread Ariadne has given him in order to leave the Daedalian structure. Theseus supposedly danced in the labyrinth,[11] and Don Quixote in the mountains "cut a couple of capers and did two somersaults in the air" (253), a dance-like action. Both men leave the labyrinth, but neither lives happily with his lady.

The double role of resurrection and death at the center of the labyrinth in the Osirian myth is also present. Don Quixote is in the Sierra Morena to do voluntary penance in order to purge and revitalize himself. He is there for three days.

Another connection between the Sierra Morena and the myth and ritual of the labyrinth is the presence of the five elements of the aforementioned Greek tragedies, which modeled themselves after the labyrinth ritual: the contest is comparable to the confrontation between Don Quixote and Cardenio before arriving at the center of the Sierra Morena; the death and resurrection correspond to the penance that Don Quixote carries out and to his leaving the Sierra Morena. The messenger is Sancho Panza, who is supposed to describe to Dulcinea what Don Quixote does for penance; the lamentations are Sancho's protests to his master's actions. The "enchantment" of Don Quixote at the end of this episode can also be related to the Egyptian labyrinth ritual, since incantations and magic spells were a part of it.

Don Quixote thinks he is enchanted when he is put in a cage like an animal. The image of Don Quixote in a cage is like that of the man/bull within the labyrinth. He is a man, yet he is being treated as an animal or a freak. His captivity recalls the coins of antiquity that Deeds examines in his essay. These coins represent a man or a horned animal at the center of a rectangular maze. This figure represents the king-god at the center of the labyrinth. The cage also evokes the labyrinth in the conversation between Sancho and Don Quixote. Don Quixote refuses to believe the reality and insists that he has been enchanted:

> it must be that those who have enchanted me have assumed
> the likeness of our friends to give you cause to think as you do

and to whirl you into a maze of fancies out of which not even
the clue of Theseus could extricate you (486).

The "maze of fancies" is a reflection of Don Quixote's own situation. It is ironic that Don Quixote directs these words to Sancho since he,
Don Quixote, finds himself in both labyrinths: the structural, represented
by the cage, and the mythical, represented by the resurrection of knight er-
rantry. These words occur almost at the end of the first part and introduce the entrance into the labyrinthical fancies of the cruel dukes, a
labyrinth that is entered not only by Don Quixote but also by Sancho
Panza.

The Labyrinth in *Don Quixote*: The Cave of Montesinos

In his article "El processo iniciativo en el episodio de la Cueva de
Montesinos del *Quijote*" ("The process of initiation in the episode of the
Cave of Montesinos in *Don Quixote*"), Augustin Redondo presents the
manifestations of these tragedies in Europe. Yet, he calls the ritual acts elements of initiation, never recognizing that they have as their origin, the
labyrinth.[12] The episode of the Cave of Montesinos has been considered
by various critics as key to the interpretation of *Don Quixote*. This
episode as well has been the object of much discussion and diverse interpretation. Redondo mentions some of these interpretations and examines
closely the initiation process in this episode, using the work of anthropol-
ogists and historians as well as that of specialists in folklore.[13] Redondo's
study complements this present one because he relates the Montesinos
episode to ritual and myth. But unlike the present work, Redondo uses
texts that are more contemporary to the cervantine text and never mentions the ritual and mythical implications of the cave as labyrinth.

The Sierra Morena was the topographical labyrinth of the first
part; the Cave of Montesinos serves the same function in the second. The
Cave of Montesinos, because it is a cave, is more directly associated with
the labyrinth as structure than is the Sierra Morena. Many descriptions
of ancient labyrinths depict them as caverns or caves with many doors.
Don Quixote thought the Cave of Montesinos a worthy challenge for a
valiant knight because there were "so many astonishing stories" (655)
about it. The connection between the cave and the labyrinth is antici-
pated, just before this adventure begins, by a discourse Don Quixote

gives on knights, in which he states that killing bulls and entering mazes are knightly activities:

> It is a fine sight to see a gallant knight . . . give effective lance thrusts at a brave bull . . . let the Knight-errant explore the corners of the world, penetrate the most intricate labyrinths, encounter at every step the impossible (646).

Here we see the knight fighting with a bull, entering labyrinths, encountering the impossible and conquering. Such action is reminiscent of the labyrinthical ritual, in which the king-god participated in the impossible task of death and resurrection, but in the end—like the knight—is victor.

There is also an important relationship between the ritual and myth of the labyrinth and the folk tales examined by Vladimir Propp. These folk tales, according to Redondo, contain rites of initiation that include a trip to the other world (the death of the king-god in the labyrinth) and the search for the beloved (marriage ceremony in the labyrinth). In these stories, the entrance to the other world is difficult, as is also the exit. Such difficulty is also true of the entrance to the labyrinth. In the Osirian ritual, fights were dramatized at the entrance and exit of the labyrinth/temple.[14] Redondo studies the characteristics of the fantastic folk tale and associates them with the episode of the Cave of Montesinos, yet he never mentions the labyrinth, a possible source of these European tales.

Deeds, on the other hand, studies the European transformations of the labyrinth ritual into tales and practices. He mentions in particular the conversion of the labyrinth dance into the European military march:

> Thus we find that when the labyrinth complex was taken over by men who were horse riders, the dance was performed on horseback. Presently the ritual origin was forgotten; but the military "musical ride" has survived to the present day.[15]

The parallels between the labyrinth ritual and the descent of Don Quixote into the cave are multiple. The first is the need for a guide. Don Quixote has as his guide the author of the book *Metamorphoses*, or *The Spanish Ovid*, and another book called the *Supplement to Polydore Virgil* (681). This is important because Ovid and Virgil (although not Polydore Virgil) both mention the labyrinth in their writings. Virgil is also a guide to the underworld in Dante's labyrinthical work *The Divine Comedy*. On another level, the fact that the book is called *Metamorphoses* is of significance because the guide of the king-god in the Osirian myth is the high priest, lord of the metamorphosis: life/death/life of the king-god.

In the Egyptian ritual, the king-god is turned into the bull and the bull into the king-god. The high priest symbolically kills the king-god, using the sacred bull. This is probably at the root of the myth of the Cretan Minotaur and labyrinth. During the ritual, the high priest uses magical words from the book of the dead, which supposedly accomplish the metamorphosis of the king-god. Montesinos is the other guide whom Don Quixote encounters in the Cave. He too is a prototype of the high priest because he dresses as a priest and carries a rosary in his hands. Montesinos as high priest takes the heart out of the body of the famous knight, Durandarte (687). To take the heart from the victim was part of traditional rituals of human sacrifice, a ritual at one time performed at the center of the Osirian labyrinth/temple.[16]

Before Don Quixote and Sancho Panza enter the Cave of Montesinos, a few other occurrences in Cervantes' novel parallel the Osirian myth ritual. Before the adventure begins, Don Quixote and Sancho are "treated and served as royalty" (680). There are also some famous lakes or ponds near the cave. Don Quixote's kingly treatment corresponds to that of the king-god, and the bodies of water near the cave are comparable to the famous canals close to the Nile river, where the death and resurrection of Osiris was said to have occurred. These canals were also very close to the temple/labyrinth dedicated to the god Osiris in Egypt.[17]

One needs a rope in order to enter the labyrinth so as not to be lost in its depths; this was also true of the Egyptian and Cretan labyrinths. Before entering the Cave of Montesinos, Don Quixote was provided with a rope. The prayer and the favors said by Don Quixote to Dulcinea before entering the cave are reminiscent of the prayer of Theseus to the gods before entering the Daedalian labyrinth and the favors conferred on him by Ariadne, the sword and the thread by which he conquered the Minotaur. Don Quixote like the king-god of the Egyptian ritual, finds hostile forces at the entrance of the cave/labyrinth. With his sword he has to cut "away the brambles at the mouth of the cave. At the noise he made, a great number of crows and jackdaws fluttered out so thickly and with such a rush that they knocked Don Quixote down"(683). In the narrative the Cave of Montesinos is called a dungeon, a burial place, an abyss and a hell. These words have also been used to describe the labyrinth. Once inside the cave, Don Quixote falls into a deep sleep. In his sleep he dreams that he is in front of "a sumptuous royal palace or castle with walls that seemed to be made of clear, transparent crystal" (687). This description is very much like that of the great labyrinth constructed by Amenemhet IV, which Pliny thought could have been a palace; its entrance was also of a clear transparent material.[18]

Inside the crystal palace, Montesinos leads Don Quixote to "a lower hall, all made of alabaster and extremely cool, there stood an elaborately carved marble tomb"; on it Don Quixote saw "a Knight stretched out full length, not of bronze or marble but of flesh and bone"(688). The body, of flesh and bone, not of bronze or marble, corresponds to the body of the dead king-god of the Osirian ritual. The Egyptians believed that the soul of the dead remained in the tombs. When the king-god entered the labyrinth, he communicated with his dead ancestors and received rejuvenating strength from them. Durandarte, a knight errant from a previous age, was thus a similar ancestor or predecessor of Don Quixote, a knight errant of the present age. The ritual procession in the cave of young women, dressed in black, lamenting the living/dead body of Durandarte is reminiscent of the processions and dances with lamentations in the annual rite of the Osirian ritual.

Belerma, the lady love of Durandarte, corresponds to the wife of the king-god in the Egyptian ritual. The women in the Cave of Montesinos wear white turbans in the Turkish style, a headdress that obviously evokes the Middle East. The enchantment of the people in the cave is another point of contact between the cave and the labyrinth because enchantments and magic were part of the ritual at the center of the labyrinth.

The beloved of the king-god played a part in the ritual, as does Dulcinea in the Cave of Montesinos. Dulcinea is enchanted and, with two other peasant girls, she roams the cave "capering and frisking like she-goats" (692). This capering and frisking evoke the ritual dance of the labyrinth, and the goats, animals with horns, the bull at the center of the labyrinth. In some archaeological excavations, stamps and coins have been found with the head of the king-god or a bull or animal with horns (representative of the king-god because they were considered sacred animals) at the center of a labyrinth design. These coins where thought to have been magical symbols or to have had a protective value.[19] Some

similar motive could be the reason that a young girl asks Don Quixote for
a dozen coins (694).

Montesinos and the stay in the cave renew Don Quixote's strength.
Montesinos tells him that he is a grand knight errant and inspires him to
pursue with greater vigor his career as a knight. When Don Quixote
awakens, he finds himself outside the cave, and he appears newly invigorated. Although Sancho assures him that he has been in the cave only a
little more than an hour, Quixote insists that in his dream three days have
elapsed—the three days of the death and resurrection myth.

To recapitulate then, the ritual of the labyrinth is a rite of initiation
and renovation. The Egyptian king-god enters the labyrinth and experiences death and renewal. The resurrection takes place on the third day.
This is almost precisely what occurs to Don Quixote in the Cave of
Montesinos. Mystery, magic, death, as well as elements of the fantastic
are present in both cases. The double, mirrored image at the center if the
cervantine labyrinth is Don Quixote/Quijano. The episodes of the Sierra
Morena and the Cave of Montesinos suggest aspects of the myth of
Osiris and the labyrinth. At the same time, they represent a microscopic
vision of the text *Don Quixote.* Alonso Quijano descends into the labyrinthical depths of himself, from which emerges Don Quixote. The adventures that he encounters are the rites of initiation and of renovating
death at the center of the labyrinth. At the end of the Quixote adventures,
Alonso Quijano re-emerges. He is a wiser Quijano because he has confronted his mirrored self and has conquered it.

Don Quixote has preoccupied scholars since its creation because of
its form and its complex hero; they have led to multiple interpretations
and regerminations of the work, which are at times paradoxical and of
course labyrinthical. Alonso Quijano, Don Quixote, is immortalized in a
new myth that has been repeated since the seventeenth century: the
labyrinthical myth of *Don Quixote.*

"The House of Asterion" and the Labyrinth

In this century, the image of the labyrinth, and the "double" or
"other" at its center, have experienced a revival in literature, as have
other ancient classical myths. The recognized father of contemporary
Latin American literature, Jorge Luis Borges (1899-1985), became obsessed
with the labyrinth as myth and structure. For Borges, this structure be-

comes an emblem for the modern world. Borges has become famous for creating his own labyrinths of time and space, and fiction within fiction. His obsession with the "other" and his metaphysical questioning leads him back to the ancient myth of Osiris and the figure of the Minotaur. In two companion poems, "The Labyrinth" and "Labyrinth," Borges gives us two views of the labyrinth. In the first the labyrinth is the center of a much awaited death, a death related to the encounter with the "other":

> I know that hidden in the shadows there/lurks another, whose task is to exhaust/ the loneliness that braids and weaves this hell,/ to crave my blood, and to fatten on my death./ We seek each other. Oh, if only this/ were the last day of our antithesis![20]

This poem presents the labyrinth as life, and its end a much awaited death. Unlike the myth of Osiris, there is no resurrection or renewal, only death. The death occurs when the "other" is encountered. In the Osirian ritual, the "other" is the sacrificed bull that represents the king-god. In the poem, the "other" is an unknown, a double that is feared yet yearned for. It is a double that devours and bellows, as does the Minotaur of the Cretan myth. In this sense, this labyrinth is close to the Cretan labyrinth—but not really. In Borges, the Minotaur is not a monster. He is both monster and victim. The Minotaur is man, and the labyrinth the world he inhabits.

This is also the view presented in "The House of Asterion," where we encounter the Minotaur from within. The narration is in the first person, and we do not at first perceive that the narrator is the Minotaur himself. The point of view of the Cretan myth has been turned around. We are made to relate to the creature, not to his victim. The epigraph that begins the story is an excerpt from Apollodorus: "And the Queen gave birth to a child who was called Asterion."[21]

There is no mention of the monstrous shape of the child, no clue as to his unnatural conception. He is simply "Asterion," the name Ovid gave to the Minotaur. Without this previous knowledge, one would discover the nature of the speaker only gradually, piecing together the clues, and having one's suspicion confirmed at the end, when Theseus comments to Ariadne: "Would you believe it, Ariadne?. . . The Minotaur hardly defended himself."[22]

The ambivalence Borges creates by using the lesser-known name, Asterion, and the word "house" in the title, instead of "labyrinth," is directed at lessening the distance between the reader and the creature. The reader is not presented with the mythological Minotaur—the monster, half-man half-bull, who feeds on human flesh. We are presented instead with a sad, perplexed, pensive, infantile Minotaur. He does not inspire fear, but on the contrary, pity. He is trapped, but not in a physical prison. His prison is the prison of his thoughts, a prison that he has chosen, inasmuch as the doors of his house are open and he is free to leave if he wishes. He opts to remain in the labyrinth, even if doing so means condemning himself to solitude and monotony:

> Another ridiculous falsehood has it that I,/Asterion, am a prisoner. Shall I repeat/ there are no locked doors, shall I add that/ there are no locks? Besides, one afternoon/ I did step into the street; if I returned/ before night, I did so because of the fear/ that the faces of the common people inspired/ in me (138).

The Minotaur is afraid of what is outside his house, outside of his world. That is why he is a prisoner. He is also a bit of a snob. He reminds the reader that he is the son of a queen and that he is unique. His royal ancestry connects him with the Egyptian king-god, as does his voluntary inhabitation of the labyrinth. The labyrinth of ancient Egypt, as we have said, was probably temple, palace and tomb. In a similar way, the House of Asterion fulfills the same functions. It is his palace and also a temple, because a sacrificial ritual is performed there regularly. It is also his tomb. When talking about his house, he says that there is none like it and denies the existence of a similar house in Egypt—yet another allusion to the Egyptian labyrinth.

The ritual that occurs in the house of Asterion is reminiscent of both Osirian and Cretan ritual. Nine youths arrive every nine years so that Asterion "can deliver them from all evil" (140). Asterion, with these words, changes the violent act of their deaths into a redemption, which is at the same time what he hopes for himself. The sacrifice of the youths is similar to that of the Cretan myth, but the theme of death and resurrection reverts back to the more ancient myth of Osiris. Asterion delivers his victims from the evil of life. He in turn expects to be redeemed from his loneliness:

> my loneliness does not pain me, because I know/ my redeemer
> lives and he will finally rise above/ the dust. . . . I hope he will
> take me to a place/ with fewer galleries and fewer doors.
> What/ will my redeemer be like? I ask myself. Will he be a bull
> or a man? Will/ he perhaps be a bull/ with the face of a man?
> Or will he be like me? [23]

The redeemer is the "other" of Borges' poem "The Labyrinth." He is
the awaited one. It is a bleak redemption, far removed from the joyous
resurrection of the Osirian myth. The redemption is death by the sword of
Theseus. Yet Borges goes even further in the destruction of the myth, in
his second poem, "Labyrinth." Here he offers not even the hope of encountering the "other" and the yearned death at his hands:

> Forget the onslaught/ of the bull that is a man and whose/
> strange and plural form haunts the tangle/ of unending inter-
> woven stone./ He does not exist. In the black dusk/ hope not
> even for the savage beast.[24]

The Minotaur in "The House of Asterion" is a symbol for modern
man—the monster/victim at the center of the labyrinth, confused, alienated, and imprisoned by the modern world. He has no hope of renewal,
or of resurrection, or of redemption. The myth of Osiris and the Cretan
myth of the Minotaur are transformed by Cervantes in *Don Quixote*, and
in literary works by many other writers. In Borges, the myth is not only
transformed, it is also parodied, and ultimately destroyed. The world is
itself a labyrinth, and its inhabitants are confronted with its bifurcations,
twisted paths, wrong turns, dead ends, and eternally hopeless wanderings. There is no exit and no hope, not even that of "the savage beast"
and death.

Notes

[1] Jorge Luis Borges and Margarita Guerrero, *Manual de Zoología Fantástica* (Mexico: Fondo de Cultura Económica, 1975), p. 102.

[2] O. Kimball Armayor, *Herodotus' Autopsy of the Fayoum: Lake Moeris and the Labyrinth of Egypt* (Amsterdam: J. C. Gieben, 1985), p. 135.

[3] See C. N. Deeds, "The Labyrinth," *The Labyrinth: Further Studies in the Relation between Myth and Ritual in the Ancient World*, ed. S. H. Hooke (New York: The Macmillan Company, 1935), pp. 30-35.

[4] See Penelope Reed Doob, *The Idea of the Labyrinth from Classical Antiquity Through the Middle Ages* (Ithaca: Cornell University Press, 1990), pp. 157-158.

[5] See Deeds, p. 4.

[6] See Deeds, pp. 23-25.

[7] See Deeds, pp. 41-42.

[8] See Deeds, pp. 30-32.

[9] Salvador Jiménez Fajardo, "The Sierra Morena as Labyrinth in *Don Quixote*," *MLN* 99 (1984), pp. 214- 234.

[10] Miguel de Cervantes Saavedra, *Don Quixote of La Mancha*, trans. Walter Starkie (London: MacMillan and Company, 1957), p. 252. All subsequent quotations come from this edition, and will be followed by the page number of the material cited.

[11] See Deeds, p. 30.

[12] Augustin Redondo, "El proceso iniciativo en el episodio de la Cueva de Montesinos del Quijote," *Cervantes: su obra y su mundo*, dirección, Manuel Criado de Val (Madrid: EDI-6, S.A., 1981), pp. 750-53.

[13] See Redondo, p. 749.

[14] See Redondo, p. 755.

[15] See Deeds, p. 36.

[16] See Deeds, p. 27.

[17] See Deeds, pp. 22-23.

[18] See Deeds, p. 19.

[19] See Deeds, pp. 6-11.

[20] Jorge Luis Borges, "The Labyrinth," trans. John Updike, in *In Praise of Darkness,* ed. Norman Thomas di Giovanni (New York: E. P. Dutton and Co., 1974), p. 37.

[21] Jorge Luis Borges, "The House of Asterion," in *Labyrinths: Selected Stories and other Writings,* ed. Donald A. Yates and James E. Irby (New York: New Directions, 1964), p.138.

[22] Borges, "The House of Asterion," p. 140.

[23] Borges, "The House of Asterion," p. 140.

[24] Borges, "The Labyrinth," p. 39.

Erich Wolfgang Skwara

Don Juan as Myth

Excerpts from the novel *Plague in Siena* by Erich Wolfgang Skwara, translated by Derk Wynand. *Pest in Siena* (German title) was originally published in 1976; subsequent definitive German edition by Ullstein Verlag, Berlin, 1983. English translation to be published in 1992 by Ariadne Press, Riverside, California. *For my dead* was translated by H.F. Broch de Rothermann.

for my dead

When
you switch off the light,
within you
the stars arise
all around.

They draw blood
from the presence
of undoable
bodies.

But you,
you hunt what is falling,
you ravish
blazing cheeks.

You, a stranger,
seek
life and hand.

He was leaning over the rail of the boat. Half on solid footing, half hanging over the waves, almost in a horizontal position, he surrendered his body to the arbitrariness of the water, to these intimations of sinking. He was on his way yet remained motionless. He had already left his Venice too often just to be able to escape from this city. As everywhere else, Don Juan was at home here too, and as everywhere else he was at home nowhere. The ride across the lagoon revealed to him new insights: outlooks really, across the sea, over the banks, and he perceived the curvature of the earth from the diagonal view of his nearly horizontal body. He finally had a presentiment of the patience that the water has to achieve to join itself into a sphere, and he received knowledge of the accumulated tension that inheres in creation so that it doesn't collapse into fragments.

But this knowledge adorned Don Juan, and people were friendly toward him so long as they didn't know his name. He happened to meet young women and to sense how easy it would be to bring his old arts of seduction into practice again in this world. But then he remembered that people are always much too young; the women's youth caused him pain, and with a sigh he let the beautiful beings pass. He knew that all devotion and all talent the others had for loving could be nothing but a game in his life, heavy breathing, while he would have liked to become vulnerable finally in closeness to another. An ambition to become smaller filled him. But he had never mastered devotion, and neither did he have to die. We calculate only inaccurately how old Don Juan is today, would have to be today, but we know from dependable sources that he was one of the few survivors of the great plague in Siena, and we know also that he had maintained good relations with the Saracens in Moorish Spain. Historical events encompass Don Juan like fences. They speak their own language.

Don Juan met people, but he didn't need encounters. What he needed was the one encounter, a certainty of loving, but he failed miserably in the satisfaction of this particular hunger. He learned to see that in all the centuries he hadn't obtained the slightest knowledge of the soul. No worse psychologist existed than Don Juan. He had certainly acquired a rough understanding of his victims, but he didn't know human beings. They remained as unpredictable for him as for all of us.

*

He had really aged. He had finally run through the ordinary phases of his life, which are spread out for us in literature, and nothing had remained except possibly a trace of disgust and of longing for purity. He consoled himself with the idea that true innocence wasn't the childlike kind but what is gained only through living, and in his exhaustion he flirted with this speculation. At the same time Don Juan distrusted his convictions and, now that he was getting old, he was certain of only one thing, namely of having led a chaste life. To be sure, he couldn't deny that he had seduced 1003 women and girls in Spain alone, but in the new and better balance that Don Juan was beginning to establish for himself, the women's bodies turned into cold walls of cloisters. His early immoderation had been a kind of incorruptibility that's somewhat difficult to understand. For the first time Don Juan was longing for his first love in order to escape his loneliness.

He knew he was in a hurry and that this love that he needed to find could still give some meaning to his life after all, a meaning that it had lacked up to now. He even intended to agree to the stipulations of love; he wanted to become shy, embarrassed, anxious, simply a different person than he had been before. But above all he finally wanted to learn to cry and not merely to see other people's tears. Don Juan was curious about so-called pure happiness. However, until he had reached the point of longing for the values of simplicity, so much time had already passed that Don Juan was living among us in this century. Like all of us he was compelled to participate in this world, at least with regard to externals. He had a driver's license and used credit cards; he wore suits and ties, of course. Nevertheless, he lived apart and out of touch. Many learned and — still worse — literary works had been written about him. Don Juan had certainly always had to tolerate fabricated books which purported to understand and to see through him, but this flood had become increasingly worse in the last hundred years. Unqualified authors came along more and more frequently who hadn't even known Don Juan in the past. Men of some stature at least had come to an understanding with him, and that was always a consolation. Although even those men had all too often overlooked what mattered; despite all the misinterpretations there was something flattering about being perceived inaccurately and being damned a trifle unjustly through the boldest music by a certain Mr. Wolfgang Mozart. It was acceptable to be sent to hell by Signor da Fonte, but sometimes it hurt that the musical score, too, directed him to hell. However, all these small horrors were overcome by the glory of being a famous European. Should we say having been, because much else had changed in the meantime? Everyone who was still writing about Don Juan reduced him to a pathological case.

But Don Juan was well, had at least recovered his health, and above all he had always been European in spirit. When this Europe was still split into a thousand principalities and kingdoms, he already felt at home in all of them. His life, confusing only in appearance but in reality ordered mathematically, had borne for centuries the seal of great Europeanism and humanism. Don Juan liked to pronounce these words to himself in a low tone when he walked through the streets alone: Europeanism, humanism. The ring of their syllables robbed him of hope. Being a celebrity had a beneficial effect for that very reason.

All too often applause distracts unhappy and depressed people from the menacing clouds. But fame has its shady sides; everyone, almost everyone, misunderstood Don Juan, and it was totally without foundation that he had become an allegory for the skirtchasing rabble. As if it weren't simply a question of who is seducing, who is pulling the strings. Don Juan didn't care about symbols because he was virtually immortal.

Hardly anyone has been informed that Don Juan had tried for centuries to write an autobiography. He didn't want to do it out of vanity but to snatch the lie from the mouths of the intruders who made his life the titles of their books. Every time he had begun to write, however, the first pages had immediately withered in his hands. He was a virtuoso in giving pleasure to the bodies of others, but just because he knew about lust and joy, his hands recoiled from the boredom of the written record. Secondhand living was not for Don Juan. Nevertheless, he would have liked to know that his affairs were in order and would have liked to place the memory of his crystal-clear life into just hands. But just hands are not the hands of artists nor the hands of scholars, certainly not the hands of love. Don Juan knew that, but he didn't want to draw the consequence of resignation so long as he was waiting for his—admittedly quite improbable—transformation into a human being. It depended on a word that could convince him. He was hard to satisfy because he was, we know, an aging man.

*

This day was not nearly over but was already filled with great experiences. In the morning, after Don Juan had drunk his tea on the Piazza, as always at the Caffè Florian in the room with the putti lamps, and when all of the city's bells suddenly began to ring under the pretext of a completed hour, he sensed that an important day was in the making. Among these sounds of bells flowing from all directions, even dissonance turned into harmony. The former greatness of this city, which Don Juan had shared and which was preserved visually in his memory as if related to the Holy Grail, seemed to have been preserved into this century only in the bells of the churches on the islands and in the freedom of their ringing. A beneficent spirit, a gentle breeze, which promised a favorable journey to humankind and their ships, emanated from the vibrations that rang across the lagoon.

In that hour Don Juan had discarded all recollections, the orgiastic ones and the spiritualized ones. The city of Venice, which he thought he had exhausted, was still preserving everything for him: after its fables, now its reality.

On the boat he cultivated his unreal nausea. While he watched the foaming water being cut into green streaks like fish gliding past and being lost in the boat's wake, he was dreaming, though wide awake, of the great contract, of the compromise that was agreed upon here silently but also very openly. The hard and the soft yielded to each other, both gave up a little of their souls, and the result was this gliding that enabled the spirit to stretch out horizontally in unison with a body and to play. That was surely something, oh yes, and Don Juan, becoming more daring now, considered whether all that happens in and outside the world didn't depend on a compromise with harshness and whether the necessity of creation wasn't this: to weaken, to harmonize more softly, to make things more fluid, in short to moderate.

When he leaned over the side of the boat, he could enjoy the gliding along and the cool wind like precious nourishment. But what if, he thought, the boat runs into a sandbank or sinks? The quiet day will end in horror, people will scream and sink as they scream, pieces of wreckage will float on without feeling. The wind won't be caressing the frail people any longer, it won't dishevel our hair any more because with the death of one there really won't be any humans left.

Don Juan feared everything that moved fast. The gentle getting-ahead-of-oneself, the seductive hurrying that turns malicious, could lose its own structure before it found time to bid farewell. Dying wasn't really bad if it only allowed bidding farewell in advance. An airplane and a human face were subject to the same laws, and they were beautiful if they only remained themselves. So long as the gentle gliding was preserved, the world was saved too. But with increasing frequency, crude acts of violence were committed everywhere, which exhausted Don Juan even if he was only reading about them in his newspaper. Gentleness seemed to be vanishing, and its disappearance threatened Don Juan's existence. He was determined to continue, to go on living as long as water remained soft and permitted sinking.

In the past he had found compensation for harshness in the soft bodies of women, then later in music, but now Don Juan learned to understand that the softness that matters doesn't set any conditions. The world with its corners and edges was above all soft. Softness could be found in gaps and unevenness rather than on the easily travelled streets. That's why Don Juan no longer plunged deeply into art and music exclusively but also into confusing cities, statistics, and ordinary people. Everywhere he suddenly found himself in tune, and he comprehended that the conditions for harmony expand if we expand ourselves. He no longer loved youth in order to sleep with them but for the sake of that gentleness that was lacking in their hearts, and because it was only a question of seeing the faint lines in their faces sink deeper, become engraved, and trickle into life through living.

When the boat glided past a dead dog floating in the water, Don Juan found nothing about the animal ugly. The spongy cadaver proved that here solid material was patiently becoming softer, and what proof was more valid for this experience than death? So the passengers finally reached the bank, where the captain docked with routine care. The images penetrated still more deeply into Don Juan as he stepped onto firm ground again.

*

He met the girl and spoke with her — a few sentences, a few overtures, allusions to the summer festival.

For the summer festival, the girl had invited guests who knew the great sadness in which the gardens were enveloped. The girl had not merely planned her summer festival; she had rather raised it as others bring up their children, with all possible care, with all possible love. When the summer festival finally took place, when it rolled across the stage of the garden, the laughter was too loud and too distinct. The girl had had to recognize that some guests weren't sad: these happy ones ruined the celebration. "Don Juan should be content that he did not appear at the festival," said the girl. "The shabby pleasure of those thoughtless guests had actually set the flowers ablaze. Up to today nobody could find out who had perished at the summer festival. The next morning only ashes and daylight had remained, and nobody knew who was hidden in there. Nor was it possible to look around for survivors because the crowd had dispersed when the flames were flying highest. The summer festival had turned into the darkest night," said the girl, with a voice lacking tone.

But Don Juan replied that he had more friendly thoughts about the summer festival and that he had enjoyed very much being one of the guests. He had worn his silk suit and had observed precisely how pleasure had ignited the flowers. It had been the fault of the flowers, not a crime committed by pleasure. He said that the flowers had refused for a long time the rain of cheerfulness; they burned brightly for that reason only. The summer festival had been splendid, a success even for the dead. But the girl cried and didn't believe a word of it.

Don Juan was glad to see the beautiful hostess again. During the summer festival she had been too busy to find time for conversation. They had merely noticed each other so fleetingly that the young girl had already forgotten the old man. But this forgetting is not accomplished so quickly in the other direction. Now there was a nice opportunity to walk a short distance together.

*

>>It shouldn't astonish you that we know each other only in passing: we all know each other only slightly. For example, when I walk around the lake, I wonder whether there is any human being at all that I know better than you, my girl, my so brief acquaintance. I think about the summer festival too when I walk around the lake. And because I'm getting older, the lake seems to me bigger and bigger in circumference, whereas my life appears to me narrower and narrower. The curves stretch out into straight lines. Nobody knows my lake, Lake Compounce; before anyone finds it and gets to know it, its waters will have dried up.

>>I have bathed in Lake Compounce. I didn't take the warning about poisonous snakes seriously. I swam in the middle of the lake and struggled back onto land again at a different place. Wherever I approached the bank, I found the rails of a miniature train and beyond that the big forest. Anyone who would like to find Lake Compounce needs

good maps and good eyes. But I am on intimate terms with my lake and imagine that I know it better than even Sevilla, my hometown. Lake Compounce really belongs to me.

>>Why do I mention the lake? Because it's so terribly unimportant, because I want to hold onto it, because it should be important. Maria Obolensky, whose love I never knew, unfortunately didn't know the lake. She would surely have liked it. Nevertheless, I fear sometimes that I stray into madness, that Maria Obolensky wouldn't have accepted me or the lake into her life. She kept everything inside her and didn't need anyone. But Lake Compounce needed me. People have always refused to travel to the lake with me. Most of them called it boring, but a few admitted the real reason: they considered Lake Compounce dangerous. They knew that its waters put me into a sad mood. The banks of the lake were actually very closely associated with the death that I didn't die. I was Lake Compounce; it was one with me. Today, when for a long time I haven't been the real me any more, when I have almost forgotten this me, only this lake remains me from now on. It has a strange reflecting surface that preserves what is lost. Nobody who is unwilling to accept permanency should bend over Lake Compounce.

>>I admit that I have rarely told about that over there, about my real country, and I will preserve the "over there" for myself from now on too. I will keep quiet. It annoys me, to be sure, that public opinion wants to keep me in Spain right up to this very day although I have suffered through only a tiny part of my lust in Spain. Spain, this wretched proud land, means to me only my dusty childhood, my palace that's been lost for centuries. Certainly the people in Sevilla still point out my tavern, but couldn't any inn in the world be my tavern? I have stopped everywhere.

>>The roads avoid Lake Compounce, of course, and anyone who wants to go down to the bank has to find the right approach. A sharp left turn which even the skilled driver takes too fast again and again. Then the tires squeal and throw the stones up high. Using the access road is forbidden, and most people probably turn back because of the no-trespassing sign. To reach the lake you need a little audacity, you need a little courage.

>>Then the road ends in the amusement park. A Ferris wheel rises high into the air behind the low booths. The haunted house is barred by padlocks, like everything else. The restaurant is built entirely of boards, which wait hungrily for a bolt of lightning. The lake stretches out behind

that. Its waves are only suggested; their splashing shows little enthusiasm. Nobody celebrates major festivals here any more, but the place carries within itself the possibilities of holding a festival. A few keys should suffice to unlock the huts. A few burning torches to chase away rats and spiders and a few cans of fresh paint to repaint a marvelous world should do. The festival would have to dim the beauty of the lake. But Lake Compounce lies in shade; the mountains are too close and too high. By three in the afternoon the sun sinks behind the woods.

>>Long ago, Indians lived there. According to legend their princess drowned in the lake. The people in the vicinity of the lake know this story, but they hardly know the road to the water.

>>As a destitute newcomer I didn't own a vehicle to get to the lake. So I started to hike, hour after hour, always alone. But footsteps don't lead to anything. Motorists stared at me; dogs ran after me furiously. There were neither fences nor boundaries; everyone lives exposed there. After I had tired myself out with walking, the low sun forced me to stop. I looked around and froze; I was still at the same point. Despite that, I had to brave the walk back, many hours in darkness. When I finally reached my bed, I fell asleep in tears.

>>I would have liked to meet that princess. I loved the quiet lake as her second, larger body. Sleeping alone is a torment if you hear the clock tick. But most people are blind and deaf; they don't recognize the curse of time wasted.

>>The first time I grasped the lake I finally knew where I was meant to be. That September was outrageously hot, and Lake Compounce soothed me. The insanity of walking by myself received its sense around the banks of the lake. Not all is lost in a country where there's a Lake Compounce. A world in which walking remains futile will definitely drive anyone crazy who can't find the lake. But the lake had saved my life. I could walk only on the railroad track because there was no other open space in the forest. The train on the narrow track had probably amused children in the past. A ride around this lake may have cost a quarter, and it was worth it, worth it.

*

>>Behind this forest rise the mountains—rugged and rocky, and behind them again the Sunday hunters are aiming their guns at wild ducks. One cringes at every shot. Today this lake has played its role to the

end. I will prove my gratitude to it. I had completed the circuit again and again on my own feet, had reached the Ferris wheel, my starting point. My steps had become steps again in defiance of the continent. Each circuit of the lake validated a feeling, and every arrival validated a lonely pleasure, until I finally recognized the car that came to pick me up and take me back to the others, who called my walks insanity, who never understood my arrivals.

>>When the mute encounters remained on the streets as bluish smoke, I thought of the girl while I was accustomed to the cold. There are no proofs of her death, as there is also no evidence of her life. Words fail, and mathematical formulas fail. A diagram of her life lacks the green of the commonest trees. Maybe anyone who places flowers on her stony arm is violating the right of someone closer. Thus Maria Obolensky lives on, and she hasn't cried or laughed for so many years. "She and I and what we miss: pardon this *we*, my girl."

>>Everything about this story is correct with the single exception that I will remember it and tell it. It is probably a mistake to tell it. Besides, I wouldn't like to remember anything, anything at all, and certainly not this story. I would like to spare myself and my topic, but in this instance I don't matter, and certainly the weakness of sparing doesn't matter either.

>>Because less and less remains expressible, because a word can hardly exist any more, our languages become poorer, but our silence doesn't become richer. We search again for possibilities of reaching Maria Obolensky, and we search for new dignity to qualify as her friend. But the winged seeds fall from the cypresses, fall and explode— a sharp sound that would be impossible to locate, and nothing more is left for us.

>>There had been painters; poets had lived. Some had composed music; others had produced thoughts. We learn these accusations far and wide in our schools, and the cemetery proves these propositions. People have lived who dined on terraces in the evening, where the wind cooled their brows. The terraces were constructed of marble, and the gardens displayed themselves with grace. We have heard this a hundred times, and we have also believed it. At that time the aroma of the flowers was unquestioned, and even love wasn't always denied. School matter, fear of a test.

>>Maria Obolensky believed in words that made her eyes larger and her lips softer. We don't know whether she could kiss well. Maybe

she wasn't a technician of love; after all, she died at eighteen, but she surely possessed a certain talent for tenderness. Her softness was appropriate for the city in which she died. To be born in Russia and to die at eighteen in Rome produced a notable obituary in the newspapers even then.

>>The small emptiness that her dying tore open lasted eternally and yet was soon filled. We may presume discreetly that the sculpture of the girl at her grave, this respectable work of art, was like a tooth-filling for the sadness of those left behind, silencing the pain quickly. But we may likewise assume that nobody really knew the girl. People like her remain aloof. Maybe her life was meaningless; maybe it was also of the greatest importance. Thus you could get into a dispute about Maria Obolensky. But who would be helping her by quarreling over her? And finally a person would have to love her to quarrel about her. Who could love her, though, since no one at all knows her? Who knows Maria Obolensky? Who knows her anyway?

>>To find her grave, a sister would have to come along who doesn't know anything about their kinship. Only where silence lives is there a sudden flash of lightning that sets something on fire. Sometimes the lightning, too, strives for a reflection of speech. One should think that a bloodline is not dead while a sister still lives. However, the flowers around Maria Obolensky wilt, and the marble of the sculpture fades. The question about the right moment withers before the face of time.

>>If I, Don Juan, live longer than others, if I'm immortal to small minds, that's only because I have wasted my life and because dissipation is eternal. A person must undertake evil and senseless things to be certain of permanence. Now, while I talk about Maria Obolensky, about the love that was missed, I feel my age already, my very imminent death. Just thinking seriously is enough to cause death. How serious, then, when we start doing something serious. . ., I'm thinking of this girl again. She died because she was ready for love; her face of marble betrays the readiness, but I live because I'm incapable of devotion. If my crime of belatedness didn't stand between us, your monument would be without flowers now.

>>Maria Obolensky: this forbidden thought, this repetitious mention of her name, is taking place behind the wall that separates her grave from the noisy street. A few more years and this wall will be torn down too. Man builds on the world really only to be able to destroy it more successfully. To raze a cemetery is a child's game, simpler than destroying a

city. Where the living who lack all self-restraint begin to scream inarticulately, the dead remain silent, of course. Maria Obolensky, who says much, would keep silent too if someone moved her grave away. That is the great and only superiority of the dead and the most momentous distinction between them and us, that they don't gripe when something insignificant happens.

>>At her grave, a sound is sometimes audible that is not seeking communication. It is imprecise and resembles the sighing of lovers. Of course it's the humming of the dead, who cuddle into this earth, which is theirs, and it welcomes us tenderly without conditions because we don't matter to it. The humming of the dead soothes us.

>>Where Vincent, the painter, another friend that I have missed, where this Vincent had the strength to despair of some stars and cypresses, Maria Obolensky musters only the weakness of being without motion and without longing. Nevertheless, strong death has nothing to do with weakness.

>>Vincent's world hadn't turned dark suddenly; his mind darkens here today, looks for shadows among the unbearable stars, whereas Maria Obolensky died only that one time. Poor victims of their rotting aristocratic lungs, those dedicated to death became so marvelously beautiful, and their demise sounded like chamber music. Maria Obolensky's dying hardly applied the cosmetic of despair. If we no longer cry about her today, it's only because our grief has become greater than her absence. That our grief has become greater. . ., for some words there is no measure, and there will soon be no mouth any more to call after the dead.

>>The aged grandee dreams of Maria Obolensky as his lover. The girl is still loyal to us. Artificial flowers are still blooming at her grave. This tastelessness is a good sign.

>>And don't fear the familiar *Du!* I will definitely not become maudlin and cry; I will definitely not demand substance. At the most we'll stroke your stone hair, but life and caresses are too impatient and brief to threaten your marble. Although we know that every stroking hand converts a tiny particle of marble to dust and steals it away, the amount lost doesn't increase fast enough to endanger your hair. Thieves are harmless, Maria Obolensky; only the disinterested are dangerous, who don't stroke you, who let the dust grow on you.

>>I perceive that I have surrendered hopelessly to these words, which are not loyal and which betray me. Because we can't cry, because

we can't love, we want to talk and find language to justify ourselves for what makes us go mute. I notice on the streets that human beings are becoming more beautiful, to be sure, that my body craves them, but that relationships to human beings are becoming uglier and more absurd. I do desire these bodies, but if I had them, I wouldn't know what to do with them. I possessed many people; some I had to besiege for a long time; they were beautiful victories for me, but they don't carry any weight in my memory. I, Don Juan, have no memories; as far as Maria Obolensky is concerned, I have missed her and everything.

* * *

Rushing over the fields, a ruddy man approached, silently as a wing-beat; more ugly than pleasant, he did not look like anyone in particular; though exhausted and breathless from hurrying, he began to speak at once.

>>Wherever we turn—limits, increasing bitterness— but something within us won't be deceived, won't be killed, and hence, wherever we turn—sweetly flowing life, radiance everywhere that we take in and miss for all that. I haven't painted my real pictures. Standing on the main square in Ghent, streaking through the fields in Provence, are intermediate phases, and there is no fundamental phase. The grief killing us is an intermediate phase, and consider this: discotheques, that easy music, that extreme grief so popular and current, is only an intermediate phase. Limits: painting.

Disguised, Don Juan was unsure whether he had really fled the closed sanatorium or not. What this man in front of him said, or rather, what this man poured forth, could no doubt be called right, correct, but nevertheless — or for that very reason — remained hospital speech, institutional jargon.

>>And we're in the middle of my craft, of the little lines I've drawn, which have become efficacious without my agency. All of us must realize that it's a matter of describing unbearable circumstances, of natural riddles, the enumeration of which is the only thing we still have to do. You assume I don't know you, but you're wrong, Don Juan, for I know you very well. Not only did we mutually feel the southern fall wind, which the wine-growers love as they fear it, but we also heard the same stories: Spanish, Moorish, desert tales, and among all of these, the one story that

concerns you—you, good sir—about the small tavern with the dark wal-
nut benches. You look at me, you stare with astonishment, but you
shouldn't be astonished, since I've already confessed that I failed to paint
the true pictures, just as you did. Yes, I'm a painter, and I often use this
little word, yes, which makes you flinch, flinch time and again. . . . I em-
ploy this little word "yes" at the beginning, in the middle, at the end of
sentences, for I've forfeited the right to a "no" long ago, in those days not
too far from Paris, in Auvers-sur-Oise. It was quite a valid no, a long-
term contract, much too long for an artist in any case. An artist —and
aren't we both artists, good sir? — shouldn't enter into such permanent
contracts. But what's done is done, and so we're standing face to face
here, you and I, having come out of the night of fugitives into the day of
the frustrated. My pictures hang in The Hague, hang in Arnhem, hang all
over the planet, yet most of my pictures are hoarded in Amsterdam. I've
appeared widely for some time. Basically, Don Juan, you too are a
painter. You only think you're better than that, and you tense your neck
muscles for a reply. Save your reply, good sir, and believe me: you too are
a painter. I've seen the faces twisted with joy, and also the souls twisted
with pain, which bore your insignias, in all the museums to which I — to
which the likes of us — have access. Although your fame, Don Juan, is
known to all, you know little about it; you can't analyze your own significance. Maybe that explains your purity.

The one who spoke, spoke wildly, but the style of his speech led Don
Juan to believe that he was dealing with a man of his own stature. So he
listened out of politeness. With the silence of a Spanish grandee, the thin
smile of one drowned in lust, and the candid gaze of a knight of the Grail,
he listened to the stranger's words.

>>The function of lighthouses bothers me, this myth of their light.
Lighthouses, they say, still cast their light when we, you or I, walk
through city streets or when we've long lost sight of the shore.
Lighthouses are said to be concerned with salvation. Here we're dealing
with belief once more, which has come hard to me all my life, especially in
the days when I was still preaching. Those doubts about the blowing
grass, whose gentle dancing weighs more than unshakeable certainty.
Whether we consider the certainty of God or merely the certainty of our
brush-strokes, neither of them counts any more, nor anything else, once
we park on the dunes and let the wind freeze us in. Today, everyone can
afford to watch the setting sun's last mimicry in his own fashion, as a fan,

as a poet—whatever— because we're backed up by computers we don't consistently believe in, while we consistently make them indispensable.

His words rang with familiarity. The morning had advanced; the sun maintained its course toward the zenith.

>>Sheet-lightning, good sir, wading through life, cold-water treatment for the soul, lightning-quick emigration. You or I — and it's a kind of bond — will have to say no to darkness so long as we're dead, so long as we live. Say no to it and to the clouds, these monstrous perversions on the pale horizon. . ., sunsets as in America . . ., I wonder. . . whether stars and liberation aren't one and the same. . ., liberation being a somewhat more ordinary death. But this question leads to the empty chair with candle that's in Amsterdam now.

>>When Paul left me, going away from Arles, going back into his despair, because my own didn't have room for two, an empty chair remained behind, an empty chair and a great deal of night. But chairs don't want to be empty; they cry out for people to sit on them and grow older on them. That's why Paul left a candle behind, and a book as well: two signs of a solitude even greater than mine was and is no longer. . . . The candle was threatened by the icy pain of Paul's departure. Thus I had to paint the candle, and the book too, and the chair on which both lay. . ., and so saved the candle from being blown out. Now the candle glows, and its light finally lit my way to Auvers-sur-Oise, that glowing point which taught me how to say no and to avoid empty chairs in the future. But, good sir, though it seems easy to say now, it's not. What's terrible after a long journey is the inevitable arrival in some room, having to set foot in the hostel or the destination, and this arrival frightens us so much that we secretly hope for an accident, some tragedy that will spare us the arrival in the room.

>>I, too, the renowned fugitive answered, know what it is to listen for the tragedy, know what it is to wait for some fatal disease. When I was staying at the sanatorium from which I've just. . . departed to hurry toward our chance encounter, I saw faces, saw evenings looming, quivering with tension. I should have observed them and fixed their form, but I thought there was still time. Repeatedly, I began to write, but I stopped just as often. Now, after my terrible night march, I'm tired. Wherever I turn —you see, caballero, your speech has become my speech; your paintings are embellished by the frame of my past —wherever I turn, I see fields, I see plains, I see no possibilities for a beginner. In the suitcase I'm

carrying, there are manuscripts certainly, successful beginnings, contem-
plated torsos, but now that everything's at hand— will, thought, reader
and light— my work is missing its base; I can't find the desk anywhere.

So they talked to each other in riddles, taking a turn they did not
choose, that they did not recognize. They listened to each other more at-
tentively now, and yet knew that in the final analysis they were speaking
nonsense, that their journey and their words were leading them further
and further into abstruse impropriety. But one is not called Don Juan and
Vincent with impunity: the judgement carried out against these names
was their grotesque passage not only through various countries, but also
through the centuries. The encounter between the two was no encounter
at all, since personalities such as they were incapable of an encounter.

>>Wherever you begin, it's a bad beginning. Spare me my own
story, my life, which doesn't even consist of strokes, as my pictures. There
are only strokes; even my ravens above the field are two black strokes.
Strokes, too, Saint Remy's silence, that endless silence interrupted only by
laughter.

Now the two reached a tree, a solitary tree in the fields. Vincent
asked for indulgence for his incoherent words, which he thought of as off-
spring of his illness. He was thirsty, he remarked, and he wanted to drink
in the blue sky. But Don Juan, who was a man of the world, preferred
champagne. They thirsted, and neither of them received what he desired.

>>Absorbed in moss and ferns and sky, we lie stretched out here. We
have a yearning that's expressed in fragments of speech, and usually in-
audible, we whisper: names, coffee in summer cups, love, Gulbenkian
Foundation, Reginald Turner, simplicity. . . . We see moths flutter around
candles, and we fear for our dirty brushes that suffer from mange and
have become almost bare. When we consider the oncoming afternoons too
closely, Mozart's music strikes us like death. Whoever looks up into the
tree-tops won't believe in the blossoms, for we don't believe in what's
real. I've painted both, good sir: landscapes that are good and exude
peace, and landscapes that become entangled, that kill us. They're moods,
it's said, humours, but ultimately the two of us know we must take these
moods seriously. All around, wherever I turn, there's the fatal landscape.
I won't be able to record this hour, since I'm too poor a painter for that.
These fields suck me dry. So my work and I are a singular contradiction.

>>Please listen to this story! Once there was a girl who believed
that I had appeared to her in her sleep and had asked her to paint where I

had left off. This girl had a bit of talent; she wanted to become a painter. Now, when I consider that I stopped because there is no going on, then I have to laugh about the girl with the false dream, but on the other hand, I don't know whether I didn't really appear to her in her dream and encourage her to continue. . . . It's possible. Although the likes of us never find successors, the natural creativity of youth sometimes simulates a future for us that's lost before the night is over. Though I entertain no hope, I believe in the dreaming girl then, in her talent, in her reputation, which will ultimately be that of lying in bed with men.

>>Those, good sir, are my walks that, should they take place in the city, lead to the neurologist, whom I beg for Nembutal, even though I know he won't prescribe the begged-for poison. So I demand what's outrageous because I'm completely apathetic. The doctor who says no becomes a man I believe in, one who shies away from me because he's healthy and senses the danger I represent. This danger, which beings like us embody for society, is our great, old-fashioned, burning intensity.

>>Odd, the Spaniard reflected, that this man whose face reminds me of Vincent, must despair of the power of colours, while the wall of fog annihilates me. In both cases, it's not a bright, but a somber death. (Thinking about his past, he realized that his stay at the sanatorium had been wasted. Even at the moment of flight, his situation had become what it had been before. He had to bear the reversal majestically; after all, Don Juan was known as a bon vivant, as an optimist. Marked by a small tree's network of shadows, the beaten man sat there and kept silent, kept silent or talked, both of which amounted to nothing.)

>>These endless possibilities for enjoyment, growing like the universe itself, from which no one who knows about them is excluded. . . . the Spaniard stressed slowly. But then he suddenly trusted the ruddy man, who for his part seemed to have ended his monologue. Because the landscape all around lay waste, waste even if in borrowed fecundity, Don Juan began to talk.

>>You turn your head and see one of those pale faces, like a Spaniard's, like an Italian's, and you go on and don't think, as you once did, that these faces are beautiful. You're standing on the corso of the city Almeria, and you hear intensive bird-song from the palm trees. You remember the stretch of park in front of the Casino in Monte Carlo, where the birds sing even in winter. You think of the oases of Palm Springs, with their yellow and blue hummingbirds. But most of all you think about

Monte Carlo, with its lackluster Casino. As you recall, you entered the gambling halls with your escort, where she immediately became the centre of attention, and felt right at home, as she said, while you, who are not at home in gambling halls, who cannot stand coincidences, urged that you go. Whenever you referred to a light, she, and others, thought they saw darkness; in your life, whenever you mentioned the night, others accused you of denying the light. Through these misunderstandings, you became you.

>>You grew old too quickly, and although the world calls you young, young or immortal —it's all the same— it cannot delude you as to your real age, even if you for your part are an expert in deluding the world, for which you feel no incentive because you're too old.

>>You will travel homeward, and once you've reached your six wooden walls, you'll forget the journey more quickly than the journey will forget you. For you must leave tracks behind—and you know it—and your enemies will continue to hate you by your tracks, as your friends will continue to love you by your tracks. You're alone, and only your tracks find company.

>>In Almeria, here as everywhere else, you live in an expensive four-star hotel, and from fear of the same sun you used to pursue, you've been sitting for days in the gloomy hotel lobby, which is bustling with terrible people. Lost in silence for weeks, you haven't said a word, haven't listened to a word save for the few words with the waiter. In this loud hotel filled with speech, only you are lost in silence. You have the bad habit of muttering to yourself, picked up by degrees, and you're dominated by bad habits. Sometimes you address yourself as "thou" and sometimes as "you": your self-esteem varies. You notice how you're slowly going mad, but that's precisely what you want to be, even if you deny it in the morning.

>>You could step out into the street, onto the broad corso; you have white shoes and silk suits in your suitcase; you could be the most elegant, the most admired man on the corso. Like everyone else here, you could take part in the evening stroll— up the corso on the left, down the corso on the right— and you could cast lecherous glances like everyone else here. If today, a Tuesday, you went out alone, by tomorrow, a Wednesday, you'd be walking arm in arm with a girl. Passionately in love, like everyone here, you'd be able to forget your past; by carrying on with it, you could become younger, but you don't want that. You say you'd have to

witness all the embraces if you took part. You'd have to see that all over the world men search for women and women for men, and you'd have to admit to the lust of children, who are falling into our filth these days. Watching the young lovers looking for a bed, you'd have to include their hollow secrets, their banal wonders in your evening stroll. All that would nauseate you today, even though you yourself have participated in everything for a time, as one of the most convincing, most lively actors. If you walked the corso today, you'd have to scale obstacles, so many that you would not be walking among people, but over rooftops, or higher still, namely in your solitude, which does not pain you, which has become painlessly intolerable. Of all the possibilities, you're safest in the hotel.

>>Of course, you're wondering about all the places you've been, and you ask yourself why. Why did you dine with the world's foremost violinist in San Diego? Why did you listen to "La Boheme" in English in Glasgow? Why do you love Paris, your oyster of silence? Why do you hire a boy prostitute for five pounds in London? Why do you take poison on Capri? And why do you break an engagement in Athens? You settle back in the hotel lobby's easy-chair and don't know the answer. You count your remaining friends and are not astonished. You order tonic water with ice and lemon from the young waiter, and you can be sure you'll get what you want. Unsure as you are, you have the definite certainty that this waiter will hardly disappoint you.

>>Every night, you resolve to return to your room early, to go to bed early. But you never go to bed before midnight, and even then you cannot sleep and get up again. You step to the window and see the stars above and the sea below. You see the harbour, the long sea wall with the lighthouse at its farthest end. Beyond that, you see the so-called open sea, which remains closed to you, however. You would dearly like to go down to the harbour, would like to see the large, rusty ship with the green light on the tip of its mast being pumped dry. Two large pipes suck the oil from the ship's belly into the belly of the harbour wall, into the earth. You would like to stand there and hear the pump pulsing, troubled by no one and heeded by no one, for it is night, for even the sailors are sleeping somewhere now. You want to be there, but you're afraid of the vile smells, the harbour's worldly smells, and above all, you're afraid of the many stray dogs that rove here in the south, diseased and ownerless, that die but spread nausea before they die. For hours, the sight of mangy dogs, like the sight of begging children, gives you the urge to vomit, because the

wretched are repulsive to you, because you feel sorry for the wretched.

>>The rooms are air-conditioned; the telephone is beside the bed. Indeed, you never use it, but you feel the security streaming from this telephone into you. You think about the seductive girls that stick like flies to the bar of the Playboy Nightclub on the hotel's ground-floor. These girls seduce the men, whereupon the men are called seducers. Unsavory, these people who reduce our world to a bar. But waking or dreaming, you see beautiful people, and you think, it would be good to summon them all to your room, but then you think that the beautiful person might be wearing dirty underwear, and already your desire for human contact fades. You walk with your suitcase in your left hand, into an ever-increasing distance, which you cannot cover; emotionlessly interested in your own existence, sometimes trying to solve its riddles, you declare yourself miserably incompetent to do so.

A measure of disillusionment was calculated here, but how does one dispense with this measure? In interrogation and silent periods, in burnt-out candles, in drained bottles, in vertiginous walks? How does one dispense with them? If someone comes by and says something only to fall silent again at once, if someone never repeats anything, the listener begins to doubt his ears. Whether anything at all was said comes into question, or whether in listening we are not being deceived. That is what always happens when someone falls silent, be it Jesus or Shakespeare: what has been spoken silently we retain in our ears, without knowing what we possess in words. The greatest speeches of mankind are all too like the fleeting wind. When great epidemics that exterminate whole nations die away again overnight, then we count the dead, but without really believing in their death. The religion of the nebulous finds its saints then, and the kiss of faith, the attachment to a thou, is treacherous.

Naturally, two men like Vincent and Don Juan, two unrivalled personalities, had never learned the art of discourse. They were great rhetoricians of the soul— dictators in the field of silence— but their tongues remained awkward, and their words were likewise covered in glue. Anyone who was like the two, who could merely hear the two, should not hope for understanding, but quickly board a train and escape to any place whatever. Departure is the only solution; arrival is an impossibility.

Thomas J. Braga

Amazonian Indian Myths
in
Mário de Andrade's *Macunaíma* (1928)

The devastation of the Amazonian rain forest has caused a world-wide uproar and forced people from diverse walks of life and in different parts of the world to take a closer look at a region of Latin America too long neglected, Brazil and the Amazon. Indeed the destruction of the forest and the disappearance of its Amerindian inhabitants along with their myths and legends form part of one single tragedy that has captured the attention of Brazilian authors, from the very beginning of the twentieth century, in their constant search for ethnic identity and national unity. If it is true as the critic Vladimir Propp asserts that "myth is the most precious treasure of a people and that to deprive man of myth is tantamount to depriving him of life itself" (Campos 271), then the defenders of the forest and the protectors of Indian culture have a common cause in their defense of indigenous habitats.

Joseph Campbell in *The Power of Myth* reminds us that "myths" are metaphorical of spiritual potentiality in the human being, and the same powers that animate our life animate the life of the world" (22). It is precisely this emphasis on myth as a "return to origins" that typifies so much of contemporary Latin American literature and has gained for its national literatures, whether written in Spanish or Portuguese, such world renown.

With the publication in Portuguese of *Macunaíma* in 1928, a nondescript work labeled a "rhapsody," that is, a potpourri of subjects taken from national folklore, by its Brazilian author Mário de Andrade (1893-1945), a whole new phase of Latin American fiction was launched. Considered by critics as the most important work of fiction to emerge from Brazilian Modernism, *Macunaíma* was to become the model for what we now call "magic realism" and lead to the boom in the Latin American novel of the 1950's and 1960's.

While in no way pretending to exhaust the subject or even proposing a new interpretation, this essay will shed some light on the subject of Brazilian Amerindian myths by focusing attention on only five characters and allusions, among myriad possibilities, contained in Andrade's masterpiece.

These are: (1) Macunaíma, the mock-heroic folk protagonist without a character, of the Tapanhuma tribe, a tribe of black Indians from the Roraima region of the Amazon, where the Uraricoera River and Brazil, Guyana and Venezuela come together; (2) Ci, Macunaíma's wife, the Empress of the Forests and the Queen of the Amazon women; (3) the muiraquitã, the greenstone amulet in the shape of an alligator given to Macunaíma by Ci as a keepsake; (4) Vei, the vengeful feminine sun who causes Macunaíma to lose the muiraquitã a second time; (5) and finally Venceslau Pietro Pietra, the Peruvian river-trader syncretized with Piaimã, the evil giant, a comic figure, an eater of men and a collector of stones, into whose hands the precious muiraquitã has fallen.

Drawing upon the three major elements that form the Brazilian racial heritage—namely, the Amerindian, the European and the African—Andrade syncretizes native myths in an attempt to depict allegorically the multifaceted Brazilian national character.

In order fully to understand the scope of *Macunaíma* and its exalted position in the canon of Brazilian literature, it is important to keep in mind both the time period in which it was written and its major source of inspiration. *Macunaíma* was written in the 1920's, the decade in which Brazilian artists — including painters, poets, playwrights, novelists, composers, musicians, sculptors and architects — were collectively celebrating their second declaration of independence, from Europe in general and Portugal in particular. One hundred years after Brazil had become politically and economically independent from Portugal (on September 7, 1822), *Modern Art Week* in February 1922 inaugurated *Modernismo* and *Brasilidade* (Brazilianess).

Thus to inaugurate the future and free themselves of fixed forms of expression imposed by European models, Brazilian modernists, with Mário de Andrade as their "Pope," turned inwards towards their primeval forests, rivers, mountains, and indigenous peoples, a flirtation with the "primitive" manifestation of art in an attempt to define what the Brazilian critic Regina Zilberman calls "the representation through art of a national identity" (143).

Equally important is the fact that Andrade's major source of inspiration was the field work of the German anthropologist Theodor Koch-Grünberg's *Vom Roraima zum Orinoco*, published in 1924, which includes a collection of Arekuná and Taulipang Amerindian folk tales. Although Andrade's *Macunaíma* is original in both form and content, it draws heavily upon Koch-Grünberg's compilation, in which the mythic hero of the tribe Macunaíma appears in a vast majority of episodes.

In fact, of the five mythic characters and allusions under discussion, the eponymous Macunaíma, literally the "Big Evil," is by far the most important. Macunaíma does not have a father. It has been observed that like all true heroes of mankind he is born of a virgin mother and spends the first six years of his life without talking. Not surprisingly, he remains throughout his life in an arrested state of adolescence, symbolized by the fact that his head remains the size of a baby's while the rest of his body grows to full maturity.

He is racially distinct from his two older brothers, Jiguê and Maanape. Andrade fuses Christian and pagan myths to explain how this differentiation occurs. By bathing in the magic waters of Saint Thomas's footprint, Macunaíma emerges white-skinned, blue eyed and fair-haired. However, Jiguê bathes in the same water, made muddy by Macunaíma's bath, and he emerges bronze-colored. Jiguê, the Amerindian, is less intelligent but braver than his white younger brother, Macunaíma. By the time Maanape, the eldest brother, washes, most of the magic water has been splashed out, and what water does remain is very muddy so that he is able to wash only the palms of his hands and the soles of his feet. Maanape remains black. He symbolizes the sorcerer, the black heritage of Brazil.

Although Macunaíma is described as a hero without a true character, one should read instead "Brazil without a fixed identity." He exudes a Rabelaisian nature, demonstrating a remarkable penchant for laziness and a voracious sexual appetite, to the point of seducing every female in sight, including his sisters-in-law Sofará and Iriquí, for he is in fact amoral. In a death foretold in a dream, Macunaíma kills his mother in the form of a doe who has just given birth.

Macunaíma has a tripartite function and delineation. He is at the same time a creator, having created the animals of prey and the fishes, a transformer, turning at will trees and animals into stones, and above all a prankster, playing tricks on his brothers and changing his appearance at will. It is precisely through the "ludic," the playful quality of the hero that the folk tale presents the Amerindian "everyman" Macunaíma in three distinct phases — his birth and youth in Amazonia, his sojurn in São Paulo to retrieve the lost amulet muiraquitã, and his return to the Uraricoera habitat. Each phase allegorically underlies the transformation of his robust primitive character and his demise once he comes into contact with the mechanized white civilization in São Paulo.

Macunaíma's most memorable experience is his encounter with Ci, Mother of the Forest and Queen of the Amazons. Although Ci is a literary invention of Andrade, she represents nonetheless an attempt to syncretize an indigenous myth with a well-known Greek myth, namely that of the Amazon warrior women who burned off their right breasts in order to facilitate their use of the bow and arrow. Smelling strongly of balsam, Ci lures Macunaíma into physical combat, and only after a long bout and with the aid of his brothers is Macunaíma finally able to seduce the Mother of the Forest; he is then hailed as the new Emperor of the Virgin Forest.

Wherever he goes in the Amazon, he is protected by a panoply of parrots overhead proclaiming his regal status. Ci, moreover, makes herself unforgettable by making Macunaíma sleep in a hammock woven out of her own hair. From their sexual union is born a son who becomes the victim of a black serpent and dies in infancy. From his grave sprouts a shrub from which Brazilians make their favorite highly caffeinated soft drink, guaraná. The unforgettable Ci, Macunaíma's only true love, is overcome with grief at her only son's death and ascends into heaven to become the star Beta Centauri.

However, before becoming a star, Ci gives her greenstone amulet, her ancestral treasure muiraquitã carved in the shape of an alligator, to her beloved. The venerable greenstone muiraquitã is made into a labret, a totem, which Macunaíma subsequently loses. It is the pursuit of the muiraquitã, romancing the stone as it were, that occupies the rest of the folk tale and gives the rhapsody its only unifying thread.

On another metaphorical level, the pursuit of the muiraquitã represents Brazil's constant search for its identity, according to the Brazilian critic Gilda de Mello (91). A musician wren communicates to Macunaíma that a turtle has swallowed the muiraquitã and that a fisherman has caught the turtle and sold the greenstone to a Peruvian river trader in São Paulo. Before Macunaíma sets out for São Paulo with his brothers, he stows away his conscience on the Island of Marapatá, at the mouth of the Rio Negro, where it will not be a burden to him on his travels.

Macunaíma is dismayed by the noise, pollution and strange customs of the Paulistas; his experiences in São Paulo afford Andrade an excellent opportunity to direct a scathing attack against the superficial quality of twentieth-century life in general, as well as the detrimental effects an industrialized society can have on primitive peoples such as the Tapanhuma Macunaíma.

Upon seeing the first white women prostitutes, Macunaíma addresses them as Mani, Daughters of Manioc, referring to the magic birth to a daughter of an Indian chieftain of Mani, a white child from whose grave the first manioc plant, a staple of the Amerindian diet, sprouted. Abandoned by the panoply of Amazonian parrots, who fly back to their virgin habitat, Macunaíma is left defenseless with his brothers in a world of machines and contraptions that he fails to understand in any terms other than those pertaining to the flora and fauna of his Amazonian homeland.

Upon seeing the first automobiles, he thinks they are the jaguars of his native forests:

> The brown and black pumas leaping along the streets were really jaguars leaping on their prey. They were called Fords, Hupmobiles, Chevrolets and Dodges and were automobile contraptions. . . A regard blended with envy grew in him for this powerful goddess with such outstanding drive, whom the Daughters of Manioc called Machine, whose voice, more strident even than the Water-Mamma's, made such a contribution to the overwhelming din (34-35).

Macunaíma's final judgment on this society — where everything in the city was some kind of machine contraption and where the children of Manioc had mastered the Machine without magic and without force — was that: "It's men who are machines and machines who are men" (36).

Macunaíma's sojourn in São Paulo involves mostly his encounter with the evil giant Venceslau Pietro Pietra syncretized with Piaimã, Macunaíma's traditional foe in native folklore, another version of the monster and dragon motif common in European fairy tales. And like the hero in European fairy tales, Macunaíma must slay this eater of men and collector of stones in order to retrieve his ancestral treasure, the greenstone of Ci.

On another level, Pietro Pietra symbolizes the foreigners, the recent immigrants to Brazil with their get-rich-quick mentality and crass materialism. The cannibals Piaimã and his greedy wife, Ceiuci, entice people into their fatal garden and force them to ride on a prickly swing as a prelude to their painful death. "Blood ran down in rivulets. The greedy old hag who was Piaimã's wife was down there at the bottom of the pit, and the blood dripped into a great cauldron of macaroni stew she was cooking for her husband" (127). It is only after a long series of bouts with Piaimã and Ceiuci that Macunaíma is finally able to outwit his antagonists and retrieve the stone amulet. And in an ironic turn of events the giant Piaimã is plunged into a bubbling cauldron of macaroni and meets his end shouting "not enough cheese" (129).

While Macunaíma's tribulations with the Eater of Men end triumphantly for the Tapanhuma Emperor of the Forest, such is not the case when he faces the Old Lady Vei, the Sun. Since Macunaíma's final undoing is directly attributable to his having offended the Sun, the episode with this fiercer albeit subtler antagonist merits special attention, made all the more noteworthy because the author attempts to assign a more overtly didactic interpretation to this part of the folk tale. In the Taulipang version of the legend, the Sun Vei is masculine, but Andrade chooses an alternate Tupi interpretation that views the sun as feminine. Once again Andrade syncretizes an indigenous myth with one taken from Greek mythology, namely Helios, the Greek sun god who rode to his palace in Colchis every night in a golden chariot furnished with wings.

Similarly, Vei invites Macunaíma onto her sailing raft; but she has an ulterior motive, for she wishes him to marry one of her three daughters. As part of the dowry, Vei is prepared to grant the Amerindian Europe, France and Bahia. But he must promise to remain faithful and cease his debaucherous ways. As a keepsake, Vei gives Macunaíma a stone vató, the flint that gives fire when one needs it. Macunaíma, however, does not treasure the vató as much as he does the totem muiraquitã, and soon swaps the flint for a photograph from a daily newspaper.

The unpardonable sin, at least in the eyes of Vei, however, is his sexual indiscretion with the Portuguese fishwife. As she casts him out of her sailing raft, Vei reminds Macunaíma what he has forfeited by breaking his promise: "If you had obeyed me, you would have married one of my daughters and you would have stayed young and very handsome forever and a day. As it is now, you'll remain young just a short time like anyone else, then you'll grow old and not be attractive at all" (65).

In 1943 Andrade explained the allegorical importance of this episode with the Sun Vei. The daughters of the sun represent the great tropical civilizations: China, India, Peru, Mexico and Egypt. In choosing Portugal over the Tropics — read European civilization — Brazil missed a golden opportunity to be a great, original power in the world. As it is, it will be only an echo of other civilizations and never realize its full potential (Mello 62). This sentiment is echoed in popular Brazilian culture by the saying: "Brazil is the country of the future, and it will always be."

Once the muiraquitã has been retrieved, Macunaíma along with his brothers prepares to return to his Amazonian homeland, but not before casting a spell on São Paulo and turning that industrial giant of South America into a stone in the shape of a three-toed sloth. But Macunaíma unknowingly has been transformed by his stay in the white man's city and his contact with the Children of Manioc. His sexual prowess is gone, and now the former macho man becomes a collector of scatological words to compensate for his asexual behavior. Macunaíma, the "Big Evil," is now a carrier of all types of disease, which will eventually lead to the death of his brothers and the demise of his people.

David Haberly in his very fine study *Three Sad Races* argues that we should read *Macunaíma* as a series of ten codes, including the entomologic and epidemiological codes (150). Indeed, the text provides ample evidence of the way life in the big city has upset the balance of nature, including the overwhelming presence of vermin; as the refrain suggests: "With fewer ants and better health Brazil will lead the world in wealth" (64).

To further complicate the plight of the Tapanhumas, Maanape has introduced the coffee bug, Jiguê the cotton boll weevil, and Macunaíma, soccer—the three pests that plague contemporary Brazil. In addition to the greenstone amulet, Macunaíma brings back with him to the Amazon three souvenirs from São Paulo — a revolver, a timepiece, and a pair of guinea fowl, representing the intrusion of the white man's world into the indigenous habitat.

Not only has Macunaíma lost his physical strength and innocence by his sojourn in São Paulo, he has also lost his peace of mind and happiness itself, for the feelings of loneliness, alienation, anxiety, boredom and despair accompany his return to the Uraricoera. But most importantly the

Amerindian Macunaíma has lost his concept of identity, as symbolized by his inability to locate his conscience, which he had carefully hidden on Marapatá Island before leaving for São Paulo. "Could wild horses find it. No they could not! Then the hero decided to take to himself the conscience of a Latin American, put it inside his head and shaped himself in that mold" (144).

Vei has planned one last act of deception to avenge herself of Macunaíma's unfaithfulness. In the Vale of Tears, where Macunaíma bathes, he can see an extraordinarily beautiful fair-skinned damsel with a most seductive smile. This extremely lovely creature is Uiara, a siren syncretized with the Lady of the Lake of Arthurian legend (Mello 74). "Vei lashed the hero's back with rays of heat like cat-o-nine tails. Macunaíma felt fire run up his spine, shimmered with apprehension and dived. Vei wept with victory. It was high noon" (160). Under the water Macunaíma is engaged in mortal combat that leads to his final mutilation by piranhas, who devour his testicles. Both his leg and the greenstone totem muiraquitã are swallowed by the monster Ururau.

Most critics agree that the conclusion of the folk tale signals a defeat not only for Macunaíma personally but also for the Tapanhuma tribe, as well as for Brazil as a nation. Dispirited by the loss of everything he holds dear, Macunaíma is left to converse with a parrot, the sole survivor and last speaker of his language. "Only the parrot had preserved in that vast silence the words and deeds of the hero. All this he related to the author, then spread his wings and set his course for Lisbon" (168).

Ironically, the hero, who proclaims throughout the tale that he did not come into this world to be a stone, ascends into heaven to be a star—the Big Dipper, Ursa Major — and now joins "the useless twinkling life of the stars" (163). Although Mário de Andrade insisted throughout his life that *Macunaíma* was "desgeograficado" (Proença 82) literally "de-localized," it is in fact much like the other great masterpiece of magic realism, *One Hundred Years of Solitude* (1967) by the Colombian novelist Gabriel García Márquez, in which myth, metaphor and fantasy are the preferred techniques by which such Latin American authors choose to convey the mysteries and enigmatic modes of behavior of their people in a language and style uniquely their own.

In essence, the moral of the tale is simply to relate it as first the parrot has done and then the author himself, for as the eminent Mexican poet, essayist and critic Octavio Paz has noted: "In myth there are no dates." Yet if as Joseph Campbell asserts in *The Hero with a Thousand Faces* "mythology is eminently untragical" (269), then the bottom line of this allegorical folk tale is, according to Mário de Andrade himself, that the "Brazilian has no fixed character because he does not possess his own civilization nor a national consciousness" (Campos 77-78). In the final analysis, however, popular Brazilian folklore is less pessimistic, for it proclaims unabashedly that "God is a Brazilian."

Works Cited

Andrade, Mário de. *Macunaíma*, 17 ed. São Paulo: Martins, 1980.

Andrade, Mário de. *Macunaíma*, tr. E.A. Goodland. New York: Random House, 1984.

Campbell, Joseph. *The Hero with a Thousand Faces*. Princeton: Princeton University Press, 1973.

Campbell, Joseph. *The Power of Myth*. New York: Doubleday, 1988.

Campos, Haroldo de.*Morfologia do Macunaíma*. São Paulo: Editora Perspectiva, 1973.

Haberly, David. *Three Sad Races*. Cambridge: Cambridge University Press, 1983.

Koch-Grünberg, Theodor.*Vom Roraima zum Orinoco*. 3 vols. Stuttgart: Strecker und Schröder, 1924.

Koch-Grünberg, Theodor.*Del Roraima al Orinco*, tr.Federica de Ritter. Caracas: Ernesto Armitano, 1966.

Mello e Souza, Gilda de.*O Tupi e o Alaúde*. São Paulo: Duas Cidades, 1979.

Paz, Octavio.*El Labirinto de la soledad*. Mexico: Fundo de Cultura Económica, 1959.

Proença, Mario Cavalcanti.*Roteiro de Macunaíma*. Rio de Janeiro: Editora Civilização Brasileira, 1969.

Villas Boas, Orlando and Claudio.*Xingu,The Indians, Their Myths*, tr. Susana Hertelendy Rudge. New York: Farrar, Straus and Giroux, 1973.

Zilberman, Regina. "Myth and Brazilian Literature."*Literary Anthropology*, ed. Fernando Poyatos. Amsterdam/Philadelphia: Benjamins, 1988.

Myth and Society

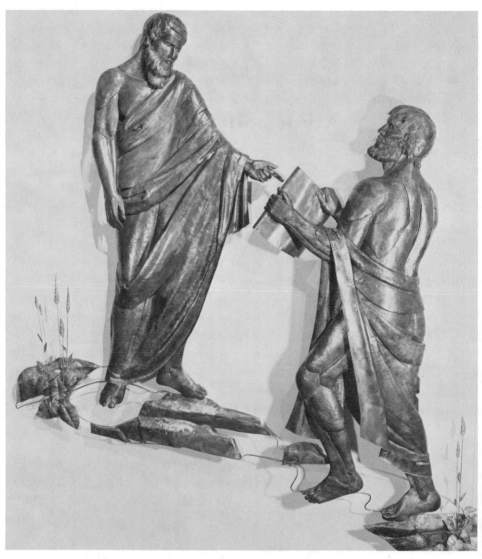

"School of Athens," left panel (1985) by Nina Winkel

Rathaus—Borken, Germany
Photo credit: Robin J. Brown

Edwin Hamblet

French-Canadian Messianism

As Quebec moves closer to political independence, traditional French-Canadian messianism remains the dominant myth that sustains her collective soul. In his book *The Presence of Myth*,[1] Polish philosopher Leszek Kolakowski emphasizes the important role of mythology in determining ethnic identity and survival. His point of departure is the sharply drawn opposition of myth and science, and he describes science as the extension of civilization's technological core. Kolakowski believes that not only the body but also the soul needs a house. Mythologies are a function of consciousness that manifests itself in all cultural phenomena, whether they be religious, political, artistic, musical, or moral.

Kolakowski describes three versions of the need for myth: first, man needs myth to rescue whatever happens from fleeting, meaningless contingency by referring it to an unconditional reality, be it God, the philosopher's absolute or other forms; second, man needs myth because he cannot live with values believed to be ephemeral, (Even if one is cosmopolitan and highly appreciative of other cultures, one cannot accept the relativity of all values. It is believed one's own values transcend the passage of time, even if reason is unable to provide such faith with justification.); third, man needs to understand the world as continuous.

Common to all three of Kolakowski's descriptions is the attempt to escape the tyranny of physical time and the terror of a world that appears to be indifferent to man's needs and hopes. Myth is born of the human inability to accept that we and all we have created someday will be past, will have vanished without a trace, unremembered and unredeemed. To feel at home in the world, we have to be able to interpret whatever presents itself in such a way that it answers to our needs.[2] The philosopher throughout the ages has attempted to provide an interpretation based on reason, but as Pascal has pointed out, the heart has its own reasons which reason doesn't know.

Individuals find their roots in the collective myths of their community or nation. Kolakowski states that universal godlessness is a utopia and that myths that teach the individual as well as the collectivity that something is good or evil cannot be avoided if humanity is to survive. All value is the work of myth, and the mythological imagination cancels the indifference of the world. However, for the smaller ethnic groups, myth is more than an evasion of reality. It is what gives meaning and identity to the members of those particular entities. For example, it is the special way of viewing life and civilization that makes the Québécois resist the temptation to become Americans and the Lithuanians from becoming Russians despite the so-called economic benefits and external pressures brought about by those more powerful nations on unwilling clients.

The founders of French civilization in the New World considered themselves to be people of God and committed Christians. They brought with them the faith and enthusiasm of the Catholic Counter-Reformation that had triumphed in France and had given rise to the ideals of French classicism. Samuel de Champlain, called the father of New France, founded Quebec City in 1608, and in 1625 invited the Society of Jesus to send missionaries and teachers to work among the Indians. The Jesuits were influenced by the writings of the Spanish prelate Bartolomé de las Casas (1474-1555), who wrote that the native peoples of the New World were human beings created in God's image and thus worthy of redemption.

The missionary accounts sent back to France inspired a devout layman named LaDauversière and Sulpician Father Jacques Olier to establish a religious colony in 1642 on the island of Montreal. They found in Paul Chomeday de Maisonneuve the ideal man to lead their group, and on May 18 of that year, the first Mass was celebrated by Father Vimont. The gospel-reading from that day's liturgy related Christ's parable of the mustard seed, which although the smallest of all seeds, grows into a tree in which the birds of the air come to nest. That parable was indeed prophetic, for the new colony would later become the second largest French-speaking city in the world. On August 15, 1642, the feast of the Assumption, the colony was named Ville Marie de Montréal in honor of the Virgin Mary. From there, the Jesuits set out to found missions in what became New York State and far into the Great Lakes region. The sedentary Hurons became the first Indian nation to embrace Christianity, and the black robes, as their new converts called them, were able to win over hundreds of natives to the faith by their zeal, example, and physical and moral courage in the face of hardships and danger. In contrast to the fur traders who followed in their footsteps, the Jesuits were totally committed to Christ, and that commitment often led to excruciating torture and martyrdom.

From 1634, for a period of forty years, the Jesuits sent annual reports, known as *Relations*, back to their superiors in France. These inspired writings fired the imaginations of devout individuals in the mother country who shared the apostolic zeal of the missionaries. The *Relations* impelled a young widow, Marie Guyard, who had become an Ursuline nun under the name of Marie de l'Incarnation, to undertake a daring adventure. She claimed to have had a vision:

> One day while I was praying in the chapel in the presence of the Blessed Sacrament I became lost in God, and that great land which I had discovered in my readings was revealed to me. The Almighty spoke these words to me: "It is in Canada that you belong— you must go there and prepare a dwelling place for Jesus and Mary." From henceforth only Canada mattered. My thoughts were in the land of the Hurons where I would accompany those preachers of the Gospel united in spirit with the Eternal Father under the auspices of the Sacred Heart of Jesus to win souls for eternal salvation.[3]

In France, Marie de l'Incarnation and her company of women were thought to be mad, but in 1639 they finally received permission to sail for Quebec, where they founded a convent school for French and Indian girls.

Thus the founders of New France were triumphant conquerors who did not flee the Old World for reasons of political or religious persecution. They, like the Spanish and the Portuguese colonizers, sought to propagate Catholic European civilization. The French made pacts with as many Indian nations and groups as possible. Apostles of the Counter-Reformation, they believed that the Church was the mystical body of Christ, and that they, as members of the Church Militant, were bound by Christ's command to preach the Gospel to every nation and to baptize all people. As orthodox Christians, they believed that baptism opened the gates of eternal life and salvation that had been won for every man, woman and child by the merits of Christ's passion, death and resurrection.

This faith explained the diligence with which the Jesuits, for example, studied the various Indian languages and cultures and their incorporation of certain native elements into the liturgy. Catholicism represented a universal point of view, which held that certain racial and cultural differences were not only to be tolerated but respected. In their undaunted messianic vision of the world, the Jesuits sincerely believed that all peoples would eventually be baptized and redeemed, and universal brotherhood and peace realized.

Their all-inclusive outlook contrasted sharply with what was going on in the English colonies on these shores. Gary Wills writes in *Under God: Religion and American Politics* [4] that the seventeenth century in Anglo-America was a time of Miliast enthusiasm. American Calvinists believed that the times were pinpointed for the dissolution of society and the end of the world. In Britain many of the best minds were on the lookout for the Anti-Christ and other signs of impending disaster. Many, including Joseph Meade, Milton's teacher at Oxford, thought the final battle of Armageddon would be fought in America, where the apocalyptic enemy would be waiting. When whole Indian villages were wiped out by plague, Cotton Mather (1673-1728) would write in *Magnalia Christi Americana* that the woods were almost cleansed of those pernicious creatures to make room for better growth.

Captain John Smith had reported earlier, in 1612, that the chief God the Indians worship is the Devil, whereas Joseph Meade stated in 1627 that the enemy of mankind had marshalled the pagans to halt the Puritan's progress. Thus the Anglo view and treatment of the Indians were colored by Miliast urgency: Indians were the living instruments of the devil, intended to try the saints and to undo God's work. The Catholic Church was the Scarlet Woman, the Whore of Babylon, and the Beast of the Apocalypse, and had a key role to play with her allies, the pagans, in the New World battle of Armageddon.

The Jesuits, especially, were seen to be the emissaries of evil power in their spreading of the "anti-gospel." The Puritans' fear of the unholy alliance would become most intense during the French and Indian Wars. Thus, it was no wonder that, in 1727, Father Sébastien Rasle would be assassinated at his Indian mission in Norridgewock, Maine, and his scalp paraded in triumph through the streets of Boston.

By the beginning of the eighteenth century, the colonists in Quebec had already distinguished themselves from the continental French and readily identified themselves as "Canadiens." The 1759 battle on the Plains of Abraham near Quebec City ended with the British conquest of New France. French Canadians began to view themselves as a conquered people whose normal evolution was thwarted by circumstances beyond their control. Although many historians considered the 1763 Treaty of Paris to be a practical dividing up of spheres of influence between the British and the French, the people of Quebec felt that they had been sold out by the mother country.

Suddenly 55,000 "Canadiens" found themselves under English rule. The Quebec Act of 1774, passed for purely pragmatic reasons, allowed them to maintain their French language and to practice the Catholic religion. Their very existence for the next three quarters of a century would prove to be very tenuous, as they struggled to survive in a Protestant Anglo-Saxon sea. However, legends and myths that sustain are hard to kill, and the conquered "Canadiens" began to glorify the halcyon days of the French regime, even though in that era there was no university, no newspaper and much neglect. In fact, when the French officials returned to Europe in 1760, they took all the liquid assets of the colony with them.

Fascinatingly, the messianic vision of the francophones did not diminish but became reinforced. Joseph Campbell discusses an interesting example of this that he found in the *Alguonquin Tales*. One of the earliest recorded is Ottawa Indian Chief Pontiac's visionary narrative entitled- *Paradise opened to the Indians*, an obvious reflex of Dante's ascent on Easter Sunday 1300 of the Mountain of Purgatory. Pontiac's account of such a visit to God's throne dates from an episode of the French and Indian Wars.

In 1760 a British force under Major Robert Rogers was sent to occupy a chain of surrendered French forts in the Great Lakes region. They needed safe passage through Ottawa territory, which was granted on condition that the Indians be treated with respect. However, the Indians soon found themselves not welcome in the forts where they had previously enjoyed the hospitality of the French. English settlers soon arrived and took their lands, and this led Pontiac to organize a "conspiracy" of almost every tribe from Lake Superior to the lower Mississippi. Thus, Pontiac's War (1763-1764) became the futile last stand of New France. The chief claimed to have received God's message to the American Indians at the conclusion of his Dantean ascent to the summit of a mountain as smooth as glass, a place of unequaled beauty. God told him to wage a just war, a holy war on behalf of the French in the name of the Master of Life.

Pontiac, as an instructed Catholic, was interpreting the global conflict and situation into which he and his people had been drawn from the point of view of the Catholic Counter-Reformation. God told him of the French:

> I love them, they know me, they pray to me; I supply their wants and give them what I bring to you. Not so with those who have come to trouble your possessions. Drive them away, wage war against them. I love them not. They know me not. They are my enemies. Send them back to the lands I have made for them.[5]

Pontiac's vision became a summons to neighboring tribes to unite in the name of God and to repel the intruders. Campbell sees this as an appeal to a thirteenth-century idea of God and his program for mankind, in contest with a seventeenth century notion of the same. The manuscript, in French, is attributed to a French Jesuit, who was one of the messengers of the Master of Life that had been accepted for almost 150 years in the region. The highest Indian mythological entity was universally a personification of the light, power and authority of the sun; the more abstract concept of a "Great Spirit" or "Master of Life" was clearly a French missionary influence. Thus, by the time of the British conquest of Canada, the mythological thinking of the Great Lakes tribes had been significantly transformed by assimilated Christian ideas.

From 1760 to 1840, during the "Canadien" period, Quebec francophones underwent the apprenticeship of British parliamentary government. The first twenty-five years of the nineteenth century saw the rise of the classical college and the return of Jesuit influence. Those schools produced a politically active elite that attempted to overthrow the British regime and to establish an independent republic with the separation of Church and state. However, their armed revolt, known as the Papineau Rebellion of 1837-1838, was brutally put down by the British army.

After this abortive attempt at political independence, the Church hierarchy stepped in to fill the void in leadership caused by the execution, imprisonment or exile of many of the political elite. The Church had always urged caution and prudence in dealing with the British and had taken a dim view of the violence of the uprising. It consolidated its power and instigated a reign of clericalism that would last from 1840 to 1960 and that marked the "French-Canadian" era.

During this long period, the Church controlled and ran virtually all of Quebec's social and educational institutions. In the eyes of French Canadians, it was a legitimate surrogate government over which they had direct control. The newly invigorated Church reaffirmed its primacy and its messianic mission in North America, and its official propaganda inspired the first group of French-Canadian poets, the "Ecole Patriotique de Québec," the Patriotic School of Quebec City, founded in 1858. Their mythology glorified the French regime and its mighty heroes, and professed fidelity to Christ the Redeemer and to the French language. These poets, like the clergy, preached a return to the soil because, as in the Old Testament example of Sodom and Gomorrah, the Canadian city was considered a place of damnation and assimilation, a cesspool of Protestant capitalism and materialism.

French Canadians viewed money with great suspicion, and their clergy admonished them to heed Christ's teachings on such matters. They were taught to lay up treasures in heaven, where neither thief can break in and rob, nor moth and rust consume. It was pointless to gain the whole world but to lose one's soul in the process, and so the kingdom of heaven became the French Canadian's pearl of great price. The English had all the money, but as far as the people of Quebec were concerned, that was all they were going to get.

In the meantime, French missionaries, especially the Oblates of Mary, took up where the Jesuits had left off and evangelized huge areas of the Canadian West in the Red River region. There, the French-speaking Métis and Indians hoped to create a new province under the leadership of Louis Riel. A Catholic mystic, Riel said that he had visions of the Virgin Mary. After two armed uprisings he was captured, brought to trial and hanged by the Canadian government, in 1885. Riel became a hero for Quebec francophones, and his execution remains even today in Canada a matter of great controversy and friction.

French Canadians became rapidly urbanized in the twentieth century, coming into direct contact with North American capitalism and technology. In the process they became more and more alienated and found themselves to be second-class citizens even in their own province. The long, stifling reign of clericalism came to an end in 1960, when the "Révolution tranquille," or Peaceful Revolution, ushered in the Quebec era and a renewed push for political and economic independence. The alienating and "colonial" term "French-Canadian" was replaced by "Québécois," as the Quebec state quietly displaced the Church from its traditional social and educational functions.

The government became the new secular vehicle of the messianic message and created a new lower-middle class of bureaucrats and functionaries who gradually replaced members of the religious orders in the administration of the province's vital institutions. But, make no mistake about it, the traditional Catholic vision of the brotherhood and salvation of all people remained intact. The Québécois began to identify with other small ethnic groups in the world, whether they be Czech, Irish, Armenian or Lithuanian.

The messianic myth brought from France so long ago can still be found in almost all of the writings and works of Quebec's contemporary writers, artists, musicians and film-makers. Two recent and internationally acclaimed films by Denys Arcand offer good examples. His 1986 *Le Déclin de l'Empire américain* (*The Decline of the American Empire*) portrays a group of brilliant but dissipated professors from the University of Montreal who are gathered for a typical French gastronomical dinner in a luxurious country setting. Their frank conversation about the kinky sex, the numerous affairs, drugs and other decadent activities that their economic well-being allows them to indulge in reveals their serious doubts and misgivings about the newly found freedom from all restraints. Tragically, the sexual revolution and the era of hedonism have left them depressed, unhappy and unfulfilled because no new values have been found to replace those that were reinforced by Quebec's traditional social and religious practices and customs. As a group, they fear for their souls and search for salvation.

Arcand's 1990 film, *Jésus de Montréal* (*Jesus of Montreal*) depicts a young marginal actor who volunteers to play the role of Christ in an avant-garde Holy Week Passion Play, on Mount Royal outside of St. Joseph's Oratory. He is taken by a successful Quebec businessman to the top of a Montreal skyscraper where the latter, much as Satan did with Christ in the desert, tempts the young idealist by offering him the wealth of the dynamic metropolis at their feet if he will compromise his principles. Like the devil in the Gospel account, the businessman is reminded that man does not live by bread alone but must also place his final trust and hope in God and in permanent moral values. The film-maker's message is clear: the amassing of great wealth solely for the sake of power and domination leads to enslavement and unhappiness.

Contemporary Québécois believe that humanity still needs salvation and that all people can be saved; one must continue to strive for universal peace and brotherhood in a world free of pollution and the threat of nuclear holocaust; all persons should be adequately fed and housed and live in dignity. The Quebec mythic salvation is collective, and not individual or personal, as one finds it in the world of American television evangelists. On this major point Quebec's messianism differs radically from the American Calvinist tradition, which preaches the salvation of the few at the expense of the many, as Philip Greven points out in *Spare the Child: The Religious Roots of Punishment and the Psychological Impact of Physical Abuse.* 6

The people of Quebec still believe that this earth is a vale of tears and that life has its share of suffering and sorrow that all must strive to alleviate. Social progress can be made up to a certain point, but the human heart will never find true peace until it rests in God or transcends the materialistic world. Passion and death must be experienced before one can know the joy of resurrection and new birth.

This message can be found in the works of Quebec's greatest living poet, Gaston Miron. It is especially eloquent in his key poem "L'octobre" ("October"),7 which, with its strong liturgical overtones, offers a powerful testimony to the messianism that has endured ever since that fateful day of July 24, 1534, when Jacques Cartier erected a cross at Gaspé.

Miron has said that each poem written in French in the New World is by its very nature a subversive act because it dares to introduce an element of difference and because it erects an effective and civilizing obstacle in the path of the overwhelming American steamroller that attempts to reduce all to a level of dreary and impersonal conformity. Arnold Toynbee substantiates Gaston Miron's views, for he has written that whatever else may happen, the people of Quebec will be present at North America's final encounter with destiny.

Endnotes

1 See Leszek Kolakowski, *The Presence of Myth* (Chicago: University of Chicago Press, 1989).

2 Karsten Harries, "Our Analgesic Culture," *The New York Times Book Review*, January 14, 1990, p. 24.

3 Edwin Hamblet, *La Littérature canadienne francophone* (Paris: Hatier, 1987), pp. 18-19.

4 See Gary Wills, *Under God: Religion and American Politics* (New York: Simon and Schuster, 1990).

5 Joseph Campbell, *Historical Atlas of World Mythology*, Vol. II; *The Way of the Seeded Earth, Part 2; Mythologies of the Primitive Planters: The Northern Indians* (New York: Harper and Row, 1989), pp. 171-172.

6 See Philip Greuen, *Spare the Child: The Religious Roots of Punishment and the Psychological Impact of Physical Abuse* (New York: Knopf, 1991).

7 Gaston Miron, *L'Homme rapaillé* (Montreal: University of Montreal Press,1970), p.62.

Edward R. Schaffer

The Myth
of
American Exceptionalism
and
Global Peace

America's Messianic Beginnings

American society was originally founded on a Messianic myth.
America is the first post-Reformation society that recreates the Garden of
Eden story. The early Puritan settlers came to the new world in order to
construct the Kingdom of God on Earth. The New Zion of the American
wilderness had to be constructed out of the self-help of extraordinary individuals who had unbounded faith in a personal God who, in turn, had a
"calling" for them.[1] The Puritans had a special covenant with their God.

> In the early years, this sense of a common calling was
> strengthened by the widely held conviction that the reforma-
> tion being carried out in the American commonwealth was
> actually a decisive phase in the final chapter of God's plan for
> his Church in this world.[2]

The messianic spirit of Puritan Calvinist Christianity would largely
exhaust itself within a century of the founding of Plymouth colony, but its
theme of special purpose remains an important part of American religious identity. The idea that America has a special mission and is guarded
by God's special providence continues to be a central theme in what
Robert Bellah calls American "civil religion." Bellah argues that the providential religious place that American colonies held in world history was
the basis of the earliest sense of a national community in America, and
preceded the Revolution by a generation of two. He sees the results of

this first Great Awakening of the 1730s and 1740s as leading to the emergence of a "civil millennialism." This sense of national community, based on America's special mission, provided the religious inspiration that made the American Revolution possible.[3]

The Protestant period of religious hegemony lasted at least until about 1870 in American life. The small town Protestant character of American society changed significantly after the Civil War with the growth of the Eastern seaport cities and the expansion of industry. After successive phases of Catholic, Jewish, Oriental and other religious and national groups' migrations to America, the Protestant empire and its "godly" way of life no longer dominated American cultural life. The second half of the nineteenth century brought with it what the religious scholar Martin Marty calls the "modern schism."[4] Religion became less an overarching public theology and more a compartmentalized aspect of private life— leaving science, politics and economic affairs to a rising class of professionals. Still, a significant number of Americans would adhere to earlier Puritanical views of America's special mission in God's historical timetable. Ironically, just as the theological views of millennial Protestantism were declining in importance in American religious culture, its resurrection as a mythic force was taking place in the form of the American Western hero.

The transvaluation of terminologies from religious to secular language can serve to conceal the similarities between religious and dramaturgical rhetorics. In the case of the American Western hero, it can be seen as a restatement in dramatic form of the early Puritan Messianic theme. Biblical themes and symbols in the secular western movie provide the viewer with the experience of Americans struggling to keep their special covenant with God. The structure of the American Western-hero film has itself undergone significant morphological changes in attempting to serve as a morality play relevant to changes in American social structure. American presidents and other national leaders have historically incorporated the redemption language of Puritanism in their attempt to depict their struggle with good and evil.[5] Most of what is good and most of what is bad in our history can be seen in the American Western film.

The Western as Puritan Morality Play

The Messianic myth of America's special purpose is, as we have seen, rooted in a new-world covenant with God. America would prosper and grow strong as a people as long as it kept its covenant with God. All God-fearing Americans would seek self improvement through moral discipline and by resisting temptation to sin, while mastering God's special calling for them. The achievement ethic or work ethic would provide the overarching moral framework that would determine who was part of the covenanted community and who was not. The poor could be divided into two groups, the deserving poor, who need community assistance for short periods because of unforeseen hardships, and the undeserving poor, who shirk redemption by work. Periodic religious revivals, or Great Awakenings, would remind the nation of its original principles and set it back on track.

The American Western-hero myth was a creation of the late nineteenth-century religious awakening. The Western-hero myth actually says little about the historical West and more about the decadence of the East of the period. The image of the Western hero was created by Easterners to be read by Easterners. The Western hero reminds the backsliders in the East of what it is like to be brave, disciplined and resourceful. As Michael Marsden observes,

> The lawlessness of the frontier required a strong sense of divine justice untempered with mercy. The coming of the Western hero is a kind of Second Coming of Christ, but this time he wears the garb of the gunfighter, the only Savior the sagebrush, the wilderness, and the pure savagery of the West can accept.[6]

According to Wright, the American classic Western-hero film has a structure, like the grammar of language, which can be recognized even though film plots differ. We will argue that the conceptual structure of the classic American Western is a restatement of the Puritan covenanted community theme. The popularity of the Western-hero film rests on a collective consciousness shared by Americans who believe in America's special purpose to establish Heaven on Earth. The effectiveness of the classic Western-hero film is that its mythic structure provides a simple but remarkably deep conceptualization of American social beliefs. Wright identifies a number of aspects of the classic Western.

It is the story of the lone stranger who rides into a troubled town and cleans it up, winning the respect of the townsfolk and the love of the school marm. There are many variations on this theme which saturate Western films from 1930 to 1955 . . . Many differences in content were apparent—railroad building, Indian wars, wagon trains, rancher barons—but the important differentiating factor. . . [is the] relationship between the hero and society.[7]

The mythic hero of the American Western is confronted with the problem of good and evil. He is concerned with the restoration of order and moral community. The community is in crisis because of its unwillingness to resist temptation. Drinking, gambling, money, sex and violence characterize in some combination the hero's and the villain's temptations. The film reveals in various temptation episodes the self control of the hero, and the villain's lack of control. The villain has a terrible power over the town and its struggle to maintain moral order in the face of temptation. The villain cannot exhibit moral constraint in the face of temptation, and this is what makes him so terrible to the Puritan. The hero does not move to confront the evil until events make it apparent that only the violent destruction of the evil one appears just and virtuous.

Peter Homans calls the process leading up to the gunfight the "inner dynamic." Homans argues that "the circumstances which force the hero into this situation are contrived. . . what is required is that the temptation be indulged while providing the appearance of being resisted."[8] Homans sees the Western as a puritan morality tale. He observes that

> Indeed in the gunfight (and to a lesser extent in the minor temptation episodes) the hero's heightened gravity and dedicated exclusion of all other loyalties presents a study in puritan virtue, while the evil one presents nothing more nor less than the old New England protestant devil—strangely costumed, to be sure—the traditional tempter whose horrid lures never allow the good puritan a moment's peace.[9]

In the gunfight there is deliverance and redemption.

The classic Western-hero image has had a strong hold on the American political leaders whose careers were shaped by the religious revivals of the 1950s. Billy Graham and Norman Vincent Peale renewed the attack on the temptations of the Protestant devil. Western heroes enacted by

James Stewart, Gary Cooper, Robert Mitchum, Alan Ladd and John Wayne depict the self-reliant Protestant individual, a direct descendent of the New Testament Christ, who went into the wilderness of human weakness only to reemerge from this encounter with temptation with a new resolve to defeat evil.

The Inner Dynamic of Presidential Virtue

The 1980s were characterized by a reassertion of Midwestern and Texas small-town Protestant values in the right-wing of the Republican party.[10] Western-hero virtues reflecting the Puritan temper and 1950s McCarthyism sought to confront modernist tendencies in the culture. Liberated women, sexual nonconformists, cultural radicals, blacks and other minority groups had emerged as a major force in American life following the McGovern campaign of 1972. Ronald Reagan successfully organized traditional Protestant interests in fundamentalist religion, censorship, and stricter divorce and anti-abortion laws, whereas the "new politics" of the period denounced the small-town mentality of Puritanism, with its emphasis on deferred gratification and respectability, in favor of a cultural consumption style based on immediate gratification and exhibitionistic display. Economic problems of inflation, lower savings and investment, imbalances of income and wealth were identified by the old right-wing with the transformation of American values from inner-worldly asceticism to hedonism. Daniel Bell sees the transformation of American values as possessing a legitimation crisis for American culture and capitalism. He observes that

> The culture has been dominated (in the services realm) by a principle of modernism that has been subversive of bourgeois life, and the middle-class life styles by a hedonism that has undercut the Protestant ethic which provided the moral foundation for the society. . . The modernism is exhausted, and no longer threatening. . . But the social order lacks either a culture that is a symbolic expression of any vitality or a moral impulse that is a motivational or binding force. What, then, can hold the society together?[11]

The Western-hero image of current-day presidential politics from Reagan to Bush is, we believe, an expression of another awakening period in American Protestantism. Its appeal is made on the grounds of American millennial thought. America, having won its historical struggle with the evil empire of international communism, is now free to apply its superior technology to extend the Protestant Revolution to the world. The concept of a new world order is congruent with the older language of Puritan values. President Bush, in his 1991 State of the Union address, sought to conjoin the defeat of the villain Saddam Hussein with the moral renewal of American society. Bush declared that

> We are resolute and resourceful. If we can unselfishly confront evil for the sake of good in a land so far away, then surely we can make this land all that it should be.[12]

President Bush's demands for the unconditional withdrawal of Saddam Hussein's army from Kuwait, and other circumstances leading up to the final showdown in the Gulf, established the basis for the hero to indulge in what he wanted all along—the violent destruction of the evil one. It remains to be seen if the Puritan morality drama, and the spirit of small-town Protestant values, played out on the screens of our electronically integrated society, can produce a new public morality that will support Bush's vision of a new world order. As Robert Bellah has cautioned,

> American civil religion with its tradition of openness, tolerance and ethical commitment might make a contribution to a world civil religion that would transcend and include it. Any archaic claims to our special righteousness or messianic mission, however, can only further the process of global disintegration.[13]

Endnotes

[1] Daniel Bell has argued this point. He states that "In the United States nature and religion intertwined to form the character of the nation. There was the awesome expanse of the land with its extraordinary variety and fertility. Equally, at the start, there was a covenant—explicit with the Puritans, implicit in the deism of Jefferson—through which God's providential design would be unfolded on this continent." See "The End

of American Exceptionalism," in *The American Commonwealth*. Special Issue. Public Interest Magazine (New York: Basic Books,1970), p. 198.

2 See Steven E. Ahlstrom, *A Religious History of the American People,* Vol. 1 (Garden City: Doubleday, 1975), p. 182.

3 Thomas Paine, in *Common Sense*, justifies the American rebellion on the grounds of a special American metaphysical destiny and mission. Ralph Waldo Emerson and the poet Walt Whitman also used manifest destiny themes to express America's millennial greatness. For a discussion of these issues, see Robert N. Bellah and Phillip E. Hammond, *The Varieties of Civil Religion* (San Francisco: Harper and Row, 1980), pp. 2-27.

4 See Martin E. Marty, "Religion in America Since Mid-Century," in *Religion and America: Spirituality in a Secular Age*, edited by Mary Douglas and Steven M. Tipton (Boston: Beacon Press, 1983), p. 277.

5 Whitman's tract *The Eighteenth Presidency* speaks of a redeemer nation and a Redeemer-President. Woodrow Wilson speaks of American soldiers "as crusaders" and "America's entry into the League of Nations is "nothing less than the liberation and salvation of the world." See Daniel Bell, "The End of American Exceptionalism," p. 202. Bell also quotes John F. Kennedy's Inaugural speech, which expresses the ideal that America is now the guardian of world order. For a discussion of the conception of American presidents from Lincoln to Kennedy who have used the rhetoric of redemption see Ernest Lee Tuveson, *The Redeemer Nation: The Idea of America's Millennial Role* (Chicago: University of Chicago Press, 1968).

6 See Michael T. Marsden, "Savior in the Saddle: The Sagebrush Testament," in *Focus on the Western*, edited by Jack Nachbar (New Jersey: Prentice Hall, 1974), p. 95.

7 See Will Wright, *Six Guns and Society: A Structural Study of the Western* (Berkeley: University of California Press, 1975), p. 59. Wright sees later revisions of the classical Western as reflecting the decline of the role of the risk-taking entrepreneur in Americans social structure and the rise of a managerial mentality reflected in the professional plot.

8 See Peter Homans "Puritanism Revisited: An Analysis of the Contemporary Screen-Image Western" in *Focus On The Western*, edited by Jack Nachbar (New Jersey: Prentice Hall, 1974), p. 90.

9 Homans, p. 91.

10 Daniel Bell argues that when members of the corporate class take stands on cultural-political issues they often divide along geographical lines. He states that "Midwesterners or Texans or those coming from small-town backgrounds display traditionalist attitudes; Easterners or products of Ivy League schools are more liberal." See *The Cultural Contradictions of Capitalism* (New York: Basic Books, 1976), p. 78.

11 See Bell, *The Cultural Contradictions of Capitalism*, p. 84. Bell wonders why the belief in American exceptionalism lingers, even when it is no longer congruent with the social structure of the society. He does not doubt that the covenant-community ideal can still be used to mobilize Americans in time of crisis and to enforce discipline or a set of social controls. President Bush's 1991 State of the Union Address, which is replete with covenant Messianic images and the struggle with the devil figure Saddam Hussein, is evidence of the continuity of the belief in Americans' millennial mission to save the world.

12 See "Text of President Bush's State of the Union Message to Nation" *New York Times*, Wednesday, January 30, 1991, A12.

13 See Robert N. Bellah and Phillip E. Hammond, *Varieties of Civil Religion* (San Francisco: Harper and Row, 1980), p. xiv.

Barbara Fischer

The Myth of Tolerance:
Historical Dimensions of a German-Jewish
Friendship

The second centennial of two Enlightenment promulgators of
Jewish emancipation — the influential Jewish philosopher Moses Mendelssohn and the most prominent literary figure of German
Enlightenment, Gotthold Ephraim Lessing — fell in the year 1929. This
well-documented friendship between a Jew (Mendelssohn) and a Luther-
an (Lessing) seemed, in their own time, to hold out the promise of a bright
future for German-Jewish interaction and acculturation.

Lessing's second centennial also provided an occasion for celebration of rationalist thinkers and thought (it was the 100th anniversary of
Goethe's *Faust*). President von Hindenburg opened the 1929 ceremonies
in Wolfenbüttel with the following words:

> May these commemorative festivities, organized by the State
> capital of Braunschweig and the city of Wolfenbüttel, in keep-
> ing with the hallowed tradition of German cities of spreading
> German culture and letters, follow the high-minded course
> which should be accorded to them; may they contribute to the
> recurring propagation and conservation among our German
> people of the imperishable works of our great cultural
> heroes.[1]

By 1933, when Hindenburg appointed Adolf Hitler chancellor of the
German Reich, Lessing's *Nathan der Weise* (*Nathan the Wise*), the play,
that only four years earlier had been praised by Hindenburg himself as
one of the monuments of German literature, as the embodiment of the
tolerance ideal and as representative of the "best of German culture," had
been banned from all German theaters. The banning of *Nathan the Wise*
appears in retrospect as a small episode in the series of humiliations and
persecutions of Jews, whose epilogue was to be gruesomely played out in

the gas chambers of Auschwitz. The collapse of the ideal of Jewish emancipation, the extinction of Enlightenment tolerance and universalism were becoming brutally evident.

Taking as a basis the assumption that "post-emancipatory" anti-Semitism[2] represents not so much a rupture as an historical and discursive consequence of Enlightenment, I shall attempt in the following analysis to re-assess eighteenth-century notions of tolerance and emancipation, and consider the historical dimensions of the private friendship between Moses Mendelssohn and Gotthold Ephraim Lessing. The process of Jewish assimilation should be understood as part and parcel of the establishment of the German bourgeoisie. The road towards German-Jewish assimilation was, in effect—as the Mendelssohn-Lessing relationship shows—paved by Jewish and non-Jewish Enlightenment thinkers alike. They both recognized in the complex new social structures an incipient mode of existence which promised Jews a way out of the ghetto.

What I shall try to determine is the extent to which both literary and political discourses professing the ideals of tolerance already contained within themselves the seeds of the failure of the tolerance project. It is in light of this project that the metonymic relationship between Mendelssohn and Lessing assumes a special place. Before turning to this friendship, I believe it useful to provide a chronological account of the development of the tolerance discussion in the context of Jewish emancipation.

The English philosopher John Locke argues, in his *Letter Concerning Toleration*, written in Amsterdam in 1685 and published in 1689, that religious denomination should be subordinated to citizenship. Consequently, a citizen who obeys the laws of the State, who is socially integrated, has the right to expect the State's protection against religious intolerance. Religion becomes therefore a private matter, a matter of personal belief, whose practice is ensured by the citizen's inalienable rights.

It is significant in this context that, in his *Letter Concerning Toleration*, Locke places Christianity at a higher level of spiritual development than Judaism. In his view, this was justified by the fact that only the Christian religion could permit a separation between Church and State. In contrast, Judaism represented an absolute theocracy, which had never allowed and could never allow for such a separation.[3] This account of Judaism would seem to lead to the inescapable conclusion that only by renouncing his own religion could a traditional Jew subject himself to the laws of a non-Jewish state.

Locke's treatment of tolerance was to find an echo in the textual production of German intellectuals in the half-century following the publication of his Letter. A 1725 speech by Johann Christoph Gottsched—a prominent figure in early German Enlightenment— discloses an apparent parallel with the Lockean discussion of tolerance. He argues that "religious zeal is highly pernicious, whereas toleration of members of different faiths would be useful and sensible."4 He later refers specifically to the Jewish question, in a September 20, 1728, issue of *Der Biedermann*.5 In an article discussing the "harshest punishment" of twelve Jews during the Portuguese Inquisition, Gottsched, like Locke, differentiates between nation and religion. The expulsion and persecution of Portuguese Jews is thus legitimated only as "a matter of national security." As for the religious judgment, the deciding factor should be moral reason, not one's adherence to a particular creed.

The statesman and historian Christian Wilhelm von Dohm took up the definition of the parameters of Jewish integration into bourgeois society in his treatise *Concerning the Amelioration of the Civil Status of the Jews* (*Über die bürgerliche Verbesserung der Juden*, Published in 2 parts in 1781 and 1783). Dohm urged that in the interest of universal human rights of the State, Jews should be converted into "useful" citizens. Like Lessing and Humboldt, Dohm ascribed the purported wretched living conditions of Jews to the legal segregation that had been constantly forced upon them. Their social "inferiority," in other terms, was in a sense the direct result of their status as non-citizens.

Along with the political emancipation of the Jews, Dohm contended, must come a process of "education" or assimilation into the dominant culture and society. In return for this process of social improvement or transformation, full citizenship and legal equality would be granted. The political emancipation of the Jewish minority is thus articulated in terms of a mercantile exchange. The transfer of tolerance into the legislative sphere does not appear to take the form of acceptance and respect for cultural and religious difference, but rather becomes a commodity for Jews to "purchase" with services rendered to the State.

Dohm acknowledges, in fact, that the Jews' religious attachment will weaken progressively with their social and political integration. To those hypothetical critics who would point out that this mode of civic improvement actually requires the dissolution of the entire fabric of Judaism,

Dohm replies offhandedly, "what if it does! Why should the State, which demands nothing else of [the Jews] but that they become good citizens, concern itself with that?"[6] Dohm is not so much contradicting the notion of tolerance here, as taking its emancipatory project to its logical conclusion. What already seems implicit in Locke's discussion of the separation between Church and State is made explicit: in order for tolerance to bridge the gulf between Judaism and Christianity, between minority and majority, in a secular social space where both Christian and Jew would enjoy full equality under the law, the minority culture would apparently have to alter itself substantially.

The liberal statesman Wilhelm von Humboldt has provided another significant political formulation of tolerance. Humboldt expresses a similar lack of concern for the disappearance of the minority culture. In "A Project for a New Constitution for the Jews" ["Über den Entwurf zu einer neuen Konstitution für die Juden"] written in July 1809, during his appointment as Director of Culture and Education for the Prussian Ministry of the Interior, Humboldt recommends an immediate conferral of civil rights upon Jewish subjects. In his view, a gradual process of social reform would tend to exacerbate Christian prejudices against Jews, since a partial legal emancipation could only reinforce prejudicial public opinion about Jews. An immediate legal emancipation of the Jewish population, Humboldt argues,

> would not introduce a new Orthodoxy among the Jews, but rather, by means of a genuine and just Tolerance, it would promote more schisms [among them] and the Jewish hierarchy would collapse by itself. Individual Jews will become aware of the fact that they actually had no religion but only a ceremonial law, and — driven by the inherently human need for a higher faith, they will turn of their own accord to the Christian one.[7]

As Locke does, Humboldt places Christianity at the top of the religious hierarchy. The legal enactment of tolerance, in other words, is to be enforced from the top, and will aim at the progressive inclusion and dissolution of the minority culture into an unquestionably higher social order. Humboldt's lack of concern for the disappearance of the Jewish tradition finds an even more forceful expression in his private correspondence. In an April 30, 1816, letter to his wife, Karoline, Humboldt states:

"But I actually also love the Jews only *en masse, en détail* I very much try to avoid them."[8]

As Moses Mendelssohn once observed: "It is our luck that one cannot press for human rights without, at the same time, remonstrating against our own."[9] Yet, in order to participate in an imminent order of civilization, to become a citizen of the future bourgeois state, the Jew was expected, in effect, to gradually shed his Jewishness. Only by renouncing the cultural identity and religious practices that marked him as an Other, only by ceasing to be traditionally Jewish, in short, could the Jew be tolerated by the German bourgeois subject.

As I suggest above, the tolerance ideal comes to be realized at the private level in the exemplary and enduring friendship between Moses Mendelssohn and Gotthold Ephraim Lessing. This metonymic concord between Judaism and Christianity seemed to ensure the possibility of a public practice of religious tolerance. As the most prominent eighteenth-century Jewish intellectual, Mendelssohn was an influential promulgator of Jewish emancipation. Lessing, on the other hand, as author of perhaps the best known literary endorsement of tolerance, *Nathan the Wise*, emerged as a strong non-Jewish advocate for the social acceptance of Jews.

The play portrays a Jewish character who is not only morally superior to his Christian and Moslem counterparts, but becomes the embodiment of tolerance. Conventional criticism has alleged that the character of Nathan is modelled on Moses Mendelssohn. If we take as a given this biographical reading of the play, then the friendship between a Jewish philosopher and a Christian poet is transposed in the play into two broader dimensions. The first involves the literary transference of this private relationship into the social sphere: the assimilation and participation of Jews in dominant German society. At the same time, Nathan/Mendelssohn projects the as-yet-unrealized social paradigm of the fully acculturated Jewish citizen of a future bourgeois state.

It was towards the achievement of this paradigm of acculturation that Mendelssohn militated, actively disseminating among Jews the notion of tolerance. For Mendelssohn, tolerance cleared the common humanistic ground between Jew and non-Jew, and permitted the interaction between the two groups as "Menschen." In a letter to Herder Mendelssohn writes: "Moses, the human being [Mensch], is writing to Herder, the human being, and not the Jew to the Christian preacher [Superintendent]."[10] Mendelssohn's use of the term "Mensch" is significant in that it points to a crucial distinction between his articulation of tolerance and those of Humboldt and Dohm. Although bridging the gap between minority and majority (Jew and Christian), the humanistic commonality signified by "Mensch" allows for the preservation of religious and cultural difference. To be a "Mensch," in Mendelssohn's sense, does not seem to preclude being Jewish.

It was after the first staging of Lessing's early play *Die Juden* (*The Jews*), in 1749, that Mendelssohn and Lessing initiated their relationship. The play represents the first instance in German literature of a protagonist who is both virtuous and a Jew. By postponing the revelation of the main character's religious identity until the end of the play, Lessing apparently intended his contemporary audience to call into question its prejudices and stereotypes about Jews, after having identified with and cheered for a Jewish hero. As in *Nathan the Wise*, the Other whom Lessing chooses to present as the worthy object of humanistic tolerance is an acculturated and wealthy Jew.[11] The encounter between German and Jew, then, would seem to be enabled primarily by the latter's "bourgeoisification," by his assimilation into dominant German society. Inasmuch as they advocate the transformation of the Jewish individual into a German bourgeois subject, both Lessing and Mendelssohn find themselves in agreement with Dohm and Humboldt. Yet, as we have seen, Mendelssohn's conception of bourgeoisification differs substantially from Dohm's and Humboldt's.

In *Nathan the Wise*, Lessing also appears to regard the humanistic practice of tolerance and the Jews' continued adherence to their minority culture as not mutually exclusive. In scene seven of the play's fourth act, Nathan observes, in response to the Lay-Brother's enthusiastic exclamation that he is a Christian: "What makes of me a Christian in your eyes, makes you in mine a Jew."[12] He affirms the common humanity shared by Jew and Christian, who simultaneously hold on to their cultural and religious identities. Mendelssohn's and Lessing's projects could therefore be subsumed to an inside/outside dialectic of theoretical articulations of emancipation— Mendelssohn on the "inside" of the Jewish community, Lessing on the "outside"— which required only political and social praxis for their legal enactment.

Although the scope of this article does not allow for a thorough analysis of Lessing's two plays in the light of Jewish emancipation, one can nonetheless put forth some general conclusions regarding the distinctions between Lessing's and Mendelssohn's notion of assimilation and that evidenced in the more overtly political writings discussed above. As I have pointed out in the foregoing analysis, neither Dohm nor Humboldt displays much interest in the Jews as an oppressed minority nor in the preservation and legal protection of Jewish culture and religion; rather their main concern is for the assimilated bourgeois citizens whom Jews must become for the good of the State.

On the other hand, Lessing's and Mendelssohn's visions of a German-Jewish encounter are founded on their individual experiences. In their articulations, the moment of complete and universal tolerance is deferred to a future and more perfect stage of human (social) development. The specific details of this process, in contrast to Dohm's and Humboldt's, do not receive the immediate attention of the two friends who have, albeit on a personal, synecdochic level, accomplished the ideal of tolerance.

As Jacob Katz argues, however, this ideal was even in Mendelssohn's and Lessing's day more a myth than a historical or social possibility:

> Mendelssohn doubtless projected into his vision of the future his own experience of tolerant mutual relationships with friends and co-workers of different faiths. He saw no reason why the harmonious atmosphere which existed among men of good will in a small circle should not be possible in society at large. In actual fact, the kind of relationship which Mendelssohn enjoyed with friends of a different faith existed among a limited circle of intellectuals only. Even for them it was but a brief social episode.[13]

A compelling example of the difficulties inherent in translating the private practice of tolerance among friends of different faiths into public policy is a contemporary assessment of Lessing's *The Jews*. Johann David Michaelis, a Göttingen professor of Oriental Studies, who was not only a paradigm of what Edward Said has called the Orientalist scholar, but also, in my opinion, a profound anti-Semite, asserts in a 1754 critique of the play that Lessing's virtuous Jew defies verisimilitude since "such a virtuous soul" could never be produced by "a people of such morals, lifestyle and upbringing."[14]

A little less than thirty years later, in a review of the first part of Dohm's *Concerning the Amelioration of the Civil Status of the Jews*, Michaelis was to revise his disparaging interpretation of the Jewish "character," qualifying as an "exception" the rare Jew who, in contrast to the general Jewish population, was virtuous and civilized. Like Dohm, he considers the question of the Jews' "usefulness" to the State, suggesting that the Jews could become "even more useful" as settlers of hypothetical "sugar plantation colonies, which have succeeded in draining the European metropoli of people, and offset the wealth they possess with an unhealthy climate."[15] On the surface, this proposed deportation appears to contradict directly the ideal of tolerance. Nevertheless, the logic of Michaelis' intolerance is not fundamentally different from that of Dohm's and Humboldt's emancipatory project. The conclusions to which they come might seem diametrically opposed— Dohm and Humboldt postulate the social desirability of Jewish emancipation, Michaelis argues that emancipation would be both impracticable and socially harmful— but their premises are quite similar: they all see as inconsistent the Jew's continued adherence to Judaism and his citizenship in the future bourgeois state.

Yet, as the development of emancipation in the next century was to show, German Jews, though they had "gone a long way in the direction of acculturation and Verbürgerlichung [bourgeoisification] . . . were clearly not losing their group character."[16] As the notion of the bourgeois state undergoes a radically nationalist redefinition in the late nineteenth century, one can see how Germans will find it possible to call for emancipation from the Jews, for eradication of the residues of Jewishness "tainting" the cultural and political center. And soon after the emancipation of German Jews had become a legal fait accompli in 1871, the myth of tolerance had been replaced by the reality of anti-Semitism.

Notes

1 Reichspräsident von Hindenburg in: *Das Buch des Goethe-Lessing Jahres 1929; 100 Jahre Uraufführung des Faust—200. Geburtstag von Lessing* (Braunschweig: Friedrich Vieweg und Sohn, 1929), fly-leaf. All translations, unless otherwise indicated, are my own.

[2] Reinhard Rürup, *Emanzipation und Antisemitismus. Studien zur"Judenfrage" der bürgerlichen Gesellschaft* (Frankfurt am Main: Fischer, 1987), p. 114: "Modern anti-Semitism is not only chronologically, but also factually a post-emancipatory phenomenon. . . The 'Jewish Question' is no longer a question of the emancipation of the Jews, but—in the words of many contemporaries—a question of the 'emancipation from the Jews.'"

[3] John Locke, *A Letter Concerning Toleration.* Ed. and trans. Mario Montuori (The Hague: Martinus Nijhoff, 1963), p. 73.

[4] Johann Christoph Gottsched, *Ausgewählte Werke IX/2.* Hg. von P.M. Mitchell, bearbeitet von Rosemary Scholl (Berlin/New York: Walter de Gruyter, 1976), p. 463.

[5] See Johann Christoph Gottsched, *Der Biedermann. Faksimiledruck der Originalausgabe Leipzig 1727-1729.* Hg. von Wolfgang Martens (Stuttgart: J.B. Metzlersche Verlagsbuchhandlung, 1975).

[6] Christian Konrad Wilhelm von Dohm, *Über die bürgerliche Verbesserung der Juden. 2 Teile in einem Band.* Im Anhang Franz Reuß. Nachdruck der Ausgaben Berlin und Stettin 1781-83 und Kaiserslautern 1891 (Hildesheim/New York: Georg Olms Verlag, 1973), part II, p. 174.

[7] Wilhelm von Humboldt, "Über den Entwurf zu einer neuen Konstitution für die Juden."*Gesammelte Schriften.* (Bd.X) Hg. von der Königlich Preussischen Akademie der Wissenschaften (Berlin: B. Behr's Verlag, 1903), p. 105.

[8] *Juden und Judentum in deutschen Briefen aus drei Jahrhunderten.* Hg. von Franz Kobler (Königstein/Ts.: Athenäum Verlag, 1984), p. 208.

[9] Quoted in: Hannah Arendt, *Rahel Varnhagen. Lebensgeschichte einer deutschen Jüdin aus der Romantik* (München: Piper, 1959), p. 19.

[10] Quoted in: Jacob Katz, *Exclusiveness and Tolerance. Studies in Jewish-Gentile Relations in Medieval and Modern Times* (Oxford: Oxford University Press, 1961), p. 170. Mendelssohn's use of the term "Mensch" points to a crucial distinction between his articulation of tolerance and Dohm's. The latter asserts in *Über die bürgerliche Verbesserung der Juden. 2 Teile in einem Band,* part II, 20: "The Jews are, like the rest of us, human beings *too*" (my emphasis). The residue, signified by the adverbial modifier "too," appended to Jewish humanity, is Judaism itself. In order to become human beings "tout court" the Jews must ascend, according to Dohm, to the status of "useful" State citizens.

[11] In a section of *Außenseiter* (Frankfurt am Main: Suhrkamp, 1975) entitled "Der Weise Nathan und der Räuber Spiegelberg," p. 339, Hans Mayer discusses the important role played by wealth and education in the emancipation of Jews in both literary and socio-historical contexts.

[12] Gotthold Ephraim Lessing, *Nathan the Wise*. Trans. Ellen Frothingham (New York: Henry Holt and Company, 1980), p. 172.

[13] Jacob Katz, *Exclusiveness and Tolerance. Studies in Jewish-Gentile Relations in Medieval and Modern Times* (Oxford: Oxford University Press, 1961), p. 180.

[14] Gotthold Ephraim Lessing, "Über das Lustspiel 'Die Juden'" in: *Werke in drei Bänden. Erster Band.* Hg. von Herbert G. Göpfert (München/Wien: Carl Hanser Verlag, 1982), p. 290.

[15] Johann David Michaelis, "Hr. Ritter Michaelis Beurtheilung. Ueber die bürgerliche Verbesserung der Juden von Christian Wilhelm Dohm," *Über die bürgerliche Verbesserung der Juden. 2 Teile in einem Band.* Im Anhang Franz Reuß. Nachdruck der Ausgaben Berlin und Stettin 1781-83 und Kaiserslautern 1891 (Hildesheim/New York: Georg Olms Verlag, 1973) part II, p. 41.

[16] Shulamit Volkov, "The Jews in 19th-Century Germany: Notes on Becoming a Minority," *Jewish Identity in the German World: Emancipation, Assimilation and Thereafter.* Proceedings of the Symposium. 16-17 March 1990. Department of German, University of California, Berkeley, p. 131.

Eberhard Görner

Socialism: Myth and Reality

The subject Myth and Socialism is so enormous that it would be sufficient to occupy several universities. So what can you expect from me? No more and no less than the experience of forty-six years under existing socialism, an experience embodied by the German Democratic Republic as the second German state in the years 1949-1989.

I was born in the Erzgebirge mountain region in 1944. My grandfather was a coal miner, my father a fitter and my mother a shop assistant, later a housewife. I received my general education at the ten-year school down the road. I went on to learn the trade of a turner, and I was still an apprentice when my instructor convinced me that, as a youngster from a working-class background, my place was in the Party of the fledgling workers' and peasants' state. So I became a candidate member and later a fully fledged member of the SED. After completing my apprenticeship I studied German and history at the teacher-training college in Leipzig. Having worked for two years as a teacher, I applied for a job with GDR television, where I was taken on as a freelance production and drama assistant. This led to my studies at the College of Film in Potsdam-Babelsberg, from which I graduated with a degree in directing and dramatic art.

Between 1972 and 1990 I worked as an editor, journalist and screenplay writer in what was then the GDR, and since January 1, 1991, I have been a freelance writer in the new larger Germany extending from the Rhine to the Oder.

Socialism as practiced at least in Europe has apparently come to an end. But a more profound inquiry into the reasons for its inability to reform and its sudden collapse seems to be only just beginning. We are, after all, living in the midst of the greatest upheaval in German and European history since 1945 and world history since 1917. Millions of people throughout the world believed in existing, and not just theoretical, socialism. They were guided by the idea that it would endure eternally and, as a system offering greater social justice, presented a genuine alternative to capitalism. Among them there were many who sought to improve socialism as far as the situation allowed, but not infrequently they had to suffer disadvantages as a result and their disappointment now is particularly bitter. . . . One of the main reasons for its demise was doubtless the Pharaonic concentration of all power in the hands of the top men in the Party.

These are the first words of a book entitled *Der Sturz*, a cross-examination of Erich Honecker, issued recently by Aufbau-Verlag Berlin and Weimar. I'll come back to this later.

Let us ask the question: what is socialism?

Socialism: a relatively distinct socioeconomic formation in the historic epoch of the transition from capitalism to communism on a world scale. Socialism constitutes a qualitatively new type of social order, because it represents the end of the exploitation of man by man. Socialism as a social system is a constantly advancing, extremely dynamic system embodying a vast range of social relations.

This is the answer to be found on page 406 of the *Dictionary of Marxist-Leninist Sociology* put out by Dietz Verlag, the Party publishers, in 1989. And that is what we learnt at school, in our days as apprentices, and at university.

And what is myth?

At school and university, in the media, the press, on radio and television, we were told time and again, under existing socialism, that Marxism-Leninism was a scientific world outlook capable of explaining with the utmost accuracy what ultimately holds the world together. A favorite way of quoting Marx was "Religion is the opium of the people," and "history is the history of class struggles."

"Only socialism has a clear programme for the future" claimed *Neues Deutschland*, newspaper of the SED Central Committee, which asserted on April 26, 1973:

Attempts at a reformist transformation of the social policy of capitalism inevitably introduce new elements into the conditions of the class struggle waged by the proletariat in the capi-

talist countries. The revolutionary workers' movement has always regarded it as one of its responsibilities to lay bare the ideology and policy of reformism. . . . The new trends in bourgeois ideology and politics, which aggravate the contradictions in the ruling camp and reveal the infeasibility of the state-monopoly management of society, reflect, in the final instance, the weakness of the positions occupied by the monopoly bourgeoisie, their inability to achieve the objectives proclaimed by their own ideologies.
Only socialism is in a position to ensure the participation of the masses in the management of society by combining science with politics in the interests of the people. Today the ideologies of capitalism are being forced by the objective requirements of social development to extend, in a manner of speaking, the framework of social demagogy and declare objectives which in reality can only be attained in the wake of the revolutionary overthrow of capitalism.

The truth is actually a mirror image of these lines— a mythical exercise if ever you saw one. I have chosen this bombastic quotation because it illustrates in striking fashion why many people no longer took any notice of such articles. Those who did so nevertheless were either caught up in the jungle of such demagogic assertions or— and they were in the majority— accepted the monopoly on the historical truth looming between the lines.

One hardly needs to be a mystic to discover what actually happened to the idea of socialism, an idea whose origins lie in Hegel and Feuerbach. Knowledge of human nature was virtually ignored when it came to practical social policy under existing socialism.

The socialist states viewed themselves as societies organized on atheist lines and had no room for the human psyche, the inner being. Starting in 1917 a power structure was developed on the premise that if the land was nationalized, the new economic realities, the socialization of the means of production, would give the people a communist awareness precisely as Marx had supposed.

But what does myth really mean? I have not yet given you an answer to this question. It is a question which one of the GDR's leading writers, Franz Fühmann, posed back in 1983. He sought an answer in his essay "Das Mythische Element in der Literatur" (Franz Fühmann, *Essays, Gespräche, Aufsätze 1964 - 1981*, VEB Hinstorff Verlag, Rostock, 1983, p.

95 ff). He wrote: "In Benseler-Kaegi's dictionary you will find the following suggestions for equivalents under the heading 'myth': 'word, discourse, dictum, mission, dialogue, conversation, counsel, resolution, reflection, narrative, news, report, legend, cause, reason' and thirteen others. More or less the same applies to any work of reference."

At another point he writes, "Myth expresses the contradiction. Myth points insistently to reality, yet moves constantly in the realms of unreality — what is its reality, or in other words: what is the occurrence it speaks of, the thing it knows; in a nutshell, what is the object specific to it?"

Fühmann describes the fundamental contradiction as lying in the fact "that myth can never occur as a prototype, but is always nothing more than the concretization of an already existing pattern, which in turn must inevitably reveal itself to be the concretization of something existing before." The older one becomes, the clearer it is that this world has a beginning and an end. No less a thinker than Thomas Mann reflected aloud on this in his biblical story *Joseph and His Brothers*. He named the prelude "Descent into Hell." Let us join Thomas Mann in this historical retrospective and go back, back to the sources which distinguish man from all other beings, the sources from which there emerged the slaveowning system, feudalism, capitalism, socialism, Christianity, Islam, Buddhism, imperialism, communism, philosophy and art. A descent into hell indeed, and its unattainable goal — heaven.

"Deep is the well of the past," Thomas Mann tells us. "Should we not call it unfathomable?"

> And this perhaps even if or just because it is man alone whose past is at issue: this enigmatic being which unites in itself our naturally joyful and unnaturally miserable existence and whose secret is—for reasons which are only too appreciable—the be-all and end-all of our talking and questioning, lends desperation and fire to all our talk and urgency to all our questions. And then it so happens that the deeper one delves, the further one penetrates down into the underworld of the past and feels one's way, the raison d'etre of the human element, its history, its ethos, prove to be quite unfathomable and, to whatever incredible lengths we extend our probe, sink again and again and deeper and deeper into a bottomless pit. "Again" and "further" are well chosen, for that which defies

inquiry makes a fool of our inquiring mind, presenting it with apparent points of focus and destinations on its route behind which, once reached, there are revealed new distances through the past. It is like someone who walks along the coast and whose journey finds no end because, behind each loamy backdrop of dunes to which he has pushed himself onwards, new expanses offer the enticing promise of new foothills.

In his four-part novel *Joseph and His Brothers*, Thomas Mann describes how a Jewish tribe created for themselves a god from whom they could ask anything and on whom they could also unload all guild and responsibility. The magic of the old Pharaonic gods was no longer sufficient to cope with the realities. A new god was needed, a new myth: "And the Lord spoke to Moses and said: You shall not turn to false gods and shall not make cast gods for yourselves; for I am the Lord your God."

If you read the Bible carefully, you will see to your surprise that with the entry of the Jewish people into the Promised Land, every step gave rise to a new law. Moses spoke with God, and from their dialogue developed one corpus of laws after another, leading to a growth in the power of Moses and his followers.

Every faith and every state has its own myth. Karl Marx and Friedrich Engels begin their corpus of laws, *The Communist Manifesto*, with the words "A specter is haunting Europe — the specter of communism." A new epoch was proclaimed, the epoch of the proletariat. Today all that remains of the promised land of the proletariat is a band of silver on the horizon. But to some it seemed within reach. Christianity has exerted a considerable influence on the world in the past two thousand years. Its institutions are places of living communication with God. And there can be no doubt that the idea of Marxism-Leninism, too, has changed the world since 1848, but its claim to represent the interests of the proletariat has been robbed of all ethical value.

In the preface of the second edition of *Quotations from Chairman Mao Tse-Tung*, published in 1966, we read: "a new era is emerging in which the workers, peasants and soldiers of Marxism-Leninism are grasping Mao Tse-Tung's thought. Once Mao Tse-Tung's thought is grasped by the broad masses, it becomes an inexhaustible source of strength and a spiritual atom bomb of infinite power."

What we have here is a monstrous vision, a threat which no longer has anything in common with the idea of a more just world.

Myth and socialism also raises the question of why certain individuals, using a party as their instrument, managed to filter out only the negative potential of Marxist-Leninist philosophy. Why was it not possible to bring the socio-ethical element of this philosophy to fruition on the economic and sociopolitical fronts? Why was unbridled idealism substituted for realism? Why was it that unreason ruled and not reason? Why were the general secretaries of the communist parties transformed into the Golden Calf that the people have now knocked from its pedestal? For the fact that the myth of socialism lies now shattered in pieces at our feet does not make the world any better.

> No being can deny its nature in its feelings, ideas and thoughts. Whatever it brings into play, it always brings itself into play. Every being has its god, its highest being, in itself. If you extol the magnificence of God, you extol the magnificence of your own being. All admiration is in essence self-admiration, all praise — self-praise, every judgement you make about others, a judgement about yourself. [1]

This thesis by the German philosopher Ludwig Feuerbach unravels in stunning fashion the puzzle as to why those who held political power in the countries of existing socialism became more and more divorced from their peoples and thus organized the collapse of their states themselves.

The former SED Politburo member Egon Krenz wrote a letter to his former boss, Erich Honecker, dealing with the interview in *Der Sturz* which I mentioned at the beginning. It includes the following words:

> I am convinced that—as far as the internal situation is concerned—the main share of the blame for the reasons which led to the demise of the GDR lies with the Politburo to which I belonged and over which you presided. In the last few years our policy vacillated between "ignoring the realities" and "political suppression." We identified the leading role of the SED with the mistaken view that only the party leadership — and there, in turn, a few leading comrades—was in possession of the truth. I can find no other explanation why there were hardly any public discussions about the substance of our policies in the latter years.

Elsewhere Krenz notes:

I am now convinced that we, the political leadership, did not appreciate the true scale of the profound crisis that had existed in our society for years. I am now aware that it affected every sphere of life: politics, the economy, morals, scholarship and culture. The credibility of the values, ideals and objectives of socialism —even if we did not recognize this in all its vividness — had been questioned for a long time. There were many who spoke one way and acted another. And there was no small number of people — including very many Party members — who lived in a conflict of conscience between what they saw and what they were actually able to influence. Helplessness and resignation spread and began to affect the ideological situation.

Violations of the principle that people should be rewarded for what they contribute meant that it did not really pay to do a good job. We lacked the productivity to back up a social policy. That was the beginning of the end of the GDR. And that was the source of subjective decisions. [2]

While claiming to grapple with the myth —and that was the way Erich Honecker saw himself and was treated—this letter creates a new myth. Its concept is facile: if Honecker had listened to me, Krenz, socialism would not have failed in the GDR. The letter itself is a piece of documentary evidence, a psychological profile of a ruling party stripped of its power. Words like "divorced from reality," "illusions," "silence or distort," "mass psychosis," "lack of prospects and hopelessness," "lack of orientation," "cynicism," "world of your own," and "shared guilt" sound like a confession from a closed institution within a closed society, and that is what was made out of socialism right from the outset. This, too, became a myth, claiming to be timeless and destined to exist for time eternal. But a myth does not emerge overnight. Successive generations are involved in building the edifice; it is supported by social forces, passed on, interpreted, analyzed, cemented. "Myth and leadership are the spirit and the shape of a simple, naive generation-drive following the same straight line," claims the linguistic philosopher Eugen Rosenstock-Huessy.[3]

There were times when the world's great minds came under the influence of this generation-drive, this idea of social justice to be achieved by way of revolution.

Writing in his diary in November 1918, for example, Thomas Mann hailed the "social republic" and put on record that the future belonged to the idea of socialism, of communism no less, and that Germany would be well advised to take the new idea on board.

The "bourgeois age" seemed outdated; the future belonged to socialism. In January 1920 Thomas Mann articulated the desire that "Marxist class socialism [should] become the intellectual property of the community of men." "It began in the East," this resistance to Western civilization, and so it is that the German road to socialism started with the October Revolution.[4]

It is now plain for all to see that, beginning with Stalin, socialism did not turn towards human beings as Thomas Mann and others had hoped, but away from them. That marked the beginning of the end of the socialist age. What was built was the scenery for the benefit of officials.

Marxism-Leninism was elevated to the status of divine liturgy. I still remember very well how greatly impressed I was, standing before Lenin's mausoleum in Moscow for the first time, in the early seventies. What magnificent things we had heard and learned at school about the founder of the world's first socialist state. What a huge number of films we had seen about the storming of the Winter Palace. What a huge number of images was associated with the name of Lenin.

Lenin talking to the peasant, Lenin in conversation with scientists, Lenin conversing with soldiers, Lenin in dialogue with artists— and there he was, a small jaundiced figure enveloped in a diffuse light and guarded by two stern Red Armymen.

Why, I asked myself, did you spend two hours standing in line, why did you tolerate being shouted at by the guards just because you wanted to sit on a brick wall in the Kremlin, why did you allow yourself to be humiliated just for the sake of seeing a wax doll? But this critical mood soon died away. For in the world outside there was the reality of that society: Lenin as a monument, Lenin in the Tretyakov Gallery, the Lenin Library, the Lenin Museum and so forth and so on. The despotism of a society is also the despotism of its priests, artists and writers who have produced alien fairy tales and traditions from historical realities.[5] The fact that form and significance did not always coincide was deliberately suppressed in the socialist states, and this suppression in turn was historically mythicized.

As I write this, it becomes apparent to me that in my own life I was a direct participant in the rise and fall of socialism in the GDR: as a school student, an apprentice, an undergraduate, a teacher, an artist.

On the artistic front, I had an early taste of freedom. I was impressed by our church, which had been inaugurated in 1904 and, so I was told, had been built with miners' money.

There was something grand about it when the sunlight flowed through the leaded glass windows into the vestry. The holy figures on the baptismal font, with whose water I too was blessed, had been carved by a miner and a carpenter.

My father, who had been a member of the voluntary fire brigade under Hitler, Ulbricht and Honecker, told me that the three bronze church bells had been removed from the tower in the winter of 1942. Nazi Germany did not need their warning peals; it needed bronze to make guns. I enjoyed singing in tune to our pleasant-sounding organ— which had been built in Rochlitz, Saxony, and inaugurated with the church— all the lovely Christmas carols, while the apostles painted in the triumphal arch cast their benevolent glances down on me.

When I think back, I must say that our church was an important place for me in terms of what was to follow. It was my first encounter with art. "For art requires a substantial form stirred by the spirit. But the first interpreter to lend more concrete form to religious ideas is art, because the prosaic contemplation of the objective world is only brought to bear when the human being as such, as spiritual self-awareness, has cast off the fetters of the world in its direct form."6

The spiritual self-awareness soon collided with the way the state saw itself. It had different symbols. The collision was not a menacing one, not existential, but tangible nonetheless. The state which was founded in 1949 as the German Democratic Republic in the wake of World War II sought to steer the individual, and the artistic individual more than most, in the direction of its desires and its goals. The ethical principle, which is always a democratic one at the same time, was subjected to constraints. To circumvent this restriction artists looked for subjects in which this principle could be articulated. In the former GDR, for example, these included the antifascist official doctrine, the concept of resistance, the fight against Hitler between 1933 and 1945, which the SED leadership claimed for itself and which formed the basis for internationally renowned works of art — of which one good example is Fritz Cremer's figure of an ascending man, which was erected in the park at UN headquarters in New York.

Film and television in the former GDR also turned to this subject, but the ideas captured in and expressed through this substance became something of a double code. The designs of those in political power to surround their antifascist past with an historical myth were bound to encounter resistance from the artistic community, and so it was that some of the films about the antifascist resistance never reached the cinema screen. Sometimes it seemed as if the Pope were demanding the image of Judas to be painted out of Leonardo's "Last Supper." No traitors must be allowed to sit at the table with the saints.

But the fact is — and such radical language is the only appropriate form —that the ideas of socialism were betrayed right from the start and with them the art that sought to give these ideas their humanitarian reflection.

Like everything in human history, this statement needs to be differentiated. Music by Dimitri Shostakovich has already earned its place among the world's masterpieces, and the books of Anna Seghers and Christa Wolf will stand the test of time. Eisenstein's film *Battleship Potemkin* —this silent work about justice and injustice revolutionized cinema. I could continue this list and tell you of pictures I have seen in Siberia which I am convinced are three times better than Andy Warhol's pop art. But I have something else to say.

There are people who regret the demise of socialism. "Now we have lost our workers' state," my mother laments. She was born in 1906 and wonders what has become of this world. As a little girl in a frilly white dress she joined her classmates in a choral welcome for Kaiser Wilhelm II: "Hail the leader in the victor's laurels!" Then came the First World War, and the teachers began dealing out more vicious blows to their pupils. Inflation and unemployment, the strike at the pit — my grandfather was a face worker — people fighting for their daily bread, the Weimar Republic, unemployment once more. Then came Hitler.

When the stormtroopers smashed the windows at Schocken, the Jewish department store in our small town in the Erzgebirge where my mother worked, and when they shot at customers who chose to do their shopping "at the Jews" despite all the warnings, when my mother lost her job, the myth of national socialism began to crumble. Marriage. The Second World War began two years later. I was born not long before it ended. The American soldiers came into the bedroom, rocked me in their arms and cried, "This is a wonderful baby." My mother was all atremble, this being the first time she had ever seen an American sergeant with a black skin.

The Americans went and the Russians came. But we had peace, we had work, and we had bread and milk. For those who — like my parents — lived a modest existence, and always took pains to ensure that the family was not left lacking, where a large circle of friends shared in the joys and pains of everyday life, and the daily routine depended on whether my father was on the early, afternoon or night shift, there was no room for inquiring into world history. After all the bitter experience of the German past, work, food and a roof over their heads were the only things that mattered. And not only were they assured these things, but they also enjoyed a humble degree of prosperity. The name of our street was changed from Gartenstrasse to August-Bebel-Strasse, which didn't really worry anyone because Bebel was a Social Democrat, as all the miners had been before Hitler came to power. The biggest mine in the coalfield, called Kaiserin Victoria Mine, was renamed Karl Liebknecht Mine and declared the property of the people. A slogan affixed in red to the gate proclaimed "Work well today and live well tomorrow."

This slogan said a lot. There was a lot of hard work needed for the mine to surrender its black gold. "Coal for the republic!" Every night a red star on the winding tower shone far into the surrounding area, and when they saw its light they knew that the plan was fulfilled. And on May Day came the celebration. You were made an "Activist of Socialist Labor" or a "Merited Miner," were given some money and a free holiday at the seaside or in the mountains.

We children of the workers' and peasants' state spent a few weeks in summer at the best holiday camps in the country and sang beside the camp fire, "The Spanish sky spreads its stars above our trenches . . . ." The books I received from my parents were full of praise for the beauties of Germany, and nobody doubted that the two German states would soon be a united German fatherland once more, so much so that this was loudly proclaimed in the words of the GDR national anthem.

There was hardly anyone in the village who spoke about the Nazis. At school we were told that the German people had put up bitter resistance to Hitler. The best resistance fighters were now in the government, workers and peasants like our parents. A myth was built up, the myth of the historic mission of the working class. We knew the village carpenter, the fitter, the roofer, the plumber and the small farmers. There were quite a few who saw justice in the fact that the political life of the country was being run by equals among equals. But the historic tragedy was such that when the GDR was no more, all these trades disappeared from the village, the restaurants and bars were closed down, the cinema walled up, the mine exhausted and turned into a museum. Our church is closed because there is no money to plaster the walls.

Another tragedy is the continuing failure to understand that the Germans in East Germany grew up with a lie, that they believed it was possible to move from national socialism to socialism as if they were just crossing the bridge from one side to the other — simply by changing the songs and the flags.

But the reality was different. The swastika was removed from the old Nazi flags and the "new" red workers' flag hung out of the windows. I remember how shocked I was on October 3, 1990, the Day of German Unity, when I saw that next door a flag was hanging with the same black circle in the middle: this time it was not the swastika, but the hammer, compass and garland of corn which had been obliterated. I cannot forget the answer my father gave me when I asked whether he felt it was all right to use a Nazi flag as a workers' flag. "Why not if the material is still good?"

My mother and father led a quiet and uneventful life in the GDR. They were satisfied with what they had. From her historical perspective she is being quite honest when she says, "Now we have lost our workers' state. Now there are rich and poor again, just like it used to be."

And the more the current of unemployment in the eastern part of Germany gathers momentum, the deeper the social rift becomes and the more people lose the possessions they had gathered together under socialism, the greater will be the tendency towards a revival of the myth of existing socialism.

"Religion and faith are two quite different things," our village pastor told me recently over the phone. "Almost as different as democracy and freedom." Under socialism we had a sense of humanity, solidarity and closeness, despite the state. Now we have the freedom but have come to rely on money. Suddenly those who are out of work find themselves alone; what use is democracy to those who have lost their jobs?

* * *

In 1979 I worked on the screenplay for *Der Leutnant Yorck von*

Wartenburg, based on the story of the same name by Stephan Hermlin. It is the story of a dream in the final few minutes before one of the leaders of the resistance against Hitler was executed. As I worked on this adaptation I understood that the men in political power in the GDR were prepared — in order to hold on to that power — to enlist certain aspects of fascist ideology, turning for help to those whom they had once fought at the risk of their lives. Such insights, like others, were submerged in the hope that it would be possible for Marxist theory, which had become an ossified official dogma in all socialist states, to serve as the basis for democratic practice.

That same year the Publishing house Reclam in Leipzig brought out Hermlin's autobiographical essay "Abendlicht," which caused raised literary and political eyebrows in both German states at the time. In the section on his early reading, Hermlin describes his intellectual encounters with Marx's *Communist Manifesto.* He writes:

> The famous work led me to more complex and weighty works of Marxist literature, but I also kept returning to it. I believed that I had long since digested it from back to front when — it must have been in about my fiftieth year — I made a strange discovery. Among the sentences which I had long taken for granted there was one which read, "In place of the old bourgeois society, with its classes and class antagonisms, we shall have an association, in which the free development of all is the condition for the free development of each." I don't know when I actually began to read the sentence as it stands here. I read it as I did and gave it the meaning I did because it fitted in with the way I saw the world at the time. How great was my surprise, my indignation indeed, when after many years I found that the sentence actually means precisely the opposite, "where the free development of each is the condition for the free development of all."
> It was clear to me that I too had read something different than was intended — with my own ideas and my own immaturity — that what was allowed and even called for was absurd in my case because it alluded to other things that were not mentioned, because in my head a realization, a prophecy had been turned upside down.
> Suddenly a work had come to my notice which I had long been waiting and hoping for.[7]

Hermlin was born in 1913. He fought in the Spanish Civil War and in the French Resistance against Hitler. He made this discovery in the *Manifesto* just after Ulbricht, in agreement with the Soviet Union, had built the Wall, which Honecker intended to stand for a hundred years, but which was to be a feature of postwar Europe for only twenty-eight. By seeing Marx's thesis in its true light, Hermlin clearly found the intellectual means to scale the Wall.

But what are the words he uses to describe this process of realization, one which transcends the boundaries of any socialist state?

He resorts to myth. The reader — or perhaps the censor? — is enveloped in a cloud of mythological diction not unlike that of the Old Testament. I quote: "the famous work"; "when I made the incredible discovery"; "How great was my surprise, my indignation indeed"; "read a different text into a text"; "because it alluded to . . . something which was not mentioned"; "a prophecy had been turned upside down."

All the people— even a man like Hermlin who is reputed to have been friendly with Honecker — tried to handle in a way appropriate to themselves their conflict with the myth of socialism in the German Democratic Republic, which had come into existence on October 7, 1949.

I was asked in an interview that appeared in the newspaper *Frankfurter Rundschau* on November 27, 1990, whether my occupation with literature and its adaptation for the screen was not perhaps a way of escaping the contradictions that surrounded me.

I answered as follows: Yes. I found a partner in literature with whom I could discuss my own problems. The more I realized about the processes taking place in the GDR in the area of cultural policy, but also in everyday life, the greater my difficulties in coming to terms with things, because I began working in this medium with a great deal of social commitment. I was brought up with a sense of social justice and an attitude of solidarity towards those around me, and I had thought that this idea of socialism, socialism GDR style, provided the framework for a social model that I was brought up to believe in. When I realized that it all amounted to an abuse of this idea, I found a home and protection in literature and film. This protective function brought me to Thomas Mann. It was a very exciting development for me; even GDR literature at the level of Christa Wolf or Christoph Hein or Stefan Heym, to mention the names that are always cited, was actually no longer able to satisfy me anymore and could no longer provide an answer to my questions, because literature always reflects the subjective feelings of a writer; while it is objectively part of society, literature always partakes of the most profound subjectivity, even if we are dealing with mendacious literature. I am always receptive to literature and am only prepared to pass a verdict after I have read it.

It is also a literary process to read literature for its suitability for filming and to decide whether it is worthy of being adapted for television. One of the deciding factors is the message— as if literature has a message to put over— and I believe that Hermlin's writings which we put on film do have a humanitarian message. They seek to give people the courage to offer resistance, they focus on the individual and his power, and I believe that this message is always valid no matter what the system.

But — the contradictions between social reality in the GDR and the prescribed view of society — that really was the fundamental contradiction, and one that constantly shook the arts along with everything else. It is a contradiction that drove many, many artists and intellectuals away from the GDR, because this very contradiction between reality and the prescribed view of reality was very difficult to bear.

Like many other artists and intellectuals who were inspired by the idea of socialism— you will recall that it began with Danton and Robespierre —even in such a sensitive prose piece, Hermlin employs an "algebra of revolution" to describe his utopia of a classless society; but what Rosenstock-Huessy once wrote in his book on the European revolutions has shown itself to be true, and the collapse of the GDR on November 9, 1989, removed all doubts on this score:

> A community of minds is easier to establish than a community
> of matter. Marx's audience extends further than the eco-
> nomic unit, the power of the word is a mighty factor in the
> world economy. Marx did not present the working class with
> Marxism, but he put it within the intellectual horizon of all
> who could read and were inclined to do so. And the horizon
> was different from what Marx expected. It was not the prole-
> tariat that read his books —apart from the *Communist Mani-
> festo* — but the intellectuals, who were known by a word of
> French and bourgeois origin in prewar Russia.[8]

Myth and socialism. Two sides of the same coin. Their mystery, their enigma, their worship were there for all to see. I asked Professor Golo Mann whether it was not an historical tragedy that there had been this failure on the part of the working class. That was during a walk in the woods in Kilchberg by Lake Zurich in June 1990. He answered that this class has not existed since the First World War and that therefore it cannot shape history. The so-called representatives of the working class surrounded themselves at their party command centers with a circle of the initiated, who believed that their doctrines and actions were of eternal value. But nothing lasts forever. Time, history, follows its own laws.

In the mid-eighties the city fathers in Dresden had two slogans taken down on the quiet: "Socialism will win!" and "Eternal friendship with the Soviet Union!" In the circles of dogmatism, the works of Marxism-Leninism were wrongly interpreted, for they were less concerned about putting socialism into practice than expanding their political and personal power. The great enigma was "The Party is always right!" — but such a prerogative would be divine, superior even to the powers of Nature.

Events with many thousands of participants employed ritualistic means to depict a pretended unity between Party and people—and not without success. Music, dance and erotic encounters were to be had at the Whitsun rallies of the Free German Youth organization, at the Sports and Gymnastics Festival in Leipzig, on Republic Day, Miners' Day, Health Service Workers' Day, Shopworkers' Day, at the celebration of the team which had been made a "Socialist Labor Collective" and whatever all the other occasions were called. The "guardian of our souls" was the state, which for good measure sent its "armed and unarmed protective and security organs" to shield the intoxicating mysticism of the prescribed and voluntary celebrations. "Inner contemplation" and "enlightenment" were not called for.

What was to be experienced was the might of the state and nothing else. The socialist ideology was made into a substitute religion, while the paradoxical face of the actual model built on its foundation was largely ignored. Instead it was suggested time and again to the members of the Party of the Working Class and their sympathizers, alluding to the words of the Polish mystic Angelus Silesius, "I know that I cannot live without the Party. If it is destroyed I must of needs give up the ghost." This myth had clearly atheistic implications: man needs no church or priest to mediate between him and God.

In place of God there appears Nature, space, world reason, the Party or even nothingness. History is the history of class struggles. Those who put themselves at the head of these struggles belong to the vanguard of humanity. It was a vanguard represented by Stalin, Mao Tse-Tung, Nicolae Ceaucescu, Valdislaw Gomulka, Todor Zhivkov and Kim Il Sung, to mention only a few. They set up closed societies in which they could indulge in their missionary-like antics to their heart's content. Under Stalin the saints on Andrei Rublyov's icons were placed face downwards for use as floorboards; churches were replaced by swimming pools; synagogues by galleries — the Church's claim to men's souls was counted with a claim on everything resulting from the historic mission of the working class. The history of the labor movement was used as the raw material for myths which were handed down. This was accompanied by the growth of an irrational hostility to all things intellectual.

Capitalism was declared the external class enemy, and anyone who dared to doubt this dictum ran the risk of being stamped the internal class enemy. The manifestations of the official experiment known as socialism differed from one country to another, but the cause-and-effect mechanism was largely the same throughout. The more it became clear that this model of socialism shaped by Stalin did not represent a suitable concept for the continued advance of mankind, the more internal pressure grew and the more rapidly political ethics were eroded. People lived in a vicious cycle marked by distrust at every point, which ate away at their creative potential. The state security service became a security risk.

Ultimately the state abolished itself, for its potential was also exhausted, and so there occurred on November 9 a mystical event which is described in the Bible (Joshua, Chapter 6, verse 20) as follows: "As soon as the people heard the sound of the trumpet, the people raised a great shout and the wall fell down flat, so that the people went up into the city, every man straight before him, and they took the city."

That this epic scene from biblical mythology would some day mark the end of the history of socialism in the GDR — who would have dared to visualize Germany's new-found unity in this way?

Permit me in closing to return to *Der Sturz*, the book of interviews with Honecker. Reinhold Andert and Wolfgang Herzberg, Honecker's interviewers, were born in the same year as I was. I share their hopes and their fears. And I also share their thoughts:

In our quest for truth, we must now proceed step by step and ask not only which individuals are morally culpable, but also expose the deeper historical causes of the flawed social realities of socialist practice, and the influences that molded the biographies of such symbols of the system as the Honeckers, who both came from a humble working-class background.

Although the outdated social structures, the level of political culture, and those persons who represented it, may not have proved historically viable in the long run— the tremendous social and global challenges which socialism has partly sought in vain to answer and which perhaps brought on its tragic downfall are here with us to stay.They are crying out for new solutions which latter-day capitalism has not been able to deliver either. What is at stake *now* is the survival of humankind no less! 9

Notes

[1] Ludwig Feuerbach, *Das Wesen des Christentums* (Berlin: Akademie-Verlag, 1974), p. 39.

[2] Egon Krenz on *Der Sturz*, "Der Spiegel," 6/91, p. 54ff.

[3] Eugen Rosenstock-Huessy, *Die Sprache des Menschengeschlechts: Eine leibhaftige Grammatik in vier Teilen* (Heidelberg: Lambert Schneider, 1964), Part II, p. 257.

[4] Cf."Thomas Mann und die russische Revolution,"*Thomas Mann Jahrbuch*, Vol. 3. (Frankfurt am Main: Klostermann,1990), p. 90ff.

[5] Cf. Georg Wilhelm Friedrich Hegel, *Ästhetik*, Vol. 1. (Berlin und Weimar: Aufbau Verlag, 1984), p. 305.

[6] Hegel, p. 311.

[7] Stephan Hermlin, *Abendlicht* (Leipzig: Philipp Reclam jun., 1979), p. 22ff.

[8] Eugen Rosenstock-Huessy, *Die europäischen Revolutionen und der Charakter der Nationen* (Moers: Brendow Verlag, 1987), p. 462.

[9] Reinhold Andert/Wolfgang Herzberg, *Der Sturz: Honecker im Kreuzverhör* (Berlin und Weimar: Aufbau Verlag, 1990), p. 9ff.

Myth and the Human Condition

"Constellation—Virgo" (1968) by Nina Winkel

Winkel Sculpture Collection
SUNY Plattsburgh Art Museum

Armelle Crouzières-Ingenthron

Terrorism and/or Sacrifice
in
Les Justes
by Albert Camus

> "Révolte. L'absurde suppose l'absence de choix. Vivre c'est choisir. Choisir c'est tuer. L'objection à l'absurde, c'est le meurtre."
>
> Albert Camus, *Carnets* (Paris:Editions Gallimard, 1964), p. 280.
>
> "One man's terrorist is another man's freedom fighter."
>
> Peter C. Sederberg, "The Meaning of Terrorism," *Terrorist Myths: Illusion, Rhetoric, and Reality* (New Jersey: Prentice Hall, 1989).

Terrorism *and* sacrifice: are these two terms antithetical or parallel? In general, terrorism—as acts of violence—presupposes and implies the death or the sacrifice of human beings whom terrorists condemn and execute. The relationship between terrorism and sacrifice is therefore one of cause and effect; hence the conjunction "and" is usually implicit between the two terms. However, terrorism can signify self-sacrifice, and then the conjunction becomes "or." In this sense, violent terrorist acts generate the sacrifice of the terrorists themselves for a political—even ideological—goal. Camus' play *Les Justes* specifically emphasizes this second aspect—terrorism*or* sacrifice—although the first aspect—terrorism *and* sacrifice—plays a crucial and decisive part in the assassination of the "grand-duc," who symbolizes tyranny.

The revealing title, *Les Justes*, originally possesses a religious—and almost sacred—connotation. Although religion seems to be absent in the play—except within the poet Kaliayev's soul—it is in fact replaced by a political ideal intrinsically linked to the concept of liberty. According to the French dictionary *Le Petit Robert*, a "juste" is "une personne qui observe les devoirs de la religion."[1] The "justes" represent in this play the socialist revolutionary people who strictly follow their ideological beliefs. When the philosopher Pascal says: "L'impie observe le juste et cherche à le faire mourir," he unveils the sense of sacrifice intrinsic in the very conception of the "justes."[2] In Camus' play, Kaliayev's hanging symbolically reflects the death of the "just" destroyed by the "impious," the tyrannical and autocratic Russian power.

"The Just" or "les justes," a simple yet powerful term, informs Camus' work from the beginning, but it will acquire its complete significance only at the end of the play when sacrifice and the "justes" merge into a single unity. The author sets the play at its very beginning in "l'appartement des terroristes,"[3] which contrasts strikingly with the play's title. The play begins immediately, therefore, with the idea of terrorism, which Robert defines as "un emploi systématique des mesures d'exception de la violence pour atteindre un but politique" and "un ensemble des actes de violence (attentats individuels ou collectifs) qu'une organisation exécute pour impressionner la population et créer un climat d'insécurité."[4] The political goal of Camus' rebels is to defeat tyranny and thereby lead the people to triumph over the tyrant; for the terrorists, the end justifies the means.

Yet, in spite of his journalistic background, which one might think would lead him to portray terrorists as unethical and violent, Camus portrays people devoid neither of sensitivity nor of souls. His terrorists are a compassionate revolutionary group suffering for the Russian people, from which emerges the idea of "sacrifice," dating back to ritual ceremonies of antiquity. If "sacrifice" can be defined as:

> une offrande rituelle à la divinité (that is, ideology) caractérisée par la destruction (immolation réelle ou symbolique, holocauste) ou l'abandon volontaire de la chose offerte (that is, life); un sacrifice du Christ, la mort du Christ pour la rédemption du genre humain; et un renoncement ou privation volontaire (en vue d'une fin religieuse, morale ou même utilitaire)[5]

then terrorism becomes self-sacrifice; the terrorists become "justes" because they accept their own deaths as a consequence of having assassinated an important political figure.

Camus' deeply-held belief in sacrifice is also found at the heart of his theatrical essay *L'Homme révolté,* in which murder is justified so long as the killer accepts his own death as a *moral*—not only a legal or logical—consequence. Camus' murderers are innocent,[6] a fact that clearly suggests the antithetical association of "terrorism and/or sacrifice" so evident throughout the drama *Les Justes.* As one critic aptly defines them, terrorists are men "epris de pureté, [qui] veulent combiner le meurtre avec le sacrifice de leur vie, payer une vie pour une vie."[7] Murder or assassination, as a terrorist act, is used to liberate the people; and sacrifice, as a decision to die, incarnates a moral death. The terrorists—like Meursault in *L'Etranger,* or Tchen in *La Condition humaine* by André Malraux—accept their actions and, therefore, their own deaths as free men. In this essay, I would like to demonstrate the ambiguity and mythic quality of terrorism and sacrifice as they unfold essentially through two sets of characters—Voinov and Annenkov, and on the other hand Stepan and Kaliayev (nicknamed Yanek)—whose lives become entangled, overlap each other, and are finally opposed in *Les Justes.*

The word "terrorists" appearing in the stage directions at the beginning of the play clearly indicates a distance between the author and his characters. The reader is immediately prejudiced against them because the connotation of this word is not flattering. Stepan projects all sorts of revolutionary ideas and doctrines normally associated with the concept of terrorism. Stepan, as the perfect dogmatic terrorist, expresses himself with violence: "La liberté est un bagne aussi longtemps qu'un seul homme est asservi sur la terre" (308). However, these words reveal the deep pain and suffering that he feels about the enslaved Russian people, and suggest Stepan's intention to fight and perhaps to die for this cause.

Blinded by his own rigorous beliefs, Stepan defines his mission well; he must kill the symbol of tyranny and liberate his fellow-countrymen: "Nous tuerons ce bourreau. . . Disciplinés nous tuerons le grand-duc et nous abattrons la tyrannie. . . [Nous sommes] un groupe de combat du parti socialiste révolutionnaire pour hâter la libération du peuple russe" (309-10). He speaks unhesitatingly with a sanguinary fanaticism: "nous sommes décidés à exercer la terreur jusqu'à ce que la terre soit rendue au peuple" (310). This leads him to experience moments of visionary madness—when considering the power of a single bomb to destroy Moscow, Stepan's comrade overtly calls him "mad": "La bombe seule est révolutionnaire. . . . Combien en faudrait-il pour faire sauter Moscou? — Tu es fou" (312).

Stepan feels bitter and hurt as a result of his imprisonment and of the living conditions in Russia. He seems to be prepared for the worst and does not know doubt. He personifies the first meaning of "terrorism *and* sacrifice" since he is ready to eliminate any person opposed to the group's mission and to their socialist revolution. Thus the lives of two children do not count in relation to the lives of millions of human beings. It is therefore imperative to sacrifice a minority in order to liberate the majority. Stepan's deeply rooted collectivism prevents him from distinguishing the individual per se: he can only conceive people as a mass. As a matter of fact, "[il] a choisi d'être meurtrier tout court."[8]

Stepan's violent maturity is opposed by Voinov's timid youth and lack of experience. Voinov is idealistic, spontaneous, and sincere: "Je disais ce que je pensais" (313). He gives up his life as a student in order to devote himself entirely to terrorist actions that will lead to the triumph of his ideals: "J'ai compris qu'il ne suffisait pas de dénoncer l'injustice" (314). Is Voinov a mirror image of Stepan when he was younger? Or does he represent the type of man that Stepan could have been?

Rather than Stepan, Voinov more closely resembles Yanek because both men are attracted by death and fascinated by words, and yet both are able to experience happiness. Yanek and Voinov illuminate the beginning of the play with their idealistic convictions. Yanek could utter Voinov's following words: "Il fallait donner sa vie pour [l'injustice]. Maintenant, je suis heureux" (314).

Camus himself mentions the similarities between the two young men in his essay entitled "Les meurtriers délicats": "Chez Voinarovski aussi, le goût du sacrifice coïncide avec l'attirance de la mort" (1829). One great difference exists, however, between Yanek and Voinov: the latter has not yet totally understood or accepted the final impact of terrorist acts—that is to say: death. Therefore, he remains profoundly vulnerable. He admits with great humility his fear—even terror—of death, which Annenkov, the leader of the group, finds ironic in a terrorist.

Voinov can deal neither with active terrorism nor with sacrifice because his character is at once more passive and more human. That is why the reader can easily identify with him, respect his choices and decisions, and admire his dignity, whereas Voinov sees only his own weaknesses. He painfully admits: "Je ne suis pas fait pour la terreur" (345). Voinov, formerly fiercely opposed to lies—although he has often lied in self-defense—finally admits: "Je mens. Mais je ne mentirai plus le jour où je lancerai la bombe" (314). At present, however, the mature Voinov no longer lies to himself and thus liberates himself from the terrorist constraints of which he disapproves.

Unknowingly and surprisingly enough, he resembles Annenkov in whom he confides; for the leader of the group also acknowledges the fear that he feels at the idea of self-sacrifice: "C'est commode après tout, d'être forcé de ne pas lancer la bombe. . . Yanek vaut mieux que moi" (328).

Thus, Camus has created two pairs of terrorists who paradoxically complement and yet oppose each other: the couple Voinov and Annenkov can be compared to the couple Stepan and Yanek in numerous ways. The former accept terrorism and the murder/sacrifice of other beings in a moderate manner— they are opposed to the sacrifice of the innocent— but they refuse self-sacrifice; the latter accept terrorism and the murder/sacrifice of other beings as well as self-sacrifice. Stepan and Yanek are separated by their view on murder/sacrifice because Stepan opposes the concept of "a life for a life" although he stands for "several lives in exchange for one life."

Although Voinov and Annenkov are pivotal characters between Stepan's and Yanek's extremes, and do not fulfill their duties as terrorists, they play a fundamental role as mediators. They create a golden mean and fill the ideological gap which separates Stepan from Yanek. Stepan and Yanek represent black and white characters of superhuman, gigantic dimensions, whereas Voinov and Annenkov exist in a gray area. Stepan is associated with hate, pride, ugliness, and realism, while Yanek incarnates love, egoism, beauty, and idealism. Can one assert, however, that the first man represents the "anti-hero" and that the second man represents the "super-hero"? Are both men unable to reconcile? These are questions that I will try to answer here.

The conflict between Stepan and Yanek starts even before the latter's arrival. When his friends refer to him as the "Poète" (311), Stepan says with irritation: "Ce n'est pas un nom pour un terroriste" (311). "Terrorist" contrasts with "poet," that is, the first being active and the second passive. For Yanek, however, "la poésie est révolutionnaire" (311) because it implies some sort of sacrifice. This idea deeply preoccupies the young man who can think only about his death for the benefit of others. Yanek idealizes in a visionary fashion his position within the group of anti-czarist militants and imagines his own sacrifice for the Russian people, equating it with Christ's.

Kaliayev's sensitivity clashes with the harshness of Stepan, who envisions only the practical elements of a terrorist's sacrifice: "Il faut une main ferme" (318). Stepan is dominated by rigor, self-discipline and, self-control; Yanek by game, fantasy, and exuberance. Camus consciously delays the latter's arrival so that the two men's personalities clash strikingly. Collectivism, an essential value for Stepan, who is profoundly somber, is in direct opposition with Kaliayev's personal signal when he rings the bell of the apartment (310); his nickname "Yanek"; his sonorous laughter; his true happiness to live as an adolescent: "Ce déguisement, cette nouvelle vie... Tout m'amusait" (316); and his lyrical outbursts: "la beauté existe; la joie existe" (316).

The poet does appear superficial on stage, in a sort of tragical theatricality. As a matter of fact, Yanek lets himself be carried away with the exaltation and the fever of revolution: for him, only self-sacrifice seems to count and makes him forget terrorism for a moment. His wish is to, "se jeter sous les pieds de chevaux" (318) with a bomb or "imiter les Japonais" (319), who are accustomed to dying for their country. The critic Carina Gadourek describes him with insight: "Kaliayev aimait la vie et, attiré par la mort, Kaliayev est double: il est révolutionnaire et égoïste."[9] Yanek embellishes the terrorist's suicide for egocentric reasons. Everything revolves around him, the "sacrificed terrorist." "Quel honneur, quel honneur pour moi! . . . Quel bonheur pour moi!" (318), he cries out.

The reader can easily understand Stepan's clairvoyance and violent reactions as he faces Kaliayev. Community and individuality square off against terrorism and sacrifice. Stepan judiciously sees Yanek's egotistic personality: "Pour se suicider, il faut beaucoup s'aimer. . . . Un vrai révolutionnaire ne peut pas s'aimer" (319). He immediately detests Yanek's futile superficiality, which is alien to their organization: "Je n'aime pas ceux qui entrent dans la révolution parce qu'ils s'ennuient. . . . Oui, je suis brutal. Mais pour moi, la haine n'est pas un jeu. Nous ne sommes pas là pour nous admirer. Nous sommes là pour réussir" (319).

"Hate," Stepan's key word, will later clash with Yanek's "love."

Stepan loves nothing, no one, not even himself. Therefore, he can experience only a desire for destruction—almost self-destruction—because he feels so profoundly anguished. "Ce qui le soutient, c'est plutôt la haine et le désir d'apocalypse."[10]

Despite their obvious differences, Yanek and Stepan's personal ideologies manage to meet unconsciously. The former says: "J'aime la vie. . . . Chacun sert la justice comme il peut" (320) ; and the latter: "Je n'aime pas la vie, mais la justice qui est au-dessus de la vie" (320). Yanek seems to live in a concrete world whereas Stepan seems to be in the abstract, which used to be the contrary. In fact, they expect to reach the same goal—justice—, but they express themselves in opposite ways. Yanek knows it: "Il faut accepter que nous soyons différents" (320). Both men act and speak as "justes" because they follow their own doctrines.

Nevertheless, the situation shifts: Stepan paradoxically reveals his selfishness as an individualist: "Je suis venu pour tuer un homme" (320). The two revolutionary men separate once again. Stepan who, at the beginning of the play, devoted himself only to the people and collectivity, is fixated in his hate of an individual: the "grand-duc."

On the other hand, Yanek, who flaunted his individuality with ostentation, is now committed to kill the "grand-duc" because of his ideology and his love for the Russian people: "Tu ne le tueras pas seul ni au nom de rien. Tu le tueras avec nous et au nom du peuple russe. . . Je veux me sacrifier. . . Mourir pour l'idée, c'est la seule façon d'être à la hauteur de l'idée. C'est la justification" (321-323).

Yanek's mission, depicted by one critic as "la grande pureté du terrorisme style Kaliayev"[11] seems to be superior to Stepan's, and to possess more political dimensions: he is able to extrapolate his personal feelings in order to serve humanity, which Stepan cannot do. "Ce n'est pas lui que je tue, c'est le despotisme" (326), says Kaliayev. Their positions remain fundamentally opposite: Yanek represents the sacrificed terrorist and Stepan the sacrificing terrorist: "Les deux terroristes sont prêts à mourir. Kaliayev meurt *pour* les hommes tandis que Stepan meurt *contre* les hommes."[12] Thus, Yanek's more significant sacrifice "a pour fonction d'apaiser les violences intestines, d'empêcher les conflits d'éclater."[13]

Kaliayev unveils again a certain religiosity of mind in his attitude or "prise de position" toward sacrifice: like Christ, he wishes that his death bring forth redemption for all humanity. "Nous acceptons d'être criminels pour que la terre se couvre enfin d'innocents" (323). This comment does not, however, imply human salvation in a spiritual world, but rather liberation in a real and material world. Yanek's religion involves man and not God. Besides, he does not believe in eternal life: before he is hanged, "il a refusé d'embrasser le crucifix et il a déclaré: 'Je vous ai déjà dit que j'en ai fini avec la vie et que je suis en règle avec la mort'" (390). Camus himself explains this behavior:

> Nous sommes donc ici en face d'une conception, sinon religieuse, du moins métaphysique de la révolte. . . Le problème de la révolte ne se résoudra plus en arithmétique, mais en calcul des probabilités. En face d'une future réalisation de l'idée, la vie peut être tout ou rien. Plus est grande la foi que le calculateur met dans cette réalisation et moins vaut la vie humaine. A la limite, elle ne vaut plus rien. Et nous sommes aujourd'hui à la limite, c'est-à-dire au temps des bourreaux philosophiques (1832).

Clearly, Kaliayev is Albert Camus' spokesman: he presents the doctrine of the philosopher, novelist, and playwright, as well as Camus' position in regard to the concepts of murder and revolt. Camus speaks through his character when Kaliayev exclaims: "Une pensée me tourmente: ils ont fait de nous des assassins. Mais je pense en même temps que je vais mourir, et alors mon cœur s'apaise" (323).

Terrorism and sacrifice cannot exist independently in Camus' universe. For Stepan, terrorism implies only a bloody revolution that announces anarchy and despotism. Yanek refuses to murder children because, on the one hand, "il ne peut pas laisser Stepan dire que tout est permis" (327) and, on the other hand, "il voit s'annoncer le despotisme" (328) in this type of sacrificial terrorism. Camus portrays Stepan as "le prototype des révolutionnaires du XXe siècle qui abandonnent les valeurs de la liberté."[14]

For Yanek, one needs to kill and to die (324), to use terrorism and/or sacrifice, to accept death, and to take "une vie et une seule" (324). Terrorism and sacrifice merge in Camus' mind as he specifies elsewhere: "Finalement, le meurtre s'est identifié en eux avec le suicide. Une vie est alors payée par une autre vie. De ces deux holocaustes surgit une valeur intacte qui devait servir le progrès de la justice" (1832).

Kaliayev wants to be considered as a "justicier" (338) for whom "il y a un honneur dans la révolution. C'est celui par lequel nous acceptons de mourir" (340), whereas Stepan represents the murderer: "La terreur ne convient pas aux délicats. Nous sommes des meurtriers et nous avons choisi de l'être" (340). Yanek, symbolizing "revolt," wins out against Stepan, symbolizing "revolution." As Georges Maire aptly specifies: "Camus pose deux termes: la Révolution qui est le Mal et la révolte qui est le Bien. Il jouera sur le mot Révolte et la louera jusqu'au bout."[15]

In his *Carnets*, Albert Camus makes the following comments on murder and revolt, which represent the foundations of *Les Justes*:

> La limite du raisonnement révolté: accepter de tuer soi-même pour refuser la complicité avec le meurtre en général. . . Pour finir, revaloriser le meurtre pour l'opposer à la destruction anonyme et froide, et abstraite. L'apologie du meurtre d'homme à homme est une des étapes sur le chemin de la révolte.[16]

Camus is opposed to gratuitous murder, as is his hero, Yanek. The murderer must accept his own death in order to make his murder meaningful; the essence of murder is the rediscovery of innocence: "J'ai choisi de mourir pour que le meurtre ne triomphe pas. J'ai choisi d'être innocent" (341), cries out Kaliayev, the "Juste." He can no longer be accused of any crimes since he accepts death: "En 1948, Camus a parlé des qualités requises du juste égyptien: 'Dans le livre des Morts, on lit que le juste égyptien, pour mériter son pardon, devait pouvoir dire "Je n'ai causé de peur à personne.""[17]

Yanek's innocence is linked to his deep love and self-sacrifice for humanity: "Mais c'est cela l'amour, tout donner, tout sacrifier sans espoir de retour. C'est l'amour absolu, la joie pure et solitaire" (351). The key word "solitude" shows the absolute uniqueness of the being in a state of revolt in Camus' world. Only this being understands the crucial significance of his or her mission on earth. Death does not count for Yanek, but matters to others.

Unlike Stepan, who utters the word "hate" (356) very well, Kaliayev finds happiness in love and, therefore, "in" death—the sole joy of which he can approve and accept after having committed murder: "Il n'y a pas de bonheur dans la haine" (350). But everything shifts again: Yanek, the egocentric and superficial poet of the beginning of the play, changes into an altruistic and sublime man in revolt. "Tout meurtre pour être justifié doit s'équilibrer à l'amour. L'échafaud pour les terroristes était la preuve par neuf de l'amour."[18]

"Yanek n'est plus un meurtrier" (392). His death purifies him. René Girard in *La Violence et le sacré* analyzes "sacrifice" in the following manner: "Il n'y pas de violence vraiment pure; le sacrifice dans le meilleur des cas, doit se définir comme violence purificatrice."[19] Yanek's self-sacrifice in *Les Justes* makes him the best of all possible heroes. A new balance has finally been restored: "Il [Yanek] paye pour ce que cet acte peut avoir de négatif, sans toutefois se repentir. Son sacrifice lui procure la paix intérieure."[20]

Like Meursault in *L'Etranger,* or Oreste in *Les Mouches* by Jean-Paul Sartre, Kaliayev feels no remorse for what he has done: the first man knows that he is free and he accepts death; the second takes full responsibility for his acts; and the latter greatly contributes to the impending liberation of the Russian people.

For Camus, terrorism alone is useless, and the terrorist's sacrifice only adds dimension to the antithesis. There is no "terrorism *and* sacrifice"—in the sense of sacrificing others—but there is "terrorism *or* sacrifice" as equivalent goals in *Les Justes.*

Let us go back to the question above: is Yanek a super-hero? Will Stepan never be able to reconcile with Kaliayev? Camus himself admits his preference for Yanek: "Je voudrais préciser. . . que j'admire donc, et que j'aime. . . Kaliayev" (1835). Although he does not hide his affection for the sacrificed poet, Camus does not condemn Stepan either because Stepan changes at the end of the play. Stepan experiences a sudden vivid emotion while narrating the death of his apparent enemy, Yanek: "Je l'enviais. . . Stepan se tait. . . Stepan détourne la tête" (390-91). His final humility renders him likeable because he has understood the true meaning of life and of their terrorist organization.

This sudden change unites his thoughts with those of Dora, Yanek's follower and lover: "Elle me ressemble maintenant" (393), Stepan says. It is Stepan who resembles Dora, however, and not Dora who resembles Stepan, for Dora has not changed. She has always believed in Yanek's ideologies. Stepan is now closer in mind to Kaliayev and consequently to Dora. Despite Stepan's efforts to "tame" Yanek, he has paradoxically been tamed by Yanek. He is no more to be condemned than Yanek, who "n'est plus un meurtrier" (392). *Les Justes* does not end with Yanek's death but with a new beginning, a new hope for the liberation of the Russian people. Stepan, the terrorist, has become another Yanek, ready to kill and to sacrifice himself for others.

Notes

1 Paul Robert, *Le Petit Robert: Dictionnaire Alphabétique et Analogique de la Langue Française* (Paris: Société du Nouveau Littré, 1973), p. 958.

2 Robert, p. 498.

3 Albert Camus,*Les Justes*, in*Théâtre, Récits, Nouvelles* (Paris: Bibliothèque de la Pléiade, Gallimard, 1962), p. 307. Page references to Camus, hereafter within parentheses following quotations, are to this work.

4 Robert, p. 1770.

5 Robert, p. 1592.

6 Carina Gadourek, *Les Innocents et les Coupables* (The Hague: Mouton and Co. Publishers, 1963), p. 143.

7 Gadourek, p.143.

8 Gadourek, p. 144.

9 Gadourek, p. 145.

10 Gadourek, p. 143.

11 Raymond Gay-Crosier, *Les Envers d'un échec: étude sur le théâtre d'Albert Camus* (Paris: Bibliothèque des Lettres Modernes, 1967), p. 195.

12 Gay-Crosier, p. 207.

13 René Girard, *La Violence et le Sacré* (Paris: Editions Bernard Grasset, Collections Pluriel, 1972), p. 27.

14 Gadourek, p. 143.

15 Georges Maire, *Hommage à Albert Camus 1913-1960* (Paris: Editions Gallimard, 1967), p. 79.

[16] Albert Camus, *Carnets 1942-1951* (Paris: Editions Gallimard, 1964), pp. 260-275.

[17] Gadourek, p. 149.

[18] Gadourek, p. 299.

[19] Girard, p. 65.

[20] Gadourek, p. 146.

Pascale Perraudin

The Modern "Myth of Incommunicability" in
Ionesco's Theater:
The Chairs and *The Bald Soprano*

The Theater of the Absurd is often associated with the Theater of Non-communication, and Ionesco's one-act plays *The Bald Soprano* (1949) and *The Chairs* (1951) are often quoted as examples of the latter. Playwright of the Absurd, a movement deeply rooted in the malaise that followed World War II, Ionesco strives to depict the picturesque nothingness and absurdity of the human condition.

The Bald Soprano and *The Chairs* provide Ionesco with a pretext to maximize the senseless and perplexing reality of incommunicability in our ordinary existence, a pretext once called a "truly heroic attempt to break through the barriers of human communication."[1] The metaphorical perspective Ionesco offers in these two plays mirrors this unavoidable deadlock of language and enables us to find in them the "modern myth of incommunicability."

Rather than a fable or an allegory in the classical sense, "the myth of incommunicability" is a notion accepted by many people of the twentieth century, and in particular of our own generation, who mistakenly assume that lack of communication is a modern phenomenon.

One might wonder, therefore, why Ionesco tackles incommunicability on the stage, knowing that the very essence of theater is speech? Why does he choose theater to express the inadequacy of language, this incommunicability between individuals?

Before answering this question, it is necessary to discuss the issue of the myth. It is quite surprising that Ionesco did not use a traditional Greek or Oriental myth. Ionesco could have taken advantage of the myth that is, as Vernant points out, an organized and coherent system of references with historical and transhistorical factors.[2]

Dealing with incommunicability as the human condition, he could have shown the inadequacy of words (of rational language) by relying on "homonumia" (in Aristotle's terms) the lexical ambiguity that pertains in traditional Greek tragedy. However, this ambiguity usually requires some sort of interpretation on behalf of the author, some sort of rational and discursive approach on his/her part, which helps the audience understand the problem.

Ionesco adopts a different strategy. He doesn't confine himself to traditional modes expressing incommunicability: "he abolishes plausible situations, he avoids resolving conflicts of passions, he disarticulates formal language, destroys traditional theater and finally outlaws psychology altogether."[3]

Instead of confining himself to some coherent, historical and transhistorical system, Ionesco creates, according to Pronko, a "primitive theater that seeks to be itself . . . [whose] essence . . . is enlargement."[4] He wants to show, amplify and exaggerate our daily reality of incommunicability.

Again according to Pronko, Ionesco thinks "[he] must exaggerate, push [his] characters, [his] stories, and even his settings beyond the bounds of the time or the likely in order to arrive at something that is truer than life itself: the amplified and theatrical image of life which strikes deep below the surface of reality."[5]

In *The Bald Soprano* and *The Chairs*, Ionesco tackles the theme of incommunicability first by giving us a realistic image, a direct reflection of our reality. The beginning of *The Bald Soprano* is meant to be reassuring. The audience finds the familiar details of a cosy English interior—armchairs, a fireplace, Mr. Smith's slippers and the ticking of a clock—everything, in fact, that suggests an almost warm atmosphere. Yet, having been put at ease, the audience will soon be baffled when confronted with the absurdity of the dialogue.

In much the same way, *The Chairs*, reveals a far more caustic or "grinçante" perception of Ionesco's. The reality he perceives assaults us brutally: the two characters, the Old Man and the Old Woman, don't even have names. Nothing distinguishes one from the other: they are reduced to anonymity. The bare, modern setting provides a context in which the characters' smallness, their insignificance, suddenly takes on a surprising dimension. Although the walls of the set contain many windows, which symbolize the opening towards the outside world, the two old characters are confronted with a terrible vision, very revealing of the post-war malaise. The world to which the openings lead seems to have disintegrated: the city of Paris, "City of light . . . has been extinguished," and everything looks dark, gloomy, agonizing, and appalling; their "sun is black".[6] Days do not distinguish themselves from nights. All landmarks or usual daily references have vanished. Immersed in this hostile and brutal reality, the characters have nothing left but problems linked with everydayness and the human condition. Moreover *The Chairs*, like *The Bald Soprano*, unfolds in one act. Ionesco does not seek to introduce any kind of temporal structure that is linear and organized, with a beginning and an end. In both plays, he stages, in the rough, a slice of life cut directly out of reality.

Then, he discloses the implacable disarticulation of language by introducing, in *The Bald Soprano*, dislocated dialogues that caricature this English bourgeois interior, an interior that is paradoxically tranquil and cosy, like that of any average home.

In *The Chairs*, the spectator is bewildered by pessimistic signals that the playwright insidiously introduces, and which lead to a theatrical language, far beyond speech: he adopts a physical language that does not rely on words. On the contrary, by taking advantage of every detail of the setting and the characters' attempts to convey some message, he seeks to reproduce, to epitomize each human being's own reality by insisting on its intrinsic problem: the problem of communication.

His strategy resembles that of Antonin Artaud, which Artaud advocates in *Le théâtre et son double*. Both Artaud and Ionesco want to create a theater that will rouse the audience's sensibility, that will transpose and transform life on stage. Here, Ionesco reproduces a "convulsive reality"[7] so that the audience will immediately be seized by its shocking and aggressive totality.[8]

But the question still remains, how can a modern "myth of incommunicability" emerge from this disturbing reality? How does Ionesco proceed? In *The Chairs*, he starts tackling the theme of incommunicability when he presents a nameless old couple, an Old man and an Old woman, who are talking to invisible people. In order to emphasize the futility of this, he creates a painful scheme in which the deadlock of language repeats itself until the end, as we shall see.

In the *Bald Soprano*, the stereotypical, senseless dialogue of the Smiths and the Martins, throughout the play, repeats interchangeably and therefore suggests the lack of meaningful communication between the couples. The messages are interchangeable, dislocated; they have lost their very essence and specificity. The audience immediately realizes how impossible it is for these people to transmit any message. Patrice Pavis says that banal and stereotyped repetitions of dialogue

> are the scarcely emphasized parody of the classical tragic play whose hero performs in the myth a liberating and meaningful action. These plays and dramaturgy indicate that the basic myth or more simply the tale to be told are relayed by the *series* and thematic variation. This is the moment of degradation of structure.[9]

Just as Pavis defines "the degradation of structure," Levi-Strauss notices that "the structural content [of these narratives] is dispersed" and is substituted by a structure of another essence: the recurring repetition of certain elements takes the place of the pre-existing and explicative structure of the traditional myths.[10]

Ionesco denies the old model of a signifying narrative. He shows our unavoidable and daily incommunicability. He reproduces a sardonic, repetitive language: people believe that they are delivering messages, but all they can do is emit sounds, or utter interchangeable phrases.

This universal problem, with its patterns repeating the past and the present, is not limited to such theatrical performance, however. Incommunicability will invariably perpetuate itself throughout the ages. Ionesco's spectator is thus made aware of what can be referred to as the modern "myth of incommunicability"; lack of communication is, of course, no more modern than it is ancient.

In spite of the metaphorical significance of these two plays, one still wonders why Ionesco uses theater to depict incommunicability. Theater defines itself by speech, by oral exchange and conversations as in *The Chairs* and *The Bald Soprano*. Why does Ionesco, then, persist in using absurd and meaningless dialogue? Why doesn't he approach incommunicability by explaining it in a rational and discursive manner?

To begin with, we must keep in mind that the theater of the absurd and the modern "myth of incommunicability" is only a pretext for Ionesco to enlarge upon the reality of the human condition. A first observation flows from this: actors exist and define themselves through dialogues and words. Within a theatrical context, words are fundamental, and inane conversations and the absence of words suggest something other than performance: without words the actor neither performs nor exists. Similarly, much like actors, we all reveal our existence through words and conversation. Theater not only displays our incommunicability but shows that it is fatally unavoidable because we need speech.

Although traditional linguistics presents language as a logical, discursive and linear system that enables us to deliver messages, translate what we have in mind and understand our interlocutors, one can always question the relevance of this "symbolic order," as Julia Kristeva calls it.

From a symbolic point of view, what Ionesco's characters say is grammatically correct; however, it is nonsensical. As we shall see, speech is a necessity by which people locate and define themselves only within a social group.

But what does this symbolic order allow us to express? Let's look at the very beginning of *The Bald Soprano*. The stage directions indicate that "the English clock strikes 17 English strokes" (p. 8). In this banal atmosphere, the characters try in vain to create an effect of spontaneity: "there, it is . . ." (p. 9). They only *platitudinize* by adding generalities side by side: the triviality of the conversation cannot be concealed: "We've eaten well this evening. That's because we live in the suburbs of London and because our name is Smith!"(p. 9). The "symbolic order," here, despite a correct and apparently well-mastered syntax remains superficial, even illogical.

We gradually realize that the "symbolic order" leads us away from our essential reality. People struggle to express as precisely as possible images they have in mind, but in vain: there is an enormous gap between reality and language. Incommunicability stems from the fact that language shrinks the global vision an individual can have of reality: "Language appears more and more as being in contradiction to reality."[11]

For example, in *The Bald Soprano*, Mr. and Mrs. Martin get into a conversation about the parallel events that mark their respective lives. At the beginning of the dialogue, they seem not to know one another, but they gradually establish that they both "reside at Number 9" in a flat located "on the fifth floor, Number 8," (p. 15), that they sleep in the same type of bed, and therefore in the very same bed. Also, they both have a pretty daughter, Alice, "who has one white eye and one red eye" (p. 15).

Obviously, this parody of logical, rhetorical speech fails to give a true picture of life. The characters are subdued by incomplete and therefore deceiving information from which they hastily draw conclusions. Sets of words that are thought to be intrinsic details of the Martin's life are incomplete and fail to translate what Sartre calls the "contingence de la réalité." Here, we later learn that the Martins are mistaken; the child they think they have in common, apparently has the same characteristics, but we learn that the two characters do not have the same vision in mind —the right eye of one child is red, whereas the right eye of the other child is white. If language, therefore, is doomed to be a deficient tool, why do human beings keep uttering platitudes? What is concealed? What does language betray?

Human speech seems to be a patchwork, a hodgepodge of words that presents a chaotic, non-linear aspect, and implies discontinuity. From a psychoanalytical point of view, this same discontinuity appears when going from the "symbolic order" to the "semiotic order." The "semiotic order" is the pre-oedipal phase, which precedes the acquisition of language in children. It is the time when we emit rhythmic sounds and have tactile sensations. One's relationship to one's mother is then qualified as "semiotic."

The difficult jump we must make to the "symbolic order" implies a gap separating these two orders, the essential reality from the reality expressed by language. Every individual is first confronted by this gap when becoming independent from his or her mother. Passing unavoidably to the "symbolic order" is accompanied by the desire of each of us to return to the "semiotic order" and to try to bridge the two by talking. Speech, consequently, which is the very expression of this independence, intends to fill this gap.

By definition, we direct ourselves toward the symbolic and semiotic orders at the same time, and thus create a dichotomy within ourselves. This characteristic dichotomy is expressed in *The Chairs* by the Old Man and the Old Woman, who try to fill the gap: they keep talking. They keep referring to the message they want to deliver to humanity through the Orator, whom they have invited. They don't address real interlocutors, however, but invisible ones, who are represented by numerous chairs. The chairs are the symbol of the Other, who allows the individual to minimize his internal dichotomy and to aspire to unity.

Permanently motivated and divided by the desire to go back to the symbiosis of the pre-oedipal order and the impossibility as well as the need to express this desire, Ionesco's characters have found a rather interesting compromise. The endless dialogues give the impression that they enter the logical, linear symbolic order. But their nonsensical dialogue argues otherwise. For example, at the end, Mr. Smith says something like:" so I have ... I told him ... certainly ... according to us ... and to *theirs* ... as to ... I told him ... a, an, the ...."

The interlocutor therefore is not important in the eye of the person who is talking, the interlocutor is only the Other, who allows the individual to connect symbolic and semiotic orders. Mouthing nonsensical speech, or talking to invisible people, as in *The Chairs*, reveals the original meaning of any attempt to communicate: people are in search of their original "me" in the "semiotic order." As a consequence, the message they try to convey is not important: what really matters is the essence of their act of talking. As a matter of fact, any individual, any of our characters, has nothing to communicate. In *The Chairs*, before committing suicide, the Old Man surprisingly tells us that somebody will come to transmit his message to humanity: at last, the long-awaited Orator arrives on stage, but as he is about to deliver his message, the audience realizes that he can pronounce only onomatopoeias: "he, mme, mm, mm ...ju ...gou ...hou .. .heu, heu, gu, gou ...." The message is actually reduced to its minimal but essential form: it is sound, resonance. The Orator is almost mute, and his handicap becomes symbolic of our impossibility to communicate, to deliver any type of message.

Ionesco's representation of our impossibility to communicate also takes on an tragic dimension: it is unavoidable and inherent in our condition. Our daily conversations are reduced to their minimal significance: dialogue or speech is perceived as mere utterance, to which we invariably and desperately try to allocate meaning by confining our speech to stereotyped, repetitive and hypocritical social codes. This pattern duplicates itself throughout the ages and contributes to the formation of what I have called the modern "myth of incommunicability."

Given this impossibility to convey messages, should we then try to avoid talking, an act we traditionally understand as communicating? The answer probably lies in Joseph Campbell's words: "People say that what we're all seeking is a meaning for life. I don't think that's what we're really seeking. I think that what we're seeking is an experience of being alive, so that our life experiences on the purely physical plane will have resonances within our own innermost being and reality, so that we actually feel the rapture of being alive."[12]

146

Notes

1 Martin Esslin, *The Theatre of The Absurd* (New York: Anchor, 1961), p. 139.

2 Jean-Pierre Vernant, *Mythe et Tragédie-Deux* (Paris: Editions La Découverte, 1986), p. 84.

3 Jacques Benay, *Panorama du théâtre nouveau 3: le théâtre de la dérision* (New York: Appleton Century Crofts, 1966), p. 2 (my translation).

4 Leonard Cabell Pronko, *Avant-garde: The Experimental Theater in France* (Berkeley: University of California Press, 1964), p. 61.

5 Pronko, p. 61.

6 Eugène Ionesco, *Four Plays*, trans. Donald M. Allen (New York: Grove Press, 1958), p. 116. Page numbers, hereafter following quotations, refer to this work.

7 "Convulsive reality" originates with the Surrealists, who believe in the "Esthétique du choc." Surrealist artists allocated great importance to Breton's famous phrase: "La beauté sera convulsive ou ne sera pas." ["Beauty will be or will not be."]

8 See Artaud's principles on the "théâtre total."

9 Patrice Pavis, *Languages of the stage: Essays in the semiology of the Theater* (New York: Performing Arts Journal Publications, 1982), p. 186.

10 Pavis, p. 186.

11 Martin Esslin, *The Theater of the Absurd*, 3rd ed. (Harrisonburg Virginia: Pelican Books, 1983), p. 407.

12 Joseph Campbell, *The Power of Myth,* with Bill Moyers, ed. Betty Sue Flowers (New York: Doubleday, 1988), p. 3.

Sylvie Debevec Henning

Writing The Body: "Qui Tient Le/La Greffe?"

In the world of Samuel Beckett's characters, the body is unruly, messy, faulty. It farts; it pisses; it shits; it even fucks when its desires are too strong for its disgust. It is subject to the ravages of time in very painful ways: disease, disintegration, disarticulation, general dysfunction. This view of the body is, unfortunately, not limited to Beckett's world. It is there because it is here with us; it is the view of the body fundamental to our Judeo-Christian-Platonic culture.

How can such faultiness be corrected? Mortification of the flesh, rational control of the instincts. These two means are graphically staged in Beckett's last novel, *Comment c'est,* especially in Part II.[1] The instrument is the "nail"—*la griffe, le greffe.*[2]

Consider the story of the Oriental wise-man, *sunnayasin* or Buddhist monk, who clenched his fists until the nails grew through his palms, so strong was his desire to subjugate his body and its unruly will. The wise-man, however, could exercise control only over the "conscious" or "voluntary" aspects of his corporeal existence. His nails continued to grow no matter how hard he clenched his fists, or how many times he would have his palms pierced. Moreover, not even the death of his conscious mind could bring an end to this dynamism. These nails, then, even when turned against the body are still part of it. Like Clov, they serve as a means of repression while participating in the repressed. Ultimately it is their inherent ambivalence that reappears to subvert the end that they were supposed to serve. Much like Buddha, the sage finally concedes victory to the phenomenal world. The mind does not have the power to dominate the body completely.

Disregarding this caveat, the narrator of *Comment c'est* will attempt to escape from the mire by painful but cleansing martyrdom of the spirit-polluting body. Rather than suffer in his own flesh, however, he would, through a sadomasochistic projection, mortify that of his companion, Pim. (Pim, "en croix de Saint André" (p. 72), is a Christ substitute, as were St. Andrew and all Christian martyrs, the X-shaped cross marking the distance that separates his suffering from Christ's.)

Pim's training or *dressage* (a term that recalls, among other things, the need to control the unruly steed of the psyche) comprises several stages. Pim's language, in which both his body and his emotions are involved, must be brought under the narrator's rational domination before it can serve as a means of communication, leading to "plus ample connaissance" (p. 69). (The Voice of *Comment c'est* Part I, already disembodied, was in principle superior, although even it had been corrupted through contact with the panting "ça.")

In the next stage of his training, Pim, like the victims of Kafka's torture machine, is supposed to learn through the pain of having the narrator engrave with his nails his autobiography on Pim's back: "quatre pleins dos de caractères serrés" (p. 87). In a profoundly carnivalized manner, Pim receives *am eigenen Leib, die Spuren* of experience. These are then sensible truths. They are, however, given to Pim by the narrator, just as God was said to have inscribed intelligible/innate truths on the mind. What this suggests is an investigation of the relation between sensible and intelligible truths. This opposition is fundamental to traditional philosophy. It implies the body/mind distinction, the former fallen, the latter united with God, as well as all other distinctions deriving from it (e.g., nature/institution, signifier/signified, analysis/synthesis, unconscious/conscience), the naive theory of representation, and the vulgar conception of time.[3]

Among the "truths" that the narrator transmits to Pim are certain catechismal articles of Christian faith. Pim has trouble at first but eventually comes to understand almost everything—the sacrifice of the Lamb, the Trinity, the Paraclete, even God (at least a little bit). More significantly, the narrator forces upon Pim the *imitatio Christi* that he himself has been compelled to relive as part of the tradition of painful atonement.

The narrator is ultimately unable to master Pim. This leads to the disintegration of his confidence and the proliferation of displaced doubles. The repression of anxiety in one domain leads, it seems, to its uncanny return in others.

The story of Pam Prim takes up, again in a carnivalized manner, the problematic intercourse between mind and body, self and other, that has already produced the adventures of Pim and the narrator. In Part I the narrator had considered union with a female body—llama, mother, young girl, (amiotic) sack—as a possible complementary solution to his longing for completion. The appearance of Pim suggested a more ideal solution because of his essential similarity to the narrator. Nonetheless, in their queer relation, Pim continued to be treated as a subservient non-*mens* (*con*/cunt, e.g., p. 93).

Pam Prim, Pim's wife above, is, as her name suggests, a curious mixture of sexuality and prudishness. In order to deny her sexuality by pretending to be prepubescent, she shaved her genital and perianal region (mound/*motte*, p. 94). Consequently, sexual conjugation occurred less and less often as desire became merely an unfortunate excess that had occasionally to be eliminated ("par-ci par-là pour se débarrasser," p. 94). Pim had tried to reestablish contact anally, but it was too late for even such "Greek" love. Finally her earthly corpus was shattered, supposedly as a result of a Fall: "colonne brisée" (p. 94). On her deathbed, she turned to religion, forgiving everyone. The "blue mound" of love had apparently acquired more Christian connotations.

This turn to non-material solace, however, does not bring any rebirth, whether spiritual or physical. Like the wintry world outside her hospital room, Pam Prim's sensual body is coldly sterile and chaste. Nevertheless, both the natural world and Pam Prim's pubic hair continue to grow back—"ça repoussait"—as had earlier the Oriental wise-man's nails (p. 95).

This pessimistic view of human life as irredeemably fragmented reappears in Pim's summary account of his life "là-haut." The immediate sources of Pim's existence, the parents he never knew, are or see themselves as shattered. His masterbuilder father was killed "éclaté," like Pam Prim, in a fall. His Bible-carrying mother believed firmly, as Psalm 103 asserts, that God endures forever in his justice, power, and love, whereas the fragments of earthly life are scattered like dust until nothing remains.[4]

The narrator's nails—*les griffes*—are at the same time the narrator's writing instrument—*le greffe*. Writing is another means employed by the narrator to overcome natural faultiness, to bring the body's unruliness under rational control.

This conception of writing was already apparent in Part I of *Comment c'est*, where the narrator first attempted to bring some order to the mess in which he found himself. Phenomena, as the narrator perceived them, could be grouped into two domains. That of the mud was continuous; that of the Voice was discontinuous, if not fragmented. In order to relate the two, he divided the former into three parts and then grouped the fragments under them. He thus introduced a certain measure of difference into the undifferentiated "mud" and extracted certain similarities from the voice's disparate *bribes*. The three parts, when arranged into the beginning-middle-end pattern of the traditional narrative, recount the story of a journey, with Pim as its reference point. So, Part I is the voyage towards him, Part II life with him, and Part III another voyage away from him (towards his inverted double, Bom).

The provider of the paradigm is the Bible, seen as the eschatological drama of the destruction of the old creation, the union with Christ, and the emergence of the new creation. Christian thought internalized this apocalyptic pattern. Its most influential example is Augustine's *Confessions*, which established the characteristic genre of Christian Europe, the spiritual autobiography. It might also be called a theodicy of the private life. It justifies the experience of wrongdoing, suffering and loss as a necessary means to the greater good of personal redemption. The tripartite division of *Comment c'est*, as given by the narrator, would seem to correspond to this fundamental design, with Pim taking the place of Christ. Without an operative *theos*, this became a secular theodicy and belongs to the distinctive Romantic genre of the *Bildungsgeschichte*.[5]

In attempting to distinguish between sections of the narrative, however, the narrator confuses them. The tripartite structure proves just as unworkable here as in Sartre's *La Nausée*. Without abandoning it, the narrator investigates other structuring strategies.

Kram, the witness, and Krim, the scribe, are yet another attempt to distinguish what would otherwise appear as gibbering chaos or *Krimskram*. The narrator, assuming Kram's point of view, describes his own actions. He divides himself, as it were, into observed object and observing subject (another body/mind variant). By adding Krim, he would personify the recording or memory function previously fulfilled by Pim's back (or Krapp's tape-recorder). Kram's task is merely to bear witness to the narrator's existence, observing his actions and repeating his murmurings verbatim to Krim, who "tenant le greffe" (p.98) notes everything in a book.

Intertwined with Kram's account of the narrator are snatches of his own story, signalling how the subjectivity of the observer (his own cultural, historical, personal baggage) affects his interpretation of observed phenomena. To fill in the "silences monstres temps énormes néant parfait" (p. 99) between mutterings, he reads his ancestor's notes (just as

Krapp listens to his tapes), his observations and readings overlapping so that actual perception and historical account interpenetrate. Indeed the narrator's voice is so feeble that Kram loses ninety percent of what is said. Consequently what appears as empirical evidence is partly excerpts from previous accounts, partly simple invention.

Kram's account (and therefore Krim's scribbling) originally jumbled together empirical observations, verbatim transcriptions, and commentary. He did not distinguish observed from recounted, or empirical from subjective, elements. Eventually he decides to separate these aspects into notebooks coded in the primary colors (blue for the narrator's bodily movements, yellow for his mutterings, red for Kram's commentary) that together would comprehend the narrator's whole life. All observations, transcriptions and commentary are to be contained in "un seul grand livre et tout dedans" (p. 103). The agreement of the three notebooks' "riche té-moignage," however, is deemed to be "contestable" (p. 102). In addition, there are intimate notes, "effusions de l'âme," that overflow its boundaries (p. 103). The narrator of Part I had tried to appropriate for himself a soul in order to mediate between mind and body. Kram, on the other hand, cannot make his fit into either his neat categorical notebooks or the comprehensive Book.

Unable to bring a satisfying order to *Krimskram*, unable to reconstitute his fragmented corpus, the narrator longs for death or, its linguistic analog, silence. Are these our only choices?

The carnivalesque aesthetic provides a conception of the body that contrasts sharply with the perfected and idealized form of classicism. It differs as well from the Christian view that denigrates corporeal life as sinful. The carnivalesque body exceeds itself in order to go out into the world. It also allows the world to enter it. Consequently it emphasizes orifices and bulges, or, in other terms, lacks and excesses, open spaces and dense passages. From the Judeo-Christian-Classical perspective, it is "faulty"; from the carnivalesque, it is implicated in a process of transformation and becoming.

This "faultiness" takes on even greater importance when it is understood as the "origin" of "entities." In order to constitute itself, an entity (e.g., body, mind) must not only set itself apart from others—both external and internal—but insist on its radical difference from them. Nevertheless, the "fault" can never be complete. The entity is always already marked by the trace of what it is not, by its alterity, by its own absence (or death). This does not mean, however, that the faultiness can ever be fully overcome either. The fault that distinguishes "entities" also keeps them irreparably apart.

Consequently such "faultiness" makes possible all dynamism by providing space for both motion and emotion. It also drives bodies ever onward. The disorder and unruliness of the narrator's desire are transformed into the painful jabs of the can-opener (another form of *griffe/greffe*) that spurs him on: "j'ai de ces sautes" (p. 108). At the close of Part I, this pain was objectified as "aie. . . dans le cul un pal ardent" (p. 45) and then projected outward as Pim. At the close of Part II, Pim disappears but not without leaving traces (*Spuren*) that remain even in the narrator's new life of Part III. These trace-effects of Pim prod the narrator to continue, for they both hold out and frustrate the promise of order and completion.

Beckett's artistic style (a *griffe/greffe* of a different sort), which I have described at length elsewhere,[6] provides an alternative means of dealing with the faultiness of corporeal existence. It draws together many coherent and meaningful elements without integrating them into a single, comprehensive thesis, schema, system, or perspective. Some groupings may suggest structures that remain (significantly) incomplete. Other components may remain outside the authority of any structuring principle.

In addition, components included within a particular design may suggest diverse meanings, and these may accordingly be understood in terms of the same design, several different designs simultaneously, or none at all. Beckett's style stages and actively engages problems that cannot be adequately dealt with by conventional generic, logical, or even linguistic forms so profoundly grounded in a cultural perspective hostile to corporeal existence.

The corpus of *Comment c'est* is internally diversified. It is, moreover, made up of "fragments" borrowed from a range of cultural and historical sources—e.g., scientific, literary, religious, philosophical—including Beckett's other works. Such borrowings of phrases, images and situations suggest that the narrative body is neither closed nor totalized. Neither is it self-contained nor self-referential. It is implicated in a network of textual graftings—*des greffes*. Its "source" is consequently a process of re-citation and re-inscription that necessarily involves differences and deferrings.[7]

In a brief 1961 comment on the painter Bram van Velde,[8] Beckett related the interplay of order and disorder to a more encompassing struggle between life and death. Death is opposed by the unruly vitality of existence, the essential "orthographic mistake [*faute*]" that continually troubles an otherwise entropic system. Van Velde's paintings neither present a formal pattern that corrects a "fallen" natural world nor describe the ground of existence as irrational disorder. Rather, they flow like lava from fissures or faults whose eruptions profoundly disrupt both the plan of death and the traditional aesthetic of perfect order that corresponds to it. This new art supplements the text of death by explicitly staging the fundamental struggle of existence: an infinite double *agon* that pits ordering against disordering processes, *both* of which are on *each* side of a similar contest between the forces that build up and those that break down.

Notes

1 Samuel Beckett, *Comment c'est* (Paris: Minuit, 1961). References will be included in the body of the text.

2 Cf. Clov of *Fin de Partie*. For a detailed discussion see my *Beckett's Critical Complicity: Carnival, Contestation and Tradition* (Lexington: University Press of Kentucky, 1988), pp. 85-121.

3 Jacques Derrida, "La Différance," *Marges de la Philosophie* (Paris: Minuit, 1972), p. 5; *De la Grammatologie* (Paris: Minuit, 1967), pp. 24-25.

4 Cf. the elimination of the narrator's turdy discourse, "floc dans le trou" (p. 94).

5 M. H. Abrams, *Natural Supernaturalism: Tradition and Revolution in Romantic Literature* (New York: W. W. Norton and Co., 1971), pp. 83-96.

6 Henning, *Beckett's Critical Complicity*, esp. pp. 1-8; 196-199.

7 Jacques Derrida, "La Dissémination, "*La Dissémination* (Paris: Seuil, 1972), pp. 321-407.

8 Samuel Beckett, *Disjecta: Miscellaneous Writings and a Dramatic Fragment*, ed. Ruby Cohn (New York: Grove Press, 1984), p. 151.

Myth, Science, and Technology

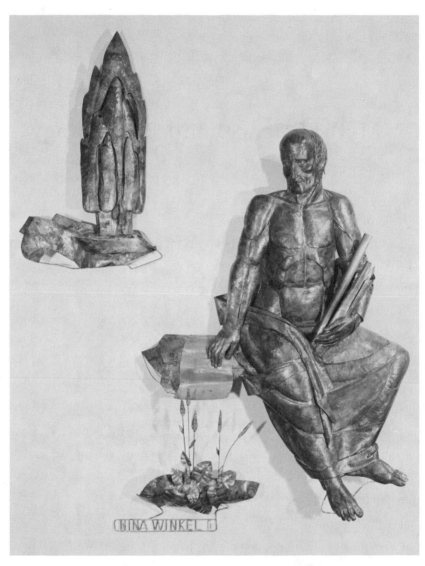

"School of Athens," right panel (1985) by Nina Winkel

Rathaus—Borken, Germany
Photo credit: Robin J. Brown

Richard D. Moore

From Science to Mythology:
A New Vision of Reality

Humanity is today at a crossroads that will determine not only our own fate, but also the fate of all life on this planet. The root of this crisis is the materialistic, mechanical world-view of the so-called modern period of Western Culture, which more and more is being recognized as not only moribund and dysfunctional, but as a threat to our very existence.

This mechanization of the world has led us to believe that we live in an essentially dead universe where life arises only by chance. The result has been a near total separation of ourselves from nature. This separation finally reached its logical extreme in the modern myth, as articulated by Francis Bacon over three centuries ago, that we can and should use science and technology to dominate, manage, and control nature for our own benefit.

But the result of this myth is the opposite of what was promised — we have just about "used up" nature — and ourselves in the process. As we near the twenty-first century, the almost unbelievable disintegration of the natural world is finally penetrating through our attempts at denial, minimizing, and avoidance.

In part a result of this devastating development, much of the "New Age" movement is rejecting science and technology in its attempt to find a new view of reality. Yet at the same time, science itself has now shown that this image of a dead nature is a false, or graven, image. Through the dynamic of science itself, a new world-view — a new picture of the nature of the universe — is emerging from the present cultural confusion and is showing the first signs of solid form.

This new scientific image is of a cosmos which is evolving. Progress is seen as more fundamental than objects are. Moreover, the secondary myth of "hard substantial matter" has evaporated under the impact of Quantum Physics, which has also shown us that everything is connected in a seamless web, and of Einstein's discovery that "matter" is only a form of energy.[1] Studies on the origin of life indicate more and more that the appearance of life was part of — not separate from — the process of cosmic evolution.[2] Thus, the new perspective suggests more than merely a new world-view. It also suggests deep connections between the universe and life. We appear to be on the threshold of a cosmic vision that suggests that life belongs in some fundamental way in this universe and hints that life may even have some fundamental role to play in the cosmic story.

Because of the potency of this new emerging cosmic vision, and the fact that science and technology provide perhaps the only basis of consensus all over the earth, this emerging vision must be considered in building the new myth for the twenty-first century.

Thus, the overarching question is: Which world-view do we accept? Do we take the modern world-view, which tells us that the fundamental basis of reality — the foundation of the universe — is some non-living material substance such as the lifeless particles, or atoms, first proposed by Democritus,[3] or do we take the new cosmic vision emerging from science itself, a vision that indicates that the fundamental basis of reality is something more like life, spirit, mind, or consciousness?

The Modern World-View: The Universe is a Giant Material Machine

What has come to be called the modern period has its roots in the origins of science (sometimes called the Copernican Revolution), which occurred during the Renaissance, in the sixteenth and seventeenth centuries. The Copernican Revolution produced a shift in perception that reinterpreted the earth not as the center of God's focus but as a tiny planet circling an average star on the edge of one among ten billion galaxies.

Moreover, in this first scientific view of reality as synthesized by Newton, everything was ruled by a deterministic law. Thus, in the modern world-view that was extracted from Newton's physics, the universe came to be seen as a giant cosmic machine. In such a universe, mankind must be elevated either to a super-natural miracle, or reduced to an accidental contingency. In either case, mankind is only a cog in this cosmic machine.

In this modern world-view, where the fate of nature is already determined, we are only spectators and hence irrelevant to the cosmos. Whereas in Eastern mythologies mankind is trapped by the cycles of time in an eternal, essentially unchanging universe, in the West the modern world-view imprisoned us in a universe of iron-clad determinism. And because such a universe can have no drama, there can be no deep cosmic story. We have no relevance to a universe, that grinds away oblivious not only to our concerns, but to our very presence. A more alienating and terrifying image is hard to envision. In such a universe, life is an absurdity. It is no wonder that in our frustration, terror, and resulting anger, our culture accepted Bacon's program of controlling and dominating nature.

In this modern world-view, reality is made up of separate objects, and all change is understood in terms of material mechanism. In this view, the reality we perceive with our senses is the primary if not the only reality, and all "objects" are made up of material atoms. As first proclaimed by Democritus, "Nothing exists but atoms and the void." This objectification of reality became embedded not only in the subconscious of the Western psyche, but in all Western languages as well. Unlike the situation in "process"[4] languages such as Hopi, in the modern languages of the West, every sentence has both a subject and an object.

During the past two hundred years of this modern period, the view that atoms are the ultimate "stuff" of which everything is made has been followed to its logical extreme. The fact that the word "atom" means "indivisible" implies that there can be no access to the interior of the smallest atomic particles, and thus that they can have no "inner" aspect.

And as the seventeenth-century French mathematician-philosopher René Descartes recognized, consciousness cannot arise from a mechanical universe that is inherently dead. As a consequence, consciousness must be grafted onto such mechanism by miracle. We do not come *out of* such a universe; we can only come *into* it through some act of God. Within this perspective, the only alternative is that life is merely an accident. Thus Descartes accomplished the final "deanimation of the world," leaving us with the image of a dead natural world — and of ourselves dead as well. In the process, this deanimation destroyed the perception that any aspect of life is sacred.

As a result of this progressive reduction of all reality to material mechanism, the idea that "consciousness," "mind," or "spirit" can exist independently from matter has, within much of Western culture, been discarded as nonsense. "Consciousness" and "mind" are now seen as a pseudo-reality, as mere "epiphenomena" of matter, and "spirit" is seen as a superstition altogether. As a mere epiphenomenon, consciousness is impotent, incapable of substantially affecting the cosmic machine. And in a world-view that does not acknowledge a consciousness founded in reality, the concepts of free-will, purpose, value, and meaning also dissolve into mere superstition.

Moreover, because human beings were thought to be composed entirely of molecules and atoms, they likewise have no interior, and therefore can be understood only as "objects" ruled by the outer forces in their lives.[5]

Another result of this "objectification" of the world, and the consequent emphasis upon externality, has been an almost exclusive focusing upon that which can be seen — material objects. This focus has resulted in what P. A. Sorokin[6] has called a "sensate culture," in which reality is defined entirely in terms of what can be seen, leading in the extreme to the view that "if you can't see it, it doesn't exist."

The impact of this sensate culture has been to degrade any concern with the future (which can't be seen), to reinforce the nihilism which denies any real values (which can't be seen), and to bias our educational philosophy towards the view that we learn only through the senses.

In uprooting consciousness from participation in the world, in denying any reality that we cannot perceive through the senses, we have destroyed any context or grounding for consciousness. And in separating ourselves from nature, we have lost our own sense of grounding. Moreover, although we have "objectified" the world, we have lost any universal context for knowing. The final irony of objectifying the world is that the resulting loss both of a universal context and of a sense of grounding has had the consequence that modern knowledge has slipped into a foggy relativism that denies any hope of "objectivity" in knowing.

The End of the Modern Era

As we approach the twenty-first century, all signs indicate that physics and biophysics, influenced by the social impact of the failure of the modern world-view — its failure to "conquer" disease, its excessive violence, its destruction of the outer world of nature and of the inner world of human nature — are launching Western culture towards a new vision of reality. This development offers the opportunity for a new scientific and cultural era: the Era of Consciousness. Thus, this new world-view may be more aptly described as a new vision of reality, a new cosmic vision.

No more profound scientific development related to the development of the new cosmic vision has occurred than the twentieth-century discoveries that have led to the dematerialization of the world.

The Dematerialization of the World

In discovering that electricity and magnetism are two aspects of the same process, James Clerk Maxwell in the 1860s showed us that physical reality consists not only of matter, but also of fields—something less "tangible" or "palpable" than material substance. Yet, the electromagnetic field discovered by Maxwell is definitely a physical reality, including not only visible light (which we can see), but also radio waves at one extreme of the spectrum and x-rays at the other.[7]

Although Maxwell's discovery weakened the materialistic view by demonstrating that something physically real does exist besides "atoms and the void," it was the development of Quantum Physics that exposed the materialistic philosophy as nothing but a false view.

In 1905, Albert Einstein published not only his first paper on relativity, but a paper in which he demonstrated that photoelectric cells could work only if light behaves not as waves, but as small discrete particles — called "photons." This paper on the "Photoelectric Effect," together with the discovery by Max Planck that all energy comes in tiny "packets" or "quanta," led to Quantum Physics.[8]

But then Louis de Broglie made the even stranger proposal that material substance, in addition to existing as a particle or atom, can also exist as a wave.[9] This radical proposal of de Broglie's was soon proven correct. Indeed, an everyday demonstration of the validity of de Broglie's idea is the electron microscope. Just as the focusing of a light microscope depends upon the wave properties of light, focusing the electron beam requires that electrons behave like a wave.

The next stage of the quantum revolution was the discovery[10]—by Erwin Schrödinger, in 1925,—of the mathematical equation[11] that describes this mysterious wave aspect of matter. The key physical parameter, called "psi," in Schrödinger's equation was initially thought by Schrödinger himself to be like any other parameter in physics — a mathematical symbol that represents some material attribute such as mass, length, or time.[12]

However, Max Born soon pointed out that although "psi" has three spatial dimensions when considering a hydrogen atom with its one electron, in general "psi" will have $3N$ dimensions (where N is the number of electrons in the system). This realization led Max Born[13] to point out that Schrödinger's equation requires that we choose between alternatives. Either we accept the radical view that the waves described by "psi" exist in spaces of more than three dimensions — or (if we remain in three-dimensional space) we must give up the common sense view that "psi" represents an ordinary material magnitude and accept the view that "psi" exists only in the realm of mathematical concepts.[14]

These strange aspects of Quantum Physics are not limited only to the equations. Perhaps no single experiment exhibits the strange world revealed by Quantum Physics more than the famous "double-slit" experiment. This experiment was invented by Thomas Young when, at the beginning of the nineteenth century, he used it to demonstrate that light behaves like a wave. When light shines through two parallel slits onto a screen, it produces a discontinuous pattern with alternating light and dark regions. This pattern can be explained only by assuming that light is a wave, and that the waves passing through the two slits interfere with each other and produce the pattern of alternating light and dark.

De Broglie's idea predicts that particles (such as electrons) behave exactly the same way when they go through two slits. Experiments confirm that this is the case. The most dramatic aspect of these results is that each electron behaves like a wave, even when the intensity of the electron beam is reduced so that only one electron at a time is fired.[15] Thus, the electron can indeed behave like a particle or like a wave, depending upon the experimental set-up as determined by the physicist.

So, it is not surprising that some physicists quickly realized that the discovery of the key relations of Quantum Theory would lead to a new world-view. In his book *The Nature of the Physical World*, published in 1927, just one year after the discovery of Schrödinger's equation, physicist-philosopher Sir Arthur Eddington wrote that "The frank realization that physical science is concerned with a world of shadows is one of the most significant of recent advances." As a result, "we have seen that substance is one of the greatest of our illusions."[16]

Since Eddington, it has become almost a truism that Quantum Theory's implications about reality seem completely unreal when compared to the common-sense view of material reality that underlies our culture.

Yet Quantum Theory must be taken seriously. For it is the most accurate theory ever developed, making predictions that differ from measurement by only two parts in a billion.[17] Richard Feynman has commented that this accuracy is comparable to determining the distance between New York and Los Angeles to within the width of a human hair. This accuracy alone would require that Quantum Theory and its implications be taken seriously.

EPR and Bell's Theorem

Perhaps more than anyone else, Einstein sensed the strange implications about reality implied by Quantum Theory. In 1935, he published a paper with Podolsky and Rosen[18] now known as the EPR paper, which so shocked Bohr's Copenhagen group that Léon Rosenfeld said, "this onslaught came down upon us as a bolt from the blue. . . A new worry could not come at a less propitious time. Yet as soon as Bohr had heard my report of Einstein's argument, everything else was abandoned."[19]

This EPR paper points out that the mathematics of Quantum Theory requires that any two objects which have tightly interacted will remain forever instantaneously correlated, or "in tune" with each other, no matter how far they become separated.[20]

Thus, the arguments advanced by Einstein, Podolsky, and Rosen clearly forced a choice between Quantum Theory and some of our most sacrosanct ideas about reality itself.

Since our ideas about the ultimate nature of reality[21] are considered metaphysical, their validation or refutation seemed beyond the ken of science: they could never be tested by experiment.

Bell's Theorem was to change all this. With Bell's Theorem, it became possible to take these arguments of Einstein out of the realm of metaphysics, and thought experiments, into the realm of real laboratory experiments. This may be the first example ever of a metaphysical, philosophical issue becoming rephrased with sufficient precision that it could become resolved by experimental measurement.

John Bell showed that if Einstein's view that instantaneous long-range effects or correlations and his view of realism ("things" such as electrons exist before they are observed) are true, it is possible to prove that a measurable parameter, S, would never be greater than 2.0: $S \leq 2$

In contrast to the classical view of Einstein, Quantum Theory tells us that the value of S, S/QT would be *greater* than 2.0 and, depending upon the experimental design, as high as: S/QT = 2.70. In the experiments on the correlation of photons, which were conducted by Alain Aspect's group[22] in France, the experimentally determined value of S, S/exp, was: S/exp = 2.697 +/- 0.015, which is not only remarkably close to the value predicted by Quantum Theory, but significantly greater than the value of 2 predicted by our classical, common-sense notions about reality.[23]

Thus, the tests of Bell's theorem indicate that the two photons — which could be light-years apart — will act together as a whole rather than as two separate objects.[24]

If we take the results of Quantum Physics quite seriously and drop all our prejudices, they clearly imply that the real action is not in the three-dimensional space of our everyday experience, but in a higher-dimensional space into which (in the words of Born) "we cannot enter" — an aspect of reality that is nonmaterial yet real. This, essentially the vision of Plato, flies in opposition to the predominant dogma of the modern period, that everything real is right here in front of our eyes.

The Rediscovery of Origins: Hint of a Cosmic Story

The revolution in our view of the cosmos as a whole began with a new view of time. From the cyclic view, which was embodied in the mechanized clocks of the early part of the Renaissance, we have rediscovered the evolutionary time of the Old Testament. First, came the confirmation by Darwin and Wallace of the ancient Greek idea of biological evolution. Then came the discovery of the Second Law of Thermodynamics — the discovery that the entropy of the universe always increases, a discovery that led Eddington to call the Second Law "time's arrow." Next came the discovery of the "Big Bang" and the expanding universe.

The Big Bang: Origin of the Universe

The "mechanical universe" of the modern world-view implied that either the universe had always existed or that the creator was a "Giant Clockmaker" who fashioned a completely developed universe "de novo" —essentially the view of present-day "creationists." Perhaps because of these alternatives, Einstein and many other scientists were convinced that the universe had eternally existed. Thus, Einstein was deeply shocked when the equations of his own "Theory of General Relativity" (1916) clearly implied that the universe had had a beginning![25]

Nevertheless, in 1929 Edwin Hubble demonstrated that all the observable galaxies in the universe were flying apart — that is, that the universe is "exploding," thus implying that all the galaxies originated from the same "place."[26] This has become known as the "Big Bang" theory.

Although the details of the origins of the universe are still uncertain, the concept that the universe had a beginning and that it all began from a tiny piece of ultradense energy is one of the most probable things we know.[27/28]

As a result of the new cosmology, we now know that the universe has expanded, and hence cooled, over its twelve to twenty-billion year history. In the process, the universe has periodically changed its form: at first, light was transmuted into subatomic particles. Then, subatomic particles became hydrogen and helium atoms. Then, hydrogen and helium atoms became stars. Then, in the thermonuclear furnaces of these first-generation stars, hydrogen and helium were converted into all of the higher elements including carbon, nitrogen, and oxygen — and all the other constituents of earth and our own bodies. Finally, planets formed, and the higher elements (carbon, nitrogen, and oxygen) began to form into living beings.

The Origin of Life — and of us

Reflecting the influence of Aristotle, academics until recently have considered biology and physics to be two separate sciences dealing with unconnected phenomena.

Now, however, we are beginning to realize that life is a "Cosmic Event" — part of the evolution of the universe. For several years scientists have known that, except for hydrogen, all of the atoms in our bodies were initially formed in first-generation stars — hence Carl Sagan's pithy comment that we are indeed made of "Star Stuff." Even more surprising is the recent demonstration that the key molecular constituents of life — amino acids, nucleic acids, and water — are formed in interstellar regions of space from the gas clouds of elements produced by exploding first-generation stars.[29] These molecules, of which all forms of life are composed, are forming in gas clouds of otherwise empty space all over the universe. The universe is like a giant incubator for the molecules of life.

Moreover, the discovery of the universality of the genetic code has also shown us that all forms of life, at least on planet earth, share the same language; thus all life is related. Now, among scientists studying the origin of life, there is a growing consensus that life is not an accident, but is a consequence of the evolution of the cosmos, just as much as the appearance of "matter," stars and galaxies. The view developing is that life did not come *into* the universe, but arose *from* the universe. Rather than a temporary contingency, life is an integral part of this new universe.

The Reexamination of "What is Life?"

Studies into the origin of life have depended heavily upon a traditional scientific definition of life.[30] Beginning with James Lovelock[31] and Lynn Margulis[32], a still small but growing number of scientists has come to the view that the earth is one living organism — hence the "Gaia"[33] hypothesis. This new view was initially based upon a more recent scientific definition of life.[34] This realization that the earth is a living planet has also been experienced by most astronauts when they looked back at their Home Planet.[35]

The idea that the earth is a living entity seems conservative compared to the suggestion that the whole cosmos is a living being. If we review our present scientific knowledge, we see that the cosmos had a beginning, grows (expands), differentiates, gives birth not only to new forms (galaxies), but to new phenomena (life and now consciousness). These are the attributes of a living being .

Moreover, Quantum Physics has clearly demonstrated that reality is not composed of entirely separate "objects." The tests of Bell's Theorem, especially, make the holistic inseparability of the world inescapable to any open and critical mind.

Thus, the universe is now seen to be more like an organism than a machine. Most importantly for our new myth, this "generative" universe, which is growing, developing, differentiating, and displaying "organic" (or "holistic") properties, does not seem inhospitable to life.

Finally, this universe is seen as a process, a dynamic web of interconnections, of which life and consciousness are inherent parts. Evolution is the overarching feature of the universe, a universe that is "going somewhere." Or to put it differently, there is a story to the universe. Just when the modern world-view, with its dismal implications, is dying, we are being presented with a a new vision of reality — a new cosmic vision — that holds promise of reuniting us with nature.

References

[1] $E = mc^2$ tells us that mass can be converted into energy and vice versa. Thus, mass is a form of energy.

[2] See *Gordon Research Conference* on "The Origin of Life," New Hampshire, August, 1990.

[3] The Greek philosopher Democritus (460-370 B.C.) was the first major proponent of atomism. In this view, everything is either space-filling matter or emptiness, the void. In order to account for the changes observed in matter, Democritus thought of matter as being made up of innumerable small particles. Since these small particles are solid they are called "atoms" or "dense bodies." See Eduard Zeller, *Outlines of the History of Greek Philosophy* (Dover, 1980), pp. 64-68.

[4] See: Benjamin Lee Whorf, *Language, Thought, and Reality* (The M.I.T. Press, 1956), pp. 51-64. In process languages, such as Hopi, there is no reference to "objects" in the sense that we use that term. Nothing is static — and therefore fixed for all time — but all is becoming. Therefore, there can be no labels. As a result, people cannot be "objectified" into static entities.

[5] In the first part of the twentieth century, this denial of an interior became the basis of behaviorism. Although psychology has backed away from this extreme materialism, today behaviorism still dominates much of American psychology, and "physicalism" says that consciousness is somehow just an emergent property of matter.

[6] P. A. Sorokin, *The Crisis of Our Age.* 1951.

7 Julian Schwinger, *Einstein's Legacy* (Scientific American Library, 1986), pp. 13-14.

8 Schwinger, pp. 38- 39.

9 A. P. French and P. J. Kennedy, eds., *Niels Bohr: A Centenary Volume* (Harvard University Press, 1985), p. 75.

10 The Schrödinger equation cannot be derived in its entirety, but can only be obtained by accepting a new vision that Schrödinger intuited. In this new "vision," we drop the assumption that what is observable is "things" and accept the inspired intuition that what is observable is an abstract concept in mathematics called "operators." The simplest example of a mathematical "operator" is the square-root symbol. For example, the square root is an "operator" in that it "operates" upon 4 to convert it into 2. An operator processes or transforms something.

11 French and Kennedy, eds., pp. 107-108.

12 Before Max Born clarified the situation, Schrödinger had initially thought that "psi" represented the density of the electron.

13 French and Kennedy, eds., pp. 105 -110.

14 In other words, unlike the usual physical parameters — mass, energy, length, time — "psi" does not refer to any material properties: "psi" has no material attributes. The correct meaning of this abstract mathematical concept, which reflects the wave properties, finally is expressed by the square of ("psi" or "psi" *"psi"), which is proportional to the probability of observing a material particle, such as an electron.

15 When one electron at a time is fired through the single slit, it scatters randomly as a baseball would through a narrow opening in a fence, with the result that after many electrons, a more-or-less smooth pattern builds up. But if one opens the second slit, the pattern completely changes: now, there are some locations on the photographic plate where the electrons never hit. In other words, opening the second slit prevents some regions from being hit which would be hit with only one of the slits open. Clearly, these electrons are nothing particulate like little baseballs: they either have the ability to know that the second slit is open, or the electron some-how "dematerializes" into a wave that can go through both slits at once.

16 Arthur S. Eddington,"*The Nature of the Physical World: The Gifford Lectures (1927)* (New York: The Macmillan Company; Cambridge, England: At the University Press,1929), pp. XV-XVI.

[17] See Roger Penrose, *The Emperor's New Mind: Concerning Computers, Minds, and the Laws of Physics* (Oxford University Press, 1989).

[18] Albert Einstein, B. Podolsky, and N. Rosen, "Can Quantum-Mechanical Description of Physical Reality be Considered Complete?" *Physical Review* 47, 1935, pp. 777-780.

[19] French and Kennedy, eds., p. 142.

[20] For example, quantum theory predicts that the polarization of two photons leaving an excited atom will always be exactly correlated across any distance, even though the two photons are moving in opposite directions. Thus, if we change the polarization of one of these photons, quantum theory predicts the polarization of the other will change instantaneously no matter how far away it has traveled.

[21] The two key ideas are realism (objects exist whether they are observed or not) and locality (no cause can be propagated from "here" to "there" except by intermediary steps). As you will recall, these ideas have their origins in Democritus.

[22] Alain Aspect, P. Grangier, G. Roger, "Experimental Realization of Einstein-Podolsky-Rosen-Bohm 'Gedankenexperiment': A New Violation of Bell's Inequalities,"*Physical Review Letters*, 49, 1982, pp. 91-94.

[23] There is, however, one possible problem with this experiment. The experimental design does not completely exclude the possibility that some heretofore undetected faster-than-light signal might pass between the two measuring devices. To rule out this remote possibility, Aspect's group conducted a second experiment, in which each of the photons is allowed to travel 6.5 meters before being measured. By an ingenious method, the choice of measurement settings was made during the flight of the photon. Therefore, in this experimental design no communication — even at the speed of light — between the two measuring devices is possible. Even in this experiment, the experimental value of S is significantly higher than the value of 2.0 predicted in the classic world-view of separate material objects.

[24] These tests of Bell's Theorem do *not* indicate that changing something here (such as the polarization of one of the two photons emitted from the same source) will *act upon* the other photon in any causal sense. One photon does not signal the other.

[25] French and Kennedy, eds., pp. 67, 186-189.

[26] Joseph Silk, *The Big Bang* (New York: W.H.Freeman and Company, 1989), p. 27.

[27] Among the evidence confirming this idea is not only its prediction by the Theory of Relativity, but especially by confirmation of two consequences of the "Big Bang" theory. One of these consequences is that the Big Bang theory predicts that the matter in the universe should be almost all either hydrogen (76%) or helium (24%). These are almost exactly the percentages observed. Only trace amounts of the elements that make up our planet and our bodies are present — and these are produced only when stars finally explode (hence, as Carl Sagan says, we are truly made of "Star Stuff"). The other prediction of the Big Bang theory is that there should be an "echo," or more precisely an "afterglow" of the Big Bang. This "afterglow" should penetrate the entire visible universe, come from all directions (be isotropic) and (at this time in the history of the universe) have the very precise characteristics of radiation emitted from an object at an absolute temperature of 2.75 degrees Kelvin. Indeed, the universe is filled with radiation characteristic of precisely 2.75 degrees Kelvin, and this radiation is isotropic to 1 part in 10,000.

[28] David T. Wilkinson, "Anisotropy of the Cosmic Blackbody Radiation," *Science 232*, June 20,1986, pp. 1417-1522.

[29] See *Gordon Research Conference* on "The Origin of Life,"New Hampshire, August, 1990.

[30] My own definition of life is developed in a forthcoming book. However, there is general agreement that living systems are out of equilibrium, yet are highly ordered, develop more order, have order that is dynamic, and develop new forms of order.

[31] See James Lovelock, *The Ages of Gaia: A Biography of Our Living Earth.* New York: W. W. Norton and Company, 1988.

[32] See Lynn Margulis, "Science's Unruly Earth Mother," *Science,* 252, April 19,1991.

[33] "Gaia" is the Greek word for "Earth Goddess."

[34] Indeed, especially as seen from space, the whole earth satisfies several of the requirements of a biophysical definition of life: it is highly ordered, out of equilibrium, dynamic, and complex. Moreover, we know that in the course of evolution, the very form of the planet is changing — and that consciousness has developed in at least some forms of life on the planet.

[35] In the words of James Irwin, as he moved farther and farther from the earth on his way to the moon: "That beautiful, warm, living object looked so fragile, so delicate, that if you touched it with a finger it would crumble and fall apart. Seeing this has to change a man, has to make a man appreciate the creation of God and the love of God." quoted in: Kevin W. Kelley (For the Association of Space Explorers), *The Home Planet* (Reading, MA: Addison-Wesley Publishing Company, 1988), p. 38.

Scott R. Smith

The Myth
of
Mind as Machine:
Mankind's Misunderstanding of Self

For several hundred years, since about the time of Descartes, a deep and pervasive myth has taken root in mankind's perception of self. The rise of science, together with the decline of the widespread belief in a "natural order" in which humans rank just below God, yet above other animals by virtue of possessing souls, has led to this century's practice of "cognitive science."

According to the dominant view in cognitive science, the study of the mind must be cast in objective terms, like those used in physics, so that human behavior is reduced to understanding mind, and man, as a machine. Subjective perspectives, including those suggesting a "reality" that is visible only from within the individual or collective consciousness, rather than in a laboratory, are regarded by many cognitive scientists as epiphenomena, not worthy of primary consideration. Many cognitive scientists seem to have adopted the working hypothesis that humans are nothing more than "meat machines."

Some historical reflection reminds us that the reductionism practiced by Isaac Newton was ideally suited to furthering our understanding of the substances of which our environment is composed. The successes of physics in discerning the basic laws of mechanics, electromagnetism, and gases could not have been achieved without the curious drive to "get to the bottom of things" and understand how the world is constructed from the atoms up. Chemistry, anatomy, and biology all owe their inspiration and methods of research to the physics model. Likewise, the applied fields of engineering and modern medicine derive their raison d'être from an essentially mechanistic view of the world.

By the time the humanities disciplines began emerging in the late 1800s, the successes of the physical sciences had captured the imagination of the intellectual community and had begun to percolate into everyday world-views, as well. To borrow from Kuhn,[1] the operative paradigm of the era was reductionism, and almost everyone came to see the world through that perspective. Thus, it is no wonder that sociology, history, and psychology began to define themselves as social *sciences*. To be credible as independent disciplines, worthy of their places in the academy, they felt obligated, and were apparently ever-so-eager, to "elevate" themselves above "merely emotive" and therefore lesser-valued endeavors such as poetry, fiction, and the visual and performing arts. The social sciences sought legitimacy, in part, by positing themselves in the image of the physical sciences, and in opposition to the humanities. And more recently cognitive science — including aspects of psychology, philosophy, and computer science — has been trying to understand the mind from within the reductionist perspective engendered by the successes of the physical sciences.

I would like to suggest that, understandable as its historical origins may be, this paradigm for cognitive science's understanding of mind, in fact constitutes a very unfortunate societal *mis*understanding of our selves. Although this essay comments largely on cognitive science issues per se, I would like to stress that neither cognitive science, nor any other science for that matter, is done in a vacuum, but is situated within a social context that defines the "problems" that academic disciplines find worthy of investigation, and so I mean to suggest that the misunderstanding of self currently implicit in cognitive science disciplines is only a consequence of the *already* societally entrenched paradigm of mind as machine.

In order to characterize the misunderstanding of self in which our culture finds itself, I first trace briefly the means by which we got where we are today. I then identify the misunderstanding, using a few examples from cognitive science perspectives on mind. Subsequently, in a more positive tone, I discuss the conception of mind offered by some alternative thinkers, in the belief that they can help us to augment the paradigm of science, which we have begun to outgrow. Finally, I suggest extensions to these alternative conceptions of mind, by sketching a rejection of the claim that an artificial intelligence rivalling our own might one day be constructed.

Before Descartes, the concept of mind was not well-defined. Considerable energy had to be invested in the tasks of daily life, and illiteracy and lack of public education effectively left reflection on the nature of the self to an educated elite. Of course, because the Church promoted a distinction between the mortal body and the immortal soul, believers had grounds for supposing that the soul was something non-physical. But it is probably safe to assert that the "man in the street" didn't get much beyond accepting this distinction at face value.

Furthermore, pre-Cartesian notions of the non-material component of personality were distinctly theological in nature. The personality was characterized by the soul, and not by the largely non-theological term "mind," which we are inclined to use today. Whether one's faith was spiritually revealed or logically reasoned, the theological argument for the mortal body and the immortal soul was the only explanation of self available at the time.

To the extent that we can identify the concept of "soul" as a precursor of our current concept of "mind," it is clear that pre-Cartesian notions of mind were distinctly non-material and non-mechanistic. Of all the many beliefs that were held about the soul at that time, *none* included a belief that the soul was a computable-function supported by the physiology of the brain.

René Descartes' writings in the seventeenth century mark an epoch in our cultural conception of "mind" as distinguished from "soul."[2] Surveying Descartes' legacy, we recall that the methodological doubt he promoted has been a catalyst for the paradigm of modern science, which has all but eliminated the mind, arguing that it derives from the body.

Descartes' well-known criterion of truth was to regard every proposition as false that one cannot know with absolute certainty to be true. It lies outside the scope of this paper to discuss epistemological considerations about the certainty and means by which one might know any proposition to be true, but modern "Science" learned its lesson well from Descartes, and has been largely content to ignore the implicit epistemological difficulties. Descartes' program of methodological doubt amounted to the beginning of a now-longstanding tradition of attempting to mechanize or formalize the process of reason. Rationality, if we take the Cartesian lesson, is to be understood as an explicit process of examining evidence and evaluating it according to rigid standards or rules so that all meaningful knowledge might be cast in the form of declarative propositions that can be said to be "true" or "false." As Descartes forged the distinction between the theological soul and the rational mind, he made abundantly clear that it is the task of the mind to serve as a mechanistic tool, yielding up knowledge where justified.

His characterization of the mind as a mechanistic tool for rational thinking, together with his effective prescription of methodological doubt as the recipe for scientific procedure, are *at least* as important as his dualistic distinction between "mind stuff" and "body stuff." Descartes may not have viewed the brain as the seat of the mind, since for him, mind-stuff was still of the more ethereal soul, but he did mechanize our conception of mind to the extent that he posited its ideal functioning in a machine-like manner. The point to take from our look at Descartes is that the process of intellectual inquiry was being rewritten to favor a brand of rationality that Descartes' successors would extend in such a way as to favor the investigation of "body stuff," and to disregard the study of "mind stuff."

Beginning with Isaac Newton, the post-Cartesian period comprising the seventeenth through nineteenth centuries witnessed incredible advances in man's understanding of the physical world. Beliefs about a flat earth and the efficacy of blood-letting began to yield to more and more accurate understanding of the elements and compounds that constitute our environment, and the laws of physics that relate these substances to one another. The mystery about the nature of things began to dissipate. Branches of physics emerged into free-standing scientific disciplines, and chemistry, biology and medicine adopted the empirical-reductionistic methodologies of physics as their model.

To evolving medical science, it became clear that one's state of health did not attribute to good or bad "humours," but rather to the state of health of each of the subsystems comprising the human body. Just as a tumor in the abdomen might affect one's digestion, so too was it discovered that if the brain were subjected to physiological damage, the effects could be seen in the patient's behavior. The notion of a physiologically, or brain-based mind was beginning to emerge.

Together with the public's growing appreciation for the wonders revealed by science and the reformations and infighting within the Church, the once-dominant theological notions of mind no longer held sway. The ensuing scientizing of mind persists in our culture as a dominant metaphor even today, to the extent that our rough-and-ready concept of mind typically makes reference to a list of properties inhering from brain-function. There is an implicit faith that the mysteries of mind will be yielded up in due course, as the allied disciplines of cognitive science analyze the brain and its behavior. It's still possible, of course, to believe in souls, but most believers are also willing to talk of minds. And others have thrown off belief in souls altogether. In any case, we have come to understand minds as aspects of our selves that are the province of science, not religion, to legitimately investigate. The notion of a brain-based mind is quite widely accepted.

So what do we understand by the term "mind" today? Rather than attempt a definition of this elusive entity, which would only test our ability to draft encyclopaedia entries, perhaps we should consider how we *use* the notion in practice, especially in those disciplines that purport to be investigating the mind.

In Western philosophy, a dominant trend throughout much of this century has been logical positivism and the analytic approach, which is a philosophical interpretation of the reductionistic paradigm we have observed in broader society for several centuries. Some have even proposed that ideal philosophizing should be conducted in the language of mathematics, with the predicate calculus as the expressive mechanism for posing and solving philosophic problems. Questions such as "Is there a God?" or "What is the right thing to do in this moral dilemma?" were regarded as essentially meaningless, since they refer to intangible realms not discernable within the reductionist framework.

Questions about how we can trust our senses in judging that one object is larger than another *were* fair game for this branch of philosophy, because one could use laboratory instruments and empirical methods to arrive at an answer (if we ignore the obvious difficulty of trusting our readings of laboratory instruments). But since neither God nor moral truths are to be found lying around the landscape like tables and chairs, adherents to the view of philosophy-as-a-formal-calculus did not feel compelled to concern themselves with such extraneous and fanciful notions as conjured up by the humanities. We must ask ourselves whether the reductionist paradigm leads to a satisfactory philosophy, when it seems to discourage discussing ethical issues on the grounds that they don't really exist.

In artificial intelligence and linguistics, meanwhile, research has been underway to construct computer programs that are claimed to understand natural language, at least in restricted domains. Roger Schank and his colleagues have developed a system that can read a newspaper-like article about some event, summarize it, and respond to questions about the explicit or implicit content of the article.[3] Consider the following passage:

> Susan was hungry for lunch, so she took a seat at the outdoor café she came upon. After ordering a medium-rare cheeseburger and a Coke, she was dismayed when the sandwich arrived charred to a crisp. Susan stormed out of the café in search of another restaurant.

"Why was Susan upset?" one could ask Schank's system, to which it could respond "Because her cheeseburger was overcooked." Further, if asked whether Susan had left a tip for the waitress, the system would respond that she had not, because she left the restaurant without eating the meal or paying her bill. At first glance, we might want to acknowledge that Schank may have constructed a computerized language-understanding system.

In the school of linguistics supported by the reductionist paradigm, the meaning of a sentence is determined by the consituent words, whose meaning in turn is determined by entries in a dictionary, of sorts. Thus, a computer program such as Schank's might be argued to convey the same meaning as a human speaker or writer might, so long as it uttered or "performed" the same linguistic string under comparable circumstances. Meaning is thus reduced to performance.

But as Searle's now-classic refutation using the "Chinese Room" thought-experiment demonstrates, understanding a natural language means much more than merely manipulating strings of words in grammatically and semantically acceptable sequences.[4] Searle, who cannot read a word of Chinese, by his own admission, proposed that we place him in a soundproof room with a "Chinese-Chinese dialog dictionary," should such a manual be possible, with which he could look up "input phrases" and find recommended "output phases" for any utterance a native Chinese speaker might care to write down and drop into Searle's "in" basket. Now no matter how impressed the native speaker of Chinese might be with the calibre of the dialog into which he might enter with the Chinese Room, Searle maintains that neither he, nor the room, could be properly said to understand Chinese, but that he would only be acting as a mechanistic agent, not unlike the computers and programs of Roger Schank.

Language-understanding is a rich and complex phenomenon, and we may not be able to characterize it easily. But understanding a language is *not* the same thing as manipulating a language, even if that manipulation may appear to be very clever indeed. In other words, Searle claims that there is a *qualitative* aspect to understanding that a formal system, even if functionally equivalent in terms of linguistic utterances generated, does not share. Meaning is not only performance, but has to do with the innards of the agent generating the performance, Searle might say.

For me, at least, Searle's interpretation seems much more appealing than the one that Schank and the reductionists offer us. Can we accept a linguistics that tells us that the dialogues in which we earnestly engage each other are nothing more than speech performances of a mechanistic nature?

Much effort has been misdirected in the pursuit of cognitive science. Furthermore, the "mind as machine" viewpoint has dominated research in these fields, for the simple reason that the "everything is a machine" paradigm continues to dominate conventional thought. However, as I discuss in the following section, alternatives are available that may help us to break the constraints of the reductionist paradigm, which can no longer claim to be universal.

So what *does* it mean for a mind to engage in moral reasoning, or to understand a natural language? Without reversing the process of enlightenment and retreating into an uncritical but cozy faith in a theological explanation of the human soul, how are we to account for the phenomenon of mind? If the mind is *not* best understood as a machine-like entity, what options are left open to us? Doesn't our culture tell us implicitly that just about anything one cares to name is best analyzed to its primitive components, if we wish a thorough understanding of it?

The phenomenological movement of this century has begun to provide an alternative to the reduction of mental phenomena to the terms of physics, acknowledging the reality of such phenomena as moral values, intentional objects such as unicorns, and the sandwich I ate for lunch, and psychological states such as jealousy and pride. In his paper "Philosophy as Rigorous Science," which appeared in 1911, Edmund Husserl addresses the problems arising from the view of mind taken by leading psychologists at the turn of the century.[5] He argues that an essential aspect of mind is its directedness towards intentional objects, and that despite the fact that some such objects are unavailable for inspection by laboratory instruments, that they nonetheless constitute a portion of reality, at least as far as the mind is concerned. Husserl further argues that if we want to concern ourselves with understanding the mind in an intellectually honest manner, we must broaden our notion of reality in order to admit all those aspects that the mind refers to.

Now, to posit that unicorns are real because the mind sometimes refers to them is regarded by many as preposterous. But Husserl does not suggest that we are even remotely likely to encounter unicorns in our wanderings on the surface of the earth. He *does* mean to argue, however, for a study of the mind that acknowledges a *mental* reality that cannot be ignored if we want to understand just what the mind is. Such a conception of mind is required not only for understanding the way we entertain thoughts about unicorns, Husserl maintains, but also for understanding thoughts about tables and other physically constituted entities that most of us already believe to exist in the traditional sense.

Husserl's successors—including Heidegger, Gadamer, and Merleau-Ponty, to name a few—have argued that ontology, the study of what exists, should precede epistemology, the study of how and what we can know.[6,7,8] Our condition of "being in the world" directs our thoughts and actions towards objects and situations that exist *for us*, independent of whether they are detectable as mass or energy. The phenomenologists want to understand the mind in its natural dimensions, uninhibited by the constraints of the traditional paradigm, which disallows the mind from referring to unicorns or formerly-existent sandwiches in any meaningful way.

Of course, the phenomenological approach does *not* claim that a comprehensive view of reality can be attained easily, if at all. Moral values are not lying around the landscape, waiting to be bumped into. At best, moral values may well prove to be species-relative, in which case we may hope for convergence in moral theory and practice. It may turn out that moral values are relative to each culture, so that there is no way to resolve differences of opinion between two cultures. Tolerance when crossing cultural boundaries may be the best prescription that a phenomenological understanding of morality can provide. But at least the phenomenological perspective permits us to talk about moral values, granting them an existential status, rather than trying to pretend that they do not exist.

Likewise, phenomenologists may not be able to give a formal description of the grammar and semantics of a natural language. In fact, they argue that the attempt to provide such a formal description is misguided in the first place, because language use and meaning are socially determined, and always in flux. To the extent that we understand each other at all, it is because we share sufficiently common backgrounds, interests, and desires to further our understanding together. Every day, we extend our understandings of words in our vocabularies, and we acquire new words from time to time, as the contexts in which other speakers introduce those words suggest clearer meanings to us.

Language *is* a complex and mysterious dance of words, and despite regularities in grammar that make it sometimes appear to be a pseudo-formal system, it is a dynamically moving target, which can be captured only in part by beings whose conditions of *being in the world* are sufficiently similar.

So if minds arise only in beings that are sufficiently alike, how can anyone seriously entertain the prospects of "strong A.I.," the claim that human-equivalent intelligence may be produced in a computer? Gradually, many of the early adherents of strong A.I. have retracted their claims, or have recast them, acknowledging that our table-top word-processors are unlikely to become our conversational partners.

The recasting of the strong A.I. claims now depends upon the use of connectionist,[9] or parallel distributed processing models, rather than the traditional serial architectures of almost all current computers. Current connectionist research is in a very early phase, but its proponents hope that by mimicking more closely the neurological system of man, they will sooner understand how the brain supports the features of the mind.

Although connectionist models are not currently well-developed enough to begin testing them on problems beyond simple pattern-recognition, control of coarse motor skills, and the like, many connectionist researchers recognize that there *are* human-relevant, and therefore real, phenomena of mind that must be accounted for, which cannot be dismissed as irrelevant concoctions from the humanities. While the connectionists may no longer simply dismiss such phenomena, they do expect to find thoughts of unicorns and ex-sandwiches supported by lower-level structures that *could*, in principle, still be explained within the reductionist paradigm.

Unless one equates the mind with a God-given soul, trying to sidestep the connectionists and plaintively mourn "but I'm *sure* we aren't just meat machines, are we?", what escape is left? Won't it just be a matter of time until the connectionist models become sophisticated enough that artificial intelligence will become a reality? If such a demonstration proof were to be presented, then no amount of phenomenological posturing would be able to deny that reductionism is the universal paradigm of human enquiry after all.

But before the connectionist researchers invest too much labor pursuing their goal, perhaps we can save them the trouble by arguing that an extension to the phenomenological movement can be used to suggest that *connectionist* artificial intelligence is also an impossible goal. In particular, we observe that the "being in the world" of which Heidegger speaks not only precludes human-equivalent intelligence arising from a brain in a vat, but also precludes it in silicone-based androids, or gene-engineered creatures with *any* physiological makeup that is other than our own.

Just as it has been recently argued that there are potentially distinct female and male ways of knowing and being, there is an even more significant *human* way of knowing and being. Although we have believed our brains to be the primary seats of our minds, our mindedness is actually distributed also over our entire neurological systems. The *way* we feel, touch, smell, look, and hear from within the constraints of our bodies, both as they enable us and as they restrict us, imparts a physiological flavor to what it means to have a mind. In other words, one's mind is dependent upon the full-physiology of one's body, and not merely upon the structure of the brain housed in the skull as if it were a brain-in-a-vat, computing the functionality of mind.

That's why a computer could not possibly understand, whether expressed in Chinese, English, or Cree, what a guest at a restaurant means when she informs the waiter that she is very hungry. Hunger is a physiologically-induced intentional attribute of mind, which cannot be meaningfully reduced to any lower-level function—the rate of gurgling of stomach juices, or blood-sugar levels, or any other quantifiable physical term. It may well be the case that certain physical conditions prevail when one feels motivated linguistically to express one's hunger, but the mental phenomenon know as hunger is qualitatively very different from an alarm bell that goes off when one's blood sugar drops below a certain level.

Furthermore, not only do the phenomena of mind depend on the physiology of one's whole body, but they also depend, in part, upon our participation in a community of members of the same species, each of whom shares a similar physical constitution, a desire to continue one's existence, a need for interaction, and a social instinct for seeking understanding in the interest of the success of the community.[10] This community-body should suggest to us why the connectionist researchers should not expect their parallel-computers to understand language, engage in moral reasoning, or acquire such human emotional states as jealousy, love, and friendship.

Thus we see that "being in the world" is a densely-packed phrase. The connectionist may be right that we *are* meat machines, but we are not *only* meat machines. We are not only the sum of our parts, because a level of reality emerges in our minds that cannot be discovered merely by understanding the functionality of the diverse components. To borrow from a quantum physics critique of Newtonian physics, in the interest of characterizing this new conception of mind and body, it is as if there is a "Heisenberg Uncertainty Principle of Mind," whereby the attempt to understand all aspects of a complex dynamic system cannot be simultaneously realized.

Of course, the reductionist approach is not altogether mistaken, nor should it be disposed of with all due haste. I rather hope that civil engineers and aircraft designers will continue to use the physics model when constructing the highway bridges and airplanes that I will be using. But bridges and airplanes lend themselves well to the reductionist approach, inasmuch as their behavior as wholes is by and large a function of their more primitive parts.

Human beings, on the other hand, despite their clear biophysical composition, have evolved a capacity for mind that is best understood from a non-reductionist paradigm. Thus, I am not arguing for the outright rejection of the reductionist approach; I only urge that we consider when its use is appropriate, and that we also make room for an alternative paradigm. The myth of mind as machine, which was born with the Age of Reason, must make way for the New Age, so that both reductionist and phenomenological paradigms can help us to better understand the physical world, the mind, and the body.

184

Notes

[1] See Thomas Kuhn, *The Structure of Scientific Revolutions* (Chicago: University of Chicago Press, 1962), p. 10ff.

[2] See René Descartes, *Discourse on Method and the Meditations* (London: Penguin, 1968), pp. 102-112.

[3] See Roger Schank and Robert Ableson, *Scripts, Plans, Goals and Understanding* (Hillsdale, N.J.: Laurence Erlbaum Associates, 1977), p. 17ff.

[4] See John Searle, "Minds, Brains, and Programs," *Mind Design*, ed. John Haugeland (Cambridge, Mass.: MIT Press, 1981), pp. 282-306.

[5] See Edmund Husserl, "Philosophie als Strenge Wissenschaft," *Husserliana* (Dordrecht, Netherlands: Nijhoff, 1987), pp. 3-62.

[6] See Martin Heidegger, *Being and Time* (New York: Harper and Row, 1962), pp. 28-35.

[7] See Hans-Georg Gadamer, *Truth and Method* (New York: Crossroad Publishing, 1986), pp. 414-448.

[8] See Maurice Merleau-Ponty, *The Primacy of Perception*, ed. James Edie (Evanston, Ill.: Northwest University Press, 1962), pp. 12-42.

[9] David Waltz and Jerome A. Feldman, *Connectionist Models and Their Implications* (Norwood, N.J.: Ablex, 1988), pp. 1-12.

[10] See Terry Winograd and Fernando Flores, *Understanding Computers and Cognition* (Norwood, N.J.: Ablex, 1986), pp. 54-69.

Thomas J. Morrissey

Myths of Re(-)Creation:
Mythology in the (Post-)Nuclear World

Given what we know about the likely effects of global thermonuclear war, the title of this essay should be a sinister, laughable logical
contradiction. There will be no post-nuclear world, not if "world" means
an earth populated by humans or human cultures. All the world's
mythologies will be silenced forever.

Many of us who grew up during the formative years of the Cold-
War —the time of the Iron Curtain, the Rosenbergs, "duck and cover
drills"— knew even then that the idea of nuclear survivability was per-
verse propaganda and that the anthem of the nuclear age is Tom Lehrer's
"We'll All Go Together When We Go."[1]

In this macabre apocalyptic satire, nuclear annihilation is the perfect
end to industrialized society, the logical extension of capitalism, mass
production, and mass murder. For a brief instant, business triumphs, for
"Lloyd's of London will be loaded when they go." Colonialism reaches
fruition with the eradication of "every Hottentot and every Eskimo." And
the greatest crime in human history, the Holocaust, is made ultimately ef-
ficient and ecumenical: "We'll all burn together when we burn/ There'll be
no need to stand and wait your turn." Universal death—no lines, no
waiting. Lehrer's song is a parody of mythmaking, the death of myth. We
can all go to our "respective Valhallas" because all belief systems, religious or secular, are now equal and meaningless.

But nearly a half century after Hiroshima, writers continue to posit
post-nuclear scenarios, and they often do so with the conscious knowledge that they are creating myths for our troubled time. The threat of
nuclear war is our principal nemesis, and science fiction is the crucible in
which the myths of science are brewed in a scientific age.

Unleashing the atom was an event of epic proportions. Global suicide became a possibility in 1945. No other human culture ever had to face
or explain the end of the world by human means. But with the bomb everything changed and, in H. Bruce Franklin's words, "having gained ac-

cess to the very forces that shape matter, we now have powers that may either extinguish all human life or grant us conscious control over our own destiny."[2] The phrase "conscious control" is crucial because it signals the transference of the locus of human evolutionary change from God, the gods, or nature to humans.

The bomb is the ultimate transference of power because its use or non use is totally dependent on our ability to abandon war as a means of solving problems, and this will not happen easily, for as Martha Bartter writes, "we can identify our values by examining what we spend the most time, effort, and attention on. History and fiction agree that this is war, not peace."[3] And science is no longer only a field of study, a way of thinking or doing, but the tool with which we shape or truncate our destiny, "the real myth of our culture."[4] Hence, it is to writers who extrapolate on science that we look for visions of our present and potential futures in the nuclear age.

The fictional mythologies of nuclear war are both recreational and re-creational; they provide strange and malleable venues for fantastic extrapolation, and they challenge our faith in rebirth and the resiliency of humanity. Thought-experiments with nuclear catastrophe are tempting. As Gary Wolfe suggests, "for all its terror, the wasteland holds a strange attraction for us."[5] So many writers have destroyed and rebuilt the earth's decaying cities that one critic has written an article entitled "Nuclear War as Urban Renewal."[6]

Destroying the world and building a better one is certainly a good way to see the faults of the one in which we live. Extrapolations of this kind tap into the tradition of cyclical myths of vegetative, spiritual or technological rebirth. If writers have difficulty accepting Tom Lehrer's grand finale, it is probably because cyclist sentiments lie at the heart of ancient vegetative myths and the notion of scientific and industrial progress. W. Warren Wagar traces the cyclical view of history from ancient to modern times and asserts that it is so much a part of human thinking that "whatever the aftermath, fictions of the endtime feed our hopes for fresh beginnings."[7]

"Fresh beginnings" spoil quickly when one considers the probable outcome of global nuclear war, and most post-nuclear stories do not have happy or fruitful endings. The fact is that the ancient cyclical myths of rebirth are inherently incompatible with the dead-end that is nuclear war. Yet writers who care about our dubious future continue to write now because, as I argue elsewhere,[8] they won't get a chance to do it later.

There are countless examples of works that struggle with the contradictions suggested above, but I have selected four recent treatments for discussion because each focuses consciously on the interaction between myth and reality in the nuclear age and because each occupies a particular spot on the imaginary nuclear-war timeline. Each of these works balances precariously between recreation and re-creation, and together they let us glimpse what we are and what we might or might not be.

1. *The Nuclear Age*

O'Brien's *The Nuclear Age* is the first-person narrative of a character whose life has been misshaped by the myths and realities of the arms race. The book is not technically a nuclear holocaust novel at all because there is no war. But the narrator, William, is a psychological victim of the holocaust even before it occurs. As a child, he built a fallout shelter under the basement ping-pong table. As an adult he digs a hole in his back yard for the ultimate shelter, the one in which he will protect his wife and daughter from nuclear war by killing them. The hole is the logical extension of the ping-pong table shelter and a metaphor for the psychic damage brought about by life with the bomb.

The cognitive dissonance that William experiences results from the principal myth of the nuclear culture,—that is, that it is only through building and deploying nuclear weapons that their use can be prevented. The nuclear culture consciously digs its own grave, and the digging is the major focus of business and government.[9] In a culture dependent on the arms race for economic equilibrium, the moral questions that William ponders are not admissible; hence, he and some of his college friends do what so many did in the 1960's — they launch their own crusade against the war in Vietnam, the arms race, and, ultimately, the prevailing culture.

As a college student, William drops out and joins the anti-war underground, but, when he tries to surface and rejoin the dominant culture, he faces his greatest moral and psychological challenges. His test is framed by two direct encounters with the stuff of which the end of the world is made, fissionable material. After his thirtieth birthday, William becomes a geologist, discovers a rich cache of high-grade uranium, and makes a fortune, which he shares with his radical friends.

In a chapter called "Fallout," he rationalizes his attempt at ultimate denial: "It wasn't a crime. It wasn't selling out. I was an adult, I said. I was able to take the world as I found it, and to use it, and to make what I could of it."[10] Unlike most people who plunder the earth for destructive purposes, William is forced to confront the product of his actions when his former comrades hide a stolen nuclear warhead in his shed. His former girlfriend seduces him into touching the Mark-24:

> "Graceful lines, don't you think? Like me. Bombshell. If you want, we can run away together, you and me and Mark. Tuck us in at night, tell us bedtime stories. Great sex, I bet."
> > "Enough," I said.
> > "Touch it, William."
> > "Not necessary, No."
> > "Your big chance. Cop a quickie. *Feel it.*"
> > "No."
> > "*Touch.*"
> She took my hand and pressed it down. The metal was cold. No surprise, I thought. Just cold and real.[11]

The sexual imagery she uses mocks the nuclear culture's worship of the weapon of ultimate destruction and forces William to experience a primal encounter with his childhood nightmare.

The hole he digs, which is both a shelter and a grave, is a response to his recognition of lost innocence. When he finally decides to spare his family, to "stop smoking," to "have hobbies," he does so because he loves his wife and daughter and because he has decided not to believe in the bomb. Even when it falls, he says, he will "be confident to the end that E will somehow not quite not equal mc^2."[12] Traumatized by the x force of the bomb, betrayed by the myths of the prevailing culture, unsuccessful at buying into those myths by selling out, O'Brien's protagonist can experience rebirth only by creating and living by his own myth, which is that despite all evidence to the contrary, maybe Einstein could have been wrong.

2. "Going After Arviq"

Michael Armstrong's story is the improbable tale of the survival of Northslope Alaskan Inupiats after the tannaks (whites) to the south have destroyed everyone else through nuclear war. The story opens with what looks like a traditional native scene—the hunting of the bowhead whale, arviq. The anomaly is that the crew-member on whom the narrator focuses is a white anthropologist, not a male Inupiat as custom would dictate. In this post-nuclear scenario the anthropologist Claudia becomes adviser to the shaman, a man who had held an anachronistic position until those who tried to kill native American culture killed themselves instead. He tells her, "We lost our past. . . We let you tannaks take it from us. And now you will give it back."[13]

Before the coming of the tannaks, the Inupiat were self-sufficient. The life of the tribe depended on the success of the whale hunt, which in turn depended on adherence to rituals to appease and please arviq, at once the mythic spirit of the bowhead and the bowhead itself. The tannaks put an end to self-sufficiency and brought in guns and explosives, forces greater than prayer or ritual.

Once Armstrong's survivors emerge after the fallout, they must learn to hunt arviq again, but they must also learn to be a people again, something they can do only by re-creating some semblance of their former culture. They knit remnants of old ceremonies and beliefs, provided by the shaman and Claudia, into a cultural fabric that binds the modernized Inupiat and the useful tannak survivors they allow to join them.

Before we get carried away with nostalgia for the Alaskan past, we must remember that Armstrong has selected the Inupiat not simply because he admires them but because their Arctic habitat and lifestyle give them a greater chance of surviving the initial blasts, the fallout, and ensuing nuclear winter. But even in this story, many die in the first year, and there is no guarantee that the plankton and other lower forms that feed arviq will continue to do so, no matter how much the people pray. As in O'Brien's novel, the happy ending depends upon blind faith and wishful denial.

3. The Gate to Women's Country

Sherri Tepper's novel is one of a number of feminist post-nuclear novels in which the survivors react against the assumptions and behaviors of the patriarchy that destroyed the earth. As in other such novels, the women in Women's Country exile the men (with the exception of servitors who do not possess the genetic propensity for bellicose machismo) and strive to create a myth that will help explain why men killed the world and how they can be prevented from doing so again.

Women's Country is composed of city-states much like the ancient Greek "polis," and the vehicle that the women choose for their mythology is an annually performed ritual tragedy, *Iphigenia at Ilium*. Like the Greeks, the women know that "myth and its tragic adaptation have, besides the authority of history, the power of poetry,"[14] and they intend to use both to shape the sentiments of the audience. Their play co-opts all of the surviving dramas about Troy, as well as the principal genres of the Greek theater.

It resembles Euripides' *The Trojan Women* in that it portrays the sorrows of the women of Troy after the Argive conquest, but it features three ghosts: Iphigenia, whom Agamemnon sacrificed to gain fair winds to sail for war; Polyxena, princess of Troy slain on Achilles' tomb; and the great hero Achilles, newly dead. Although it is dismally tragic, the play employs elements of ancient comedy too. Lusty Achilles sports the traditional exaggerated phallus of the Old Comedy, and, in the midst of the suffering, Iphigenia can deliver a line like, "you may as well forget it, Achilles. There is no fucking in Hades."[15] For Tom Lehrer and the survivors of nuclear war, black humor and tragedy are compatible.

We witness performances of the play's various scenes interspersed among episodes of the novel's main action, — the women's putting down of a coup attempt by the men. The events of the play remind us of how important it is for the women to remain dominant and of the high moral price they pay for oppressing most of the male population.

In the *Oresteia* of Aeschylus, Clytemnestra kills her husband in part because of his murder of their daughter, but when her son, Orestes, kills her, he ignores the murder of his sister and punishes his mother for Agamemnon's murder. In *The Trojan Women* we hear Hecuba's lamentation over the murder of her daughter Polyxena, but in *Iphigenia at Ilium* there can be no mistake about either the guilt of Agamemnon or the horror of these young girls' deaths at men's commands:

> Iphigenia: My father used me as he would a slave or a sheep from his flock. I think many fathers do the same. Then, having done, he claimed I'd wanted it. Perhaps it made him feel less vile. Men like to think well of themselves, and poets help them do it.[16]

And:

Polyxena: I pled for my life, Achilles. When they said they would kill me, I wet myself. My bowels opened and the shit ran down my legs. I screamed and groveled. I hated what I was doing, but I did it. Achilles, I wanted to live! I wanted to live, but they killed me, like a dung-covered animal.[17]

In the male-dominated world of the living, these girls controlled nothing, not even their bodily functions. By giving voices to the dead, the women playwrights shout down the privileged male poets who cloaked murder in sacrifice and blamed it on the victims.

Both *Iphigenia at Ilium* and *The Gate to Women's Country* are tragedies. In the play, women can escape brutality only in death. In the novel, the women of the cities can prevent another holocaust only by using violence to suppress men. Hecuba says, "Either you men kill us and are honored for it, or we women kill you and are damned for it."[18] Iphigenia's final line, "Hades is Women's Country,"[19] captures the anguish that leads to and maintains birth in this version of the post-nuclear world. Tepper plays fast and loose with the odds for survival of bands of cultured humans on the North American continent, but she has no illusions about the psychological damage that they would suffer. The women's corporate actions tarnish them; their communally performed tragic myth cleanses them through catharsis. It is a high price to pay for survival.

4. "When Idaho Dived"

The price of re-birth in this bizarre story makes survival through oppression look like a real bargain. Ian Watson's narrator, a loquacious survivor of the holocaust who remembers something of our world as it was, is our link with the new generation of humans whose genetic make-up is uncertain. The ancient narrator speaks to us as he speaks to his tribe. Even if his listeners are sick to death of the tale, we who have died before or during the nuclear war do not know the story of how an old man named Grandad, the only adult survivor in the original band of holocaust refugees, led his people to the desert where old submarines were mothballed. Miraculously, the narrator piloted the derelict craft down through the sand and discovered an underground shelter filled with foodstuffs and the remains of those who thought that they could outsmart destiny (maybe some of us were among them).

The keeper of the oral tradition, the narrator keeps a little of us alive as he preserves the history of his tribe. But he is a visionary as well as kind of bard. Seeing that the seasons have returned and that the stored food will soon run out, he offers his services to take Idaho to the stars. This boast is more than his fellow tribespeople can stomach, so they eat him. His last words are: "Alas, my tribe, you are fools. And now you will eat my brain and my heart and my liver. But first of all you will eat my tongue, which spoke to you, saying all these things."[20]

The world that the narrator inhabits is alien to us, but at least he is a storyteller and at least he remembers someone who could read our language. The faceless crowd that eyes him hungrily are our descendants, but there is little in them that reminds us of ourselves. It seems as though the lore conveyed by the narrator (once too often) will be lost, unless eating his tongue and brain will bestow eloquence and memory upon some lucky diner. But that is the kind of belief we sophisticates call primitive, so it looks as if history is doomed. However, if the storyteller is right about the changing environment, then the tribe is probably doomed too, so what's the difference? Our myths and their myths are equally perishable. They devour the keeper of knowledge as we devoured the world and damned our meager band of descendants to life in the wilderness.

These fictions, and others like them, give voice to our desire to create, even when creation is painful and re-creation doubtful. They create new myths to explore our changed role in the cosmos and to question the values and practices that have led us to the brink of the abyss. Brian Stableford writes simply and poignantly about the basis of catastrophic literature:

> In the final analysis, what these stories have in common as their fundamental assumption is the argument that we do not—perhaps cannot—care enough about one another. We are all estranged, and even when we do not find it all too easy to hate one another we still find it far too difficult to care much one way or the other what happens to people.[21]

Whatever myths we publicly honor or privately cherish, it is the indifference to one another's suffering that can kill us. The nuclear culture alienates us from ourselves and each other, and lies to us about our future. The truth to be learned from the fictions of post-nuclear mythology is that we will not be happy or secure as a species until we develop a non-nuclear mythology and live in a non-nuclear world.

Notes

1 All quotations from Tom Lehrer, "We'll All Go Together When We Go," *More of Tom Lehrer*, Lehrer Records, TL 102.

2 H. Bruce Franklin,"Strange Scenarios: Science Fiction, the Theory of Alie-nation, and the Nuclear Gods," *Science-Fiction Studies* 39:13:2 (1986), p. 117.

3 Martha Bartter, *The Way to Ground Zero: The Atomic Bomb in American Science Fiction* (New York: Greenwood Press, 1988), p. 232.

4 Gary Wolfe,*The Unknown and the Known: The Iconography of Science Fiction* (Kent, Ohio: Kent State University Press, 1978), p. 5.

5 Wolfe, p. 146.

6 See Martha Bartter, "Nuclear War as Urban Renewal," *Science-Fiction Studies* 39:13:2 (1986).

7 W. Warren Wagar, "Roundtrips to Doomsday," *The End of the World*, eds. Rabkin, Greenberg, and Olander (Carbondale, IL: Southern Illinois University Press, 1983), p. 96.

8 Thomas J. Morrissey, "Armageddon From Huxley to Hoban," *Extrapolation* 25:3 (1984), p. 212.

9 See H. Bruce Franklin, *War Stars: The Superweapon and the American Imagination* (New York: Oxford, 1988), p. 4.

10 Tim O'Brien, *The Nuclear Age* (New York: Alfred A. Knopf, 1985), p. 263.

11 O'Brien, pp. 290-291.

12 O'Brien, p. 312.

[13] Michael Armstrong, "Going After Arviq," *Afterwar*, ed. Janet Morris (New York: Baen, 1985), p. 33.

[14] Bernard Knox, *Word and Action: Essays on the Ancient Theater* (Baltimore: Johns Hopkins University Press, 1979), p. 17.

[15] Sherri S. Tepper, *The Gate to Women's Country* (New York: Doubleday, 1988), p. 50.

[16] Tepper, p. 50.

[17] Tepper, p. 277.

[18] Tepper, p. 278.

[19] Tepper, p. 278.

[20] Ian Watson, "When Idaho Dived," *Afterwar*, ed. Janet Morris (New York: Baen, 1985), p. 198.

[21] Brian Stableford, "Man-Made Catastrophes," *The End of the World*, eds. Rabkin, Greenberg, and Olander (Carbondale, IL: Southern Illinois University Press, 1983), p. 125.

Michael Johnson

Myths Doubling Back
to
Back to the Future Part II
a
II-Part Future: The Two Back-to-Back Doubling Myths

I

This study reflects its title in two respects: in structure and in message. Firstly, in the matter of structure, it may almost be read either forwards or backwards. It tries to match medium to message in the course of its seven sections. It is basically concerned with the pedagogic value of doppelgangers, and with the implications of seeing oneself in the flesh before one's very own eyes. Accordingly, it literally has a central thesis, with some reflections and reverberations on either side. Background and foreground matters will be blended as we consider the various interactions that are possible between a person and one's own self physically present in adjacent space.

The notion of the doppelganger is ancient. Saint Paul was most literal when choosing one of his most famous and striking images. He compared humanity's present state of self-awareness to seeing "now through a glass darkly (1 Cor. 13:12): in other words, all we really understand about ourselves is comparable to the dim, and perhaps distorted, reflection that was the best obtainable in the bronze mirrors then available. "But then," Paul continued, in the glorious hereafter as he envisioned it, [we shall see] "face to face." In other words, Paul reached for a fantastical notion: full self-knowledge in the hereafter is unimaginably superior to self-knowledge in the present. Now it is like having nothing better than a poor reflection in a mirror, but then it will be like seeing oneself in front of oneself, with no reflective surface in between. It will be like seeing oneself truly "face facing face," as the Greek literally has it. In fact the choice of vocabulary and an elegant variation of the voices of the Greek verb in Paul's phraseology point to this interpretation.

Secondly, this study resembles its title in the matter of message. The inelegance of the palindrome is suited to the insinuation of the subject-matter under consideration. Palindromes are self-contained with a vengeance. The words of any palindrome are both creators and prisoners; the palindrome in toto is both container and contained: a microcosm, in other words, of some aspects of human life itself.

One example may stand paramount at this juncture. You cannot escape from yourself, even by riding a time machine. This truism was recently given a vivid and amusing treatment in *Back to the Future Part II*.[1] In addition to its intrinsic entertainment value, this film can serve as a vehicle for reconsidering some of the oldest dilemmas known to man.

Insofar as myths both inform and enhance the perspective for such a study, Hollywood can send students back to the Classics with profit as they consider the implications of journeying with oneself through various time frames and dimensions.

II

Perhaps you *especially* cannot escape from yourself by riding a time machine. This motif has classical antecedents. The original time machine was, of course, the chariot of the sun. Not even Zeus himself could control its horses, but, in the ancient Greek tradition, this chariot and its counter-parts did have three riders other than Apollo.

Young Phaethon insisted on riding it to prove his pedigree: a world-wide holocaust resulted before that "day" was over. At one level, this myth can be used to support the old adage that civilization is always only twenty years away from barbarism; the generation gap is, by definition, fraught with danger.

Hercules, however, rode the cup of the Sun successfully. He was on his quest to conquer one form of death: the three-bodied monster Geryon, who lived on the island of Erythia in the far west. Einstein's physics and mythology clasp hands in maintaining that traveling at the speed of light is the necessary and sure route to becoming light oneself. Hercules tried it, but ended up being burned alive by a garment sent to him by his wife. She so wanted her husband's affections back that she somehow did not realize that the dying centaur's blood in which the robe had been steeped would retain its lethal potency. Hercules was ultimately killed by its poison: a venom derived from the tip of his own arrows. Hercules was indeed all things to all men . . . and now he can be pressed into service as the prototypical AIDS victim as well.

Medea, the sorceress, wreaked havoc at Corinth when her husband, Jason, forsook her for a younger bride. She outsmarted her enemies one by one, but ultimately she had to face herself, torn as she was between her love for her sons and her hatred of Jason. She saw him in them, and finally she killed them because in that way she could deprive Jason of his image. She subsequently appeared riding the chariot of the sun with the bodies of the children. The time machine carried her away from Corinth, but her shame still clung closely to her.[2]

Being unable to escape from oneself is not the only dilemma suggested by a palindrome. There is the closely allied problem of predestination. The first half of a palindrome determines the second half: so year "X" of a life in some sense fixes year "X + 1," etc. Yet some form of choice surely lurks behind at least one half of a palindrome. Freely chosen content can shape even the most intricately symmetrical word pattern.

The Roman poet Horace not only told us to "seize the day" ("carpe diem") but also told us to withdraw from the banquet of life graciously when the time comes, and he instructed the aspiring writer that Medea must *always* murder her children. In other words, he both supported choice and endorsed constancy.[3]

Nevertheless, as Heracleitus avowed, the only thing constant is change. The message of a palindrome is inextricable from its bidirectional wording. Neither end is intrinsically more meaningful than the other, except by the convention of a unidirectional reading of symbols. The totality conveys the meaning and, by exceeding the sum of its parts, it suggests, if it does not actually permit, little scope for randomness.

III

Humanity faces an unpleasant prospect as we approach the new millennium — the possibility that whatever alienation we feel in any cosmic sense is not only of our own doing, but is not going to be solved by even the redoubled efforts of our better selves. Even if given a second chance, we may still fail to be our own saviors in any Brave New World.

This kind of fatalistic millennialism is, of course, an outgrowth of both sacred and secular themes from antiquity.

For Saint Paul, humanity's best hope lay in the Beatific Vision of God and an accompanying realization of one's own sinful weakness. Such is the nature of his account of his Damascus road experience. He maintains that whereas most people focus so much on themselves that they are blind to their state before God, he for his part was turned around, he was "converted," because he was physically blinded by an apparition of the risen Christ Himself and soon had a vision of himself.[4]

For Boethius, a prime distinctive of God was the ability to see everything in an eternal present. Some problems of predestination melt away with this premise. Later, however, the unknown writers of the *Carmina Burana* invoked Fortune as being as mutable with her wheel as the moon in her phases.

One implicit message of the conceit of time travel is the need to divorce the mortality of the individual from the fate of the race. Why worry about dying because of the calendar? Worry about keeping the personal batteries charged up. If fatalism is one bogey of time travel, rejuvenation is the lure.

The frequent flyer through time can live in two widely contrasting manners. The traveler can live in an eternal present, presumably superimposing an aging image of oneself onto endless reruns of the greatest moments of one's life. The alternative is to live vicariously, fighting the current, so to speak, plunging further and further back into time in an attempt to put off the day of one's death forever. To be a Flying Dutchman who never berths his ship.

* * *

In theory, time travel involves a dangerous paradox: one could meet oneself at some point — that is run into one's doppelganger, the clone in some anti-universe that will explode on contact with this one.

This motif from the realm of fantasy was highlighted in the second of the three *Back to the Future* films. We shall see how this film deftly explores the various theoretical consequences of a close encounter with oneself straying somewhere in time.

The film is packed with the wizardry of special effects that the younger set demands, but it is also fleshed out with some arch social commentary that only their parents can appreciate. It has panache as well as flash.

The movie "works" because it capitalizes on the cartoonish simplicity of its characters, and it transcends the silly complexity of its plot. It does this by rehearsing all the major modes of actually coming face to face with oneself in the fullest sense, by using what is surely the ultimate strategy for risking truly stereotyped performances.

In order to do so, the film artfully blends elements drawn from the realms of science fiction and myth. As the trilogy advances, it plays with daguerreotypes as well as archetypes. It combines futuristic high-tech fantasizing with old-fashioned low-key moralizing. From this, it derives much of its entertaining impact on young and old alike.

* * *

In examining the antecedents of the movie's play with the doppelganger motif, it will be useful to distinguish first among the genres to which it is related.

There are several opinions on the crucial distinctives (if such there really be) between science fiction, fantasy, and mythology. Rather than getting bogged down in any niceties of argument on this point, I shall make a simple, albeit simplistic, working assumption.

With respect to narrative form, all three genres confront us with the unorthodox. We may decide that a particular narrative presents us with the "normal" extended and perhaps also distorted by technology. To the extent that technology alone is sufficient to explain the deviation from our present reality, we are dealing with science fiction.

If, however, a narrative presents us with elements of the abnormal that are reconceived and perhaps even normalized, often in anthropomorphic terms, then we are dealing with mythology. For as long as we are not sure which of the two obtains, we are in the realm of fantasy.

In other words, under this scheme, an android that talks because of microchip implants belongs to science fiction, at least for the present; a tin man that speaks despite a noticeable absence of lungs belongs to mythology; Frankenstein's creation hovers in between the two, in the realm of fantasy. Computers with brains the size of a planet are the stuff of science fiction; scarecrows with no brains yet the desire to have one are the stuff of mythology; Dr. Jekyll's progressively spontaneous metamorphoses lure us into the world of fantasy.

On the other hand, if we refuse to insulate "normality" from the impact of something beyond, if we categorize the here and now as more of a derivative than a source, if we locate human life a little lower than the angels, then we are in the camp of religion.

Broadly speaking, then, time machines take travelers through science fictional territory; ships with speaking prows bear heroes through a mythical Bosporus; Herbie the talking VW self-propels in a fantastical way, but chariots of fire do indeed swing low and lift prophets to bliss.

IV

Without dwelling on the point, we may note that no part of *Back to the Future Part II* posits anything other than a vaguely intrinsic wrongness about tampering with the space-time continuum. As it claims no theology, the film is susceptible to analysis as science fiction, because the DeLorean time machine is the material cause of the time traveling . . . and as mythology, because traveling through time in both directions is normalized enough to permit contact with one's younger and older selves . . . *and* as fantasy, because once the premise of bidirectional time traveling is granted, everything else follows.

* * *

Back to the Future Part II has multi-faceted charms. It includes four fantastical face to face encounters between characters and their very own selves. The time-traveling apparatus is provided by science fiction; the small-town setting is a social fantasy, and the characters' archetypes are drawn from myth: the naif, the villain, the sage, and the hero.

Two doppelganger pairs display an elegant variation on the theme of human limitations considered against human endeavor. Two players are passive insofar as the time-traveling is concerned: Jennifer and young Biff simply follow their instincts when they are in the vicinity of their older selves. On the other hand, two players are very active in the time-traveling business: Doc and Marty behave with all due precautions when in contact with their younger selves. Or is that with their former, and therefore, in a sense, with their older selves? It is all rather confusing.

III

A recapitulation of the plot should help at this point. *Back to the Future* began the series in 1985. It falls into four segments of approximately twenty-seven minutes' duration each. The action is non-stop, but the three juncture points are noteworthy and lend neat proportion to the film. The first segment ends with our hero's unplanned arrival in the past; the second ends with his use of foreknowledge to offer a way back to the future, and the third ends with the final defeat of the villain that brings the hero's own future parents together, to assure him of any future to begin with.

Marty McFly is our hero. We find him to be a member of a family with problems: Dad is a wimp, who is regularly tormented by Biff, the nemesis of his adolescent years; Mom is an overweight alcoholic; his brother is unemployed. However, Marty's biggest problem at the moment is setting up an overnight date for the weekend. He enjoys sweet talk with his girlfriend, Jennifer, in front of the town hall, where a can-shaking woman gives him a leaflet in exchange for a donation to the fund to repair the clock-tower: we learn that it was struck by lightning thirty years earlier and has never functioned since. At this point, adult viewers from the Eisenhower era may well sense an ambiguous comment on the rise of the youth culture and the consequent degeneration in morals, inter alia.

Marty is friends with "Doc," the archetypal sage and shaman of the story. With a lot of talk about "temporal displacement," Doc has Marty meet him in the parking lot of a shopping mall at midnight. There he proudly sends his dog, Einstein, on a short trip ahead of them to demonstrate that he has achieved time travel, and in a DeLorean no less. But some Libyan terrorists are after the plutonium he has stolen; they shoot Doc, and Marty makes his escape in literally a nick of time.

Marty moves back thirty years in time, but not in space. He crashes into a barn. A farm family comes out to inspect the damage. Emerging from the car in his radiation-proof suit, Marty is mistaken for an alien who has just landed from space.

The theme of tangible alienation continues as Marty explores the town center and meets George McFly, his father-to-be, in a diner. He soon witnesses the style of Biff's merciless taunting of George. He deflects the taunts onto himself, and outmaneuvers Biff by speeding on an impromptu skateboard around the town square.

When Marty finally catches up with George, he finds him playing Peeping Tom up a tree. Marty pushes him out of the way of an oncoming car, but is himself knocked down. Our hero resolutely resists the role of Oedipus, for it turns out that his grandfather-to-be was driving the car, and it his mother-to-be, Lorraine, who waits for him to recover consciousness. She greets him next morning as Calvin Klein, because his name is apparent from the tag on his underwear.[5] In the Oedipal subplot, Lorraine falls in love with him.

At the first opportunity he gets, Marty makes his way to Doc's house. Doc does not believe his story, until Marty reveals that he knows all about Doc's fall earlier that day and how it prompted the idea of the "flux capacitor" that is crucial to time travel. Marty's leaflet about the defunct clock on the town hall soon pinpoints the time when the required gigawatt of energy will be available to power the DeLorean back to the future . . . in fact the first half of the film closes with these ringing words.

In the third quarter of the film, Marty prompts George to ask Lorraine to the school dance: after all, they must kiss and fall in love, or his own future is rather bleak. Our hero's ploy involves a set-up in the school parking lot: George will rescue Lorraine from Marty's amorous advances in the car. However, when Marty discovers that Lorraine already smokes and drinks, he loses his nerve. Paradoxically it is Biff who, with genuine rough handling, rescues Marty from the situation; George soon appears and—wonder of wonders — clenches his fist and delivers it to Biff's face.

In the final quarter of the film, Marty introduces the crowd at the dance to a case of Chuck Berry meets Jimi Hendrix, and more. Meanwhile, downtown, Doc makes preparations to tap the imminent lightning discharge from the town hall clock and conduct it down to the DeLorean. Marty is safely sent back to the future, just a few minutes before he left it. From a distance, he sees the Libyan terrorists shooting Doc and he sees himself just managing to escape from them. Doc, however, took Marty's earlier written warning: he sits up and shows his bullet-proof vest. Soon he leaves for the future, to fulfill his original goal at last.

Happily, the present is not what it was, however, for Marty's fam-

203

ily is new and improved: his brother has a job, his mom is thin and fit, and his dad is a successful science fiction writer, who hires Biff to polish his cars. Just as Marty is admiring the beautiful truck that he finds waiting for him in the garage, his girlfriend, Jennifer, shows up; they are about to leave for their date when Doc arrives back in the time machine. Marty and Jennifer must come back to the future with him: it has something to do with their kids.

II

Back to the Future Part II begins with the final scene of the earlier film. Part II falls into five segments of approximately twenty-one minutes' duration each. All but the second lead up to the satisfying humiliation of the villain.

Once back in the future, it turns out that Doc wants Marty to take the place of his son, Marty Junior, to be sure that he refuses to go along with some nefarious scheme of Biff's grandson, Biff Junior. Marty does so, and a power "hoverboard" chase results in Biff's and his cronies' crashing through what is now the glass frontage of the town hall.

En route to the future, Jennifer wants especially to see her wedding dress: some sex stereotyping here, perhaps. Doc sedates her for her own protection, then he and Marty leave her sleeping in an alley, but the police pick her up and take her to the home indicated by her fingerprint ID. As she meets her (now) older relatives, Jennifer is trapped by a growing awareness of her mortality. Here the film makes amusing twists on the Oedipus and Electra complexes as Michael J. Fox plays three characters — his future son, himself as a middle-aged father, and his own daughter.

Jennifer finally sees herself as she will be thirty years later: "I'm old!" she cries, crossing her hands over her chest, just as her older self cries out "I'm young" with a mirror image gesture. Then, both Jennifers faint. Passive spectating has led to collapse. Sleeping Beauty is the antetype. Jennifer has, in fact, already bemused the police by being much too young-looking for the age that their records indicate her to be. She is even, in a sense, her own evil fairy, frightening herself into a stupor. The initial thrill of developing self-knowledge is stilled in time, but her prince will come back to awaken her.

Back to the Future Part II has a palindromic structure, at least as far as the doppelganger motif is in evidence.

The first segment features Marty literally taking the place of his future son and spitting image, Marty Junior. The second segment suggests a feminine reaction to the doppelganger: shock and collapse. After the brief prologue in 1985, the time shifts to 2005. But the rogue Biff, now an old man, sneaks into the time machine and takes an almanac with a half-century of sports results (1950-2000) back to his younger self in 1955, courtesy of the hijacked DeLorean. The net effect is to change the future, so that when Marty and Doc return to 1985, they find a town that is very different from the one they left, with Biff as the unscrupulous kingpin.

The very center of the film, in fact, presents the archetypal cemetery scene in which the hero confronts his mortality at the graveside of his father, killed in rather suspicious circumstances. Doc, as shaman, explains that time has skewed into an alternate tangent to the timeline. They must return to the point at which the deviation occurred. Old Biff's transmission of the book to his younger self must be nullified. Marty must recover the book, but not until after Old Biff thinks it has been safely delivered.

The fourth and fifth segments of the film take us back to 1955, to the same time, in fact, as the events of the original *Back to the Future*. The film constructs a crescendo of hilarity as the action plays over the previous events.

Biff, Doc and Marty all meet themselves, in suggestively different ways. The teenage thug Biff finds his seventy-year-old self in his car. He is amazed that he can start it. "Only I know how to start it," he exclaims in disbelief. As the almanac is handed over, young Biff shows no conception of its full potential. There are shades of the Greek nymph Echo here, for Biff is doomed to have no creative success of his own, but only to feed on the efforts of others. The almanac helps Biff echo victories of the future-past, and his winnings even secure a loveless marriage to Lorraine. The meeting of the two Biffs shows that the old villain has been corrupted by the power of foreknowledge; for young Biff, ignorance of oneself turns, via antagonism, into greedy opportunism.

Jennifer reacts to herself with immediate recognition, but then collapses; Biff, however, never recognizes himself, yet retains his usual aggression. The "mad" scientist, Doc, shows a third possible reaction to one's doppelganger.

With reasonable calm, he manages to sustain a conversation with his past self from the future, and he even helps him with some unique auto-repairs, on the DeLorean time machine. His younger self asks for a

5/8" wrench, but his older self suggests a 3/4" wrench, which the younger soon admits is the one he really needs for the job. Interaction and cooperation lead to restoration. Maintaining the very fabric of the universe is neatly repackaged as a wrench passing from one hand to another in a seedy downtown street. This scene presents an urban and urbane commentary on the finger of God reaching down to Adam in that recently rejuvenated ceiling in the Sistine Chapel. If one imagines God's beard removed, in fact, Christopher Lloyd's features seem almost discernible there. Doc as sage creates in his own image, with only his own wits to draw upon.

Finally the young hero, Marty, meets his own self. He admiringly watches himself play the guitar, and takes advantage of his past self's hold on the audience at the high-school dance in order to outwit his own present pursuers, by crawling along a catwalk above the stage where he is simultaneously performing. He ends up being struck on the face by a door flung open by his other self. There are echoes of Narcissus here. In this case, a healthy kind of déja vu leads to transcendence.

Ultimately, Biff is again biffed to the ground by George McFly, who thus wins the fair maiden, Lorraine; Marty recovers the almanac, and sees his nemesis once more buried under a truckload of manure. But it is a dark and stormy night, and Marty's flying guardian angel is himself zapped by lightning even further back into the past.

The doppelganger conceit is twisted still more into separation in the final sequence of the film, when the oldest Doc Brown speaks to Marty through a letter from a century earlier, now at last delivered by a Western Union agent. Marty has only one place to go for help. He finds the younger Doc in front of the town hall, just as the scientist is celebrating his success at sending Marty back to the future. But Marty is still there, and he . . . Doc . . . himself is far away. Even the sage is speechless at this concept, and it remains for our little Hercules to double back once more in time in order to save the day.

I

The four doppelgangers in *Back to the Future Part II* together provide elegant variation on the reactions that a person might well display if confronted by one's double.

The young girl faints; the young villain slowly comprehends the potential for material enrichment offered by the situation. Neither, though, initiates the encounters, whereas our prime sympathies are to lie with the two who do. The old sage assists in his own creative process; the young hero takes advantage of his own former performance.

One piece of technology presents a significant puzzle in each case. The naif is brought to confront herself when a computerized door speaks a greeting — "Hello Jennifer" — not to her, but to her double on the other side. In true Looking-glass-Land fashion, one is coming in just as the other is going out. "Mirror, mirror on the wall, who is the fairest of us all?"

Biff's car engine can be started only by Biff. Old Biff does so; the engine catches on, yet young Biff doesn't.

The older Doc is mistaken in the size of wrench he asks himself for, yet presumably without assistance from his later self he could not have survived into the future in the first place: the scientist makes himself in his own image first.

Finally, the hero doubles up in the first and final segments. Initially, in another reversal of the latent Oedipus motif, he prevents his son from being totally wiped out by taking his place in fighting the villain. The villain is ultimately worsted by being hurled through the air. Eventually, the hero is saved from his pursuers, Biff's cronies, by his own self at center stage: the puzzle of the futuristic guitar riffs distracts the young hoods long enough for Marty to dump a very symbolic load on them at the climax of his other self's playing, and ultimately to be assisted by Doc to outspeed Biff in his car. Biff's final fate is burial under manure: a fitting ignominy after he has twice been knocked out cold beside a car in earlier segments of the film. The villain's comeuppance is thus given a neat symmetry as well.

At the very least, with respect to their ages, characters and dispositions, the four doppelgangers demonstrate elegant variation to the discerning viewer. Technology is both boon and curse to each. Some of the old myths, motifs from the realm in which the abnormal is normalized, lend depth to the surface wizardry of double exposure.

Everyone's future presents variations on a basic double aspect: it is threat and enticement by turns. The traditional myths help cope with this duality: the naif can be saved from the villain, and the brains of the sage still need the guts of the hero. In this film, these wonderful double-acts from mythology are refashioned for our pleasure and take us double quick back to the future indeed.

Footnotes

1 Released in November 1989 by MCA Universal; written by Robert Zemeckis and Bob Gale; directed by Robert Zemeckis, with Steven Spielberg as executive producer.

2 For the myth of Phaethon, see Ovid, *Metamorphoses* Book 2; for Hercules, see Sophocles, *Women of Trachis*; for Medea, see Euripides, *Medea*, the earliest full source.

3 Horace, *Odes* I.11:8; *Satires* I.1:117-119; *Ars Poetica* 123, 185.

4 *Acts* 9:12.

5 Interpreting "Calvin Klein" here to signify "a little man with predestination on his mind" will be resisted as overexplication.

The Authors of this Book

Thomas J. Braga is Professor of French and Portuguese at SUNY Plattsburgh, where he founded the Campus Poets Series. Braga has published a number of essays on French and Luso-Brazilian literary figures including Tristan L'Hermite, Molière, Racine, Florbela Espanca and Castro Alves, as well as an article on liberation theology. To date he has published three chapbooks of his poetry and given readings of his works in English, French, Portuguese and Spanish. Braga received his Ph.D. from Rice University.

Armelle Crouzières-Ingenthron is a Preceptor in French at Boston University. She has published critical articles in various journals about French Literature, and she holds the M.A. in French Literature (Boston College) as well as degrees from the Sorbonne. Crouzieres-Ingenthron is a doctoral candidate at Boston College.

Sylvie Debevec Henning is an Associate Professor of French at SUNY Plattsburgh and chair of the Department of Foreign Languages and Literatures. She is the author of *Genet's Ritual Play*, and *Beckett's Critical Complicity: Carnival, Contestation and Tradition*, which received the 1987 M/MLA Book Prize. She has also written numerous articles on contemporary French Literature and Theory.

Renée Delgado teaches in the Spanish Department at the University of Houston.

Barbara Fischer is Assistant Professor of German at Concordia College, Minnesota, Institute for German Studies. She received her Ph. D. from the University of California at San Diego and has published articles on German Literature.

Eberhard Görner was screenwriter and author for East-German television (DFF) between 1972 and 1990. He has published critical articles about film and television in leading newspapers and journals. His films include: *Der Leutnant Yorck von Wartenburg, Die Zeit der Einsamkeit, Lion Feuchtwanger, Heinrich Mann, Selbstversuch* (based on the novel by Christa Wolf), and most recently *Der kleine Herr Friedemann* (based on the novella by Thomas Mann). Görner is director of the German filmstudio *Provobis* in Berlin. He is a member of P.E.N.

Edwin J. Hamblet is Professor of French at SUNY Plattsburgh. He is the past-president of the American Council for Quebec Studies. Hamblet is the author of *Marcel Dubé and French-Canadian Drama* (1970) and *La Littérature canadienne francophone* (1987). He holds the Ph.D. from the University of Pennsylvania.

Peter Hertz-Ohmes, born 1933 in Berlin, Germany, is Professor of German and Humanities at the State University of New York, Oswego. He is the translator of: *Martin Heidegger, Unterwegs zur Sprache (On the Way to Language)*. The latest of Hertz-Ohmes' numerous articles and book reviews is: "Turning the Postmodern Corner: A Personal Epilogue," in *20th Century Art Theory*, ed. R. Hertz and N. Klein, 1990. Hertz-Ohmes received his A.B. from Stanford University, his M.A. in Philosophy from Columbia University, and he received his Ph.D. in German Literature and Literary Theory from Stanford University.

Myriam Yvonne Jehenson is Associate Professor of Foreign Languages and English at SUNY Oswego. She holds the Ph.D. in Comparative Literature from Columbia University. Her publications include a book on the English and French Renaissance, as well as articles and reviews. Jehenson is currently completing a book on Latin American women authors.

Michael Johnson is the chairperson of the Foreign Language Department at SUNY Buffalo. He researches and publishes on medieval education, biblical studies, surrealism, and children's literature. Johnson holds the Ph. D. in Classics from SUNY Buffalo.

Richard D. Moore is Professor of Biophysics at SUNY Plattsburgh, and holds both Ph.D. and M.D. degrees. Moore is the co-author of *The K Factor: Reversing and Preventing High Blood Pressure without Drugs* (1986), and he has written many articles and reviews.

Thomas J. Morrissey is Professor of English at SUNY Plattsburgh. He has published critical articles and reviews in such journals as *Extrapolation*, *Science Fiction Studies*, *Eire-Ireland*, and in *Centennial Review*. His poetry has appeared in *Blueline* and *Green Fuse*. Morrissey received his Ph. D. from Rutgers University.

Pascale Perraudin has the Licence in Applied Languages from the University of Dijon, France, and is a doctoral student in French Literature and lecturer in French at the Department of Romance Languages and Literatures, Boston College.

Edward R. Schaffer is chair of the Sociology Department at SUNY Plattsburgh. His latest publication, "The Protestant Ideology of the American University," appeared in *Educational Theory* (1990). Schaffer holds the Ph.D. from the Graduate Faculty of the New School for Social Research.

Erich Wolfgang Skwara, born in 1948 in Salzburg, Austria, is Professor of German and Comparative Literatures at San Diego State University. He is a poet, novelist, essayist and critic. His novels are: *Pest in Siena* (English translation forthcoming), *Schwarze Segelschiffe, Bankrottidylle* (transl. as *The Cool Million*), *Eis auf der Brücke* (1991). Skwara holds the Ph. D. from SUNY Albany. He is a member of P.E.N.

Scott R. Smith is a lecturer in Computer Science at SUNY Plattsburgh. Smith received his B.Sc. and M.Sc. in Computing and Information Science at Queen's University, Kingston, Ontario. From 1984-1986 he was Guest Researcher at the Gesellschaft für Mathematik und Datenverarbeitung in West Germany.

Natalie Joy Woodall, formerly on the faculty of SUNY Oswego, is pursuing post-doctoral work at Syracuse University. She has published numerous articles on Greek and Roman Literature. Woodall has also written about British and Irish women authors for the *Encyclopedia of the 1890s.* She holds the Ph.D. in Classics from SUNY Albany.

The Editors

Bruce A. Butterfield is Associate Professor of English at SUNY Plattsburgh. He has written numerous articles on contemporary Canadian Literature and has done extensive editorial work. He holds the Ph.D. from the University of Illinois.

Jürgen Kleist is Assistant Professor of German at SUNY Plattsburgh. He is the author of *Das Dilemma der Kunst* (1989), and the novella *Nietzsche in Turin*. Kleist has published articles about contemporary German and Austrian literature as well as poetry and short stories in literary journals and anthologies. He studied Germanistik and Philosophy at the University Siegen (Germany), received the M.A. at the University of Houston, and the Ph. D. in German Literature from the University of California at San Diego.

Index

PLATTSBURGH STUDIES IN THE HUMANITIES

Plattsburgh Studies in the Humanities will present significant research in the fields of Literature, Philosophy, History, Sociology, Political Science and the Arts. The books in this new series include both monographs and the proceedings of Plattsburgh's annual Humanities symposium at which internationally recognized authorities, emerging scholars, writers and artists participate.

The series is under the general editorship of Jürgen Kleist, Assistant Professor of German, and Bruce A. Butterfield, Associate Professor of English, State University of New York at Plattsburgh.

Anyone who wishes to have a manuscript (200-500 pages) considered for inclusion in *Plattsburgh Studies in the Humanities* should submit a letter of inquiry with an abstract of the manuscript to either:

> Dr. Jürgen Kleist
> Dept. of Foreign Languages and Literatures
> State University of New York at
> Plattsburgh
> Plattsburgh, NY 12901

> or

> Dr. Bruce A. Butterfield
> Dept. of English
> State University of New York at
> Plattsburgh
> Plattsburgh, NY 12901